(Re)Writing Craft

Pittsburgh Series in Composition, Literacy, and Culture

David Bartholomae and Jean Ferguson Carr, Editors

(Re)Writing Craft

COMPOSITION, CREATIVE WRITING, AND

THE FUTURE OF ENGLISH STUDIES

Tim Mayers

UNIVERSITY OF PITTSBURGH PRESS

Acknowledgment is made for the following material excerpted in chapter 4:
Perelman, Bob, *The Marginalization of Poetry,* ©1996 Princeton University Press.
Reprinted by permission of Princeton University Press.

Published by the University of Pittsburgh Press, Pittsburgh, PA 15260
Manufactured in the United States of America
Printed on acid-free paper
First paperback edition, 2007
10 9 8 7 6 5 4 3 2 1
ISBN 13: 978-0-8229-5969-4
ISBN 10: 0-8229-5969-0

This is dedicated to the memory of Bernard J. Mayers, whose infectious love of books made me want to grow up and write them.

Contents

Preface

I majored in English as an undergraduate because I wanted to become a better writer. I wanted, eventually, to write poetry and fiction well enough to get published and perhaps to write persuasive nonfiction well enough that people would want to read it. I must have realized as I moved through the curriculum that it was not particularly designed to facilitate these things; instead, it was aimed at the "coverage" of major writers and time periods in English and American literature. The writing I did in my required English classes (and most of the electives) was treated almost exclusively as a vehicle for communicating interpretations of literary works. There was only one notable exception I can remember: the assignment in my "English Inquiry" course—a required first-semester course for all majors—to write a parody of a well-known poem. I chose to parody T. S. Eliot's "The Love Song of J. Alfred Prufrock," and the professor liked my parody so much that she submitted it on my behalf to the campus literary magazine, where it was later published. I also took a course in poetry writing (the only creative writing course then available at the university) and was fortunate enough to convince the faculty's lone creative writer to work with me on a directed poetry-writing tutorial. But the vast majority of my courses required me to interpret literary works and present my interpretations in five-, ten-, or fifteen-page papers. On my own time, I filled journals with fragments of poetry and fiction, occasionally imitating some of the works I had read for my classes. Although I would have preferred to have the opportunity to write more poetry and fiction for my classes, I largely accepted what the curriculum implicitly told me—that writing poetry and fiction was not really what being an English major was all about.

I am compelled to look back on these experiences quite differently now every time a student sits across from me at the conference table in my office and asks why there are not more courses like the ones I teach. As a full-time faculty member in an English department, I teach creative writing and upper-division composition courses. Some students—especially those English majors who, like me, came to the discipline with a desire to become writers—sense in my classes something dramatically different from the many literature- and interpretation-centered courses they must take to fulfill the requirements of the major. My courses, these students say, are more geared toward their desire to write than any other courses they take. These students, I think to myself as I try to offer them counsel, are already experiencing the sense of disconnection I did not fully experience until I began graduate school, where academia's culture of specialization becomes more apparent and where those in English studies seem compelled to choose both an area and a professional identity with which to ally themselves. I usually tell my students these days that more writing courses are being proposed as future offerings, but many will graduate before these courses make their way completely through the approval process. Sometimes I tell students that a few other schools around the country have developed, and currently offer, quite extensive curricula—and even majors—in writing. But these answers do not alter some basic facts: At the vast majority of English departments in U.S. colleges and universities, literature dominates the curriculum. Those relatively few schools that offer extensive writing curricula usually do so separately from a literature-intensive "English" curriculum. Sometimes the writing curriculum is an option or track within an English department, and sometimes the writing curriculum is offered from a separate academic department or unit that was once part of the English department before it split away.

Many of the problems explored in this book began presenting themselves to me when, as a graduate student in creative writing, I discovered deep antagonisms between students and professors identified with creative writing and those identified with literary study. What had struck me, when I was an undergraduate, as a sensible and natural (even if relatively lopsided) arrangement suddenly seemed strained, forced, and ready at any moment to disintegrate. Dismayed by the dismissive and even at times contemptuous attitude some literary scholars exhibited toward creative writing, and later by the anti-intellectual extremes of some creative writers, I set out to discover whether any scholars had written about these tensions. And my initially unsystematic investigations revealed that some had. A few merely reinforced the tensions and stereotyping I had already witnessed. Creative writers like J. D. McClatchy, for instance, argued that literary scholars, while skilled at theoretical exegeses of poems, have no real idea of how poems get written and therefore need to be reeducated (23–24). Other creative writers, like Eve Shelnutt, were quicker to blame their own colleagues, arguing that creative writing had been severed from "intellectual discourse" and that creative writers needed to study up on literary theory (20). Some literary and cultural theorists, like Donald Morton and Mas'ud Zavarzadeh, dismissed creative writing (especially the fiction workshop) as a mere tool of capitalist hegemony (qtd. in Fromm 227–28). Others were a bit more conciliatory, like Jonathan Monroe, who sought to explain some of the tensions between creative writing and literary theory by tracing the history of these two enterprises within the institutional framework of English studies (6).

Eventually—dissatisfied with some aspects of the available academic identity of "creative writer" but unwilling to cast it aside completely, and not wanting to assume the identity of a literary scholar or teacher—I came to composition studies. There were many reasons for this, not the least of which was that composition studies, more than any other strand of English, seemed to be home base for most scholarship examining the institutional history, structure, and politics of English studies. On a basic level, composition studies seemed—and still seems—a much more natural "fit" with creative writing, though there are a number of fissures between these two subdisciplines. Nonetheless, in the border area between composition and creative writing lies the work of several scholars to whom this book owes a great deal. Wendy Bishop's pioneering work, of course, relentlessly explores connections—especially in the realm of pedagogy—between composition and creative writing. Mary Ann Cain's adroit reading of student fiction writing and the spoken discourse of creative writing workshops opens new ground for creative writing by employing techniques and theories hitherto reserved for composition scholarship. Interesting hybrid creative writing/composition scholarship has also appeared recently from established scholars like Patrick Bizzaro and emerging voices like Kelly Ritter. My task in this book will be to build upon such scholarship and provide an extensive and systematic consideration of past, present, and possible future relationships between composition and creative writing in the realms of theory, pedagogy, and institutional/disciplinary structures.

This book, then, should be of interest to several potential audiences. My arguments move through various discursive territories, and thus many readers, depending on their distinctive disciplinary identities and affiliations, may find this book at times moving from familiar to unfamiliar territory and vice versa. This, I believe, should serve as yet another reminder of how the organization of English studies has become so fragmented. Nonetheless, this book should appeal to scholars, practitioners, and teachers of creative writing, poetry, and poetics—especially those who are dissatisfied or disillusioned with the traditional "workshop" model of teaching. It should also interest teachers and scholars concerned with the potential connections between creative writing and composition pedagogies and theories; those broadly concerned with the shape and direction of English studies, especially theoretically and historically oriented compositionists (and perhaps even a few literary scholars) who have some stake in "refiguring" the discipline; perhaps also those interested in the functions and purposes of "criticism"; and possibly even those concerned with general issues of literacy in American higher education. Perhaps, though, this book will appeal most to those new to the field(s) of English studies, especially graduate students and new assistant professors, who are struggling with issues of disciplinary identity formation and wondering whether they must abandon certain interests in order to pursue others. Certainly anyone embarking on a career in English studies, and anyone not nearing the end of such a career, will have to deal with ongoing changes in the discipline in the coming years, and this book addresses some specific strategies for enacting change.

This book develops a series of interrelated arguments. For reasons I hope will become clear to readers, these arguments cannot be neatly separated from each other and therefore are not always neatly "contained" within particular chapters. Still, I believe it will be helpful to sketch these arguments briefly at the outset. I number them here simply for the sake of convenience, not to suggest any hierarchy or order of importance.

1. The separation of composition and creative writing into different "camps" within English studies is as much the result of historical accident as it is of any intrinsic differences between the two fields of study. However, once the lines had been drawn, they rapidly solidified due to institutional factors. Problematic assumptions about the "differences" between composition and creative writing embedded themselves into the "common sense" of English studies for many reasons, not the least of which is that composition is almost always a required course while creative writing is almost always an elective. So simply pointing out that the differences may not make sense is

not enough to "undraw" the lines between the two fields. In other words, the *theoretical connections* between composition and creative writing mean very little unless they are considered in light of the *institutional differences* between composition and creative writing.

2. The available histories of English studies (at least as I read them) account for two parallel battles that were fought—at times fiercely—during the twentieth century and that continue to be fought today. The first is the battle *within* English studies for institutional power and prestige, which each strand fought (and fights) in its own way. To put the matter as briefly as possible here, proponents of literary study, beginning early in the twentieth century, fought hard to establish literature—understood as a collection or "canon" of "great" texts—as the legitimate content of English studies: content about which professionals could acquire, and subsequently dispense, expertise. In a sense, these professionals defined their expertise in terms other than the primary "business"—the required composition course—of the departments in which they were housed. Proponents of creative writing, a field that had its professional "beginnings" early in the twentieth century but did not flourish until the second half of the century, fought for prestige mainly by capitalizing on notions of the mystical, special, and rare nature of creativity. These professionals argued, both explicitly and implicitly, that creative writing is something only a few "gifted" individuals can do. They maintained that creativity is something impervious to analysis and defined their task as the recognition and nurturing of those rare "real writers" who might show up in creative writing classes. Proponents of composition studies, which emerged, according to various accounts, around the late 1950s and early 1960s, began to forge a place for composition as a scholarly discipline much like any other, not merely a collection of techniques for teaching required composition courses. Compositionists developed rich and varied theories of composing processes and also explored the relevance to composition of theories from numerous other academic disciplines. Compositionists proved, in other words, that they could "do theory" just as well as their colleagues in literary studies. Unlike creative writing, then, which attempted to distinguish itself as something *different from* an academic discipline, composition attempted to distinguish itself as *a new kind of* academic discipline.

The second of these battles found (and finds) English studies continually struggling to justify the need for its existence. In this battle, English studies has often been at odds with (and at times in uneasy alliance with) various publics both within and outside the university. But perceived problems with students' literacy skills have always seemed to provide enough "justification" for English departments, which are often among the largest on campus and which often come into contact with virtually every student who matriculates at any given school. Through much of the twentieth century, professionals in English studies were shrewdly adept at capitalizing on the public sense of "need" for college-level instruction in reading and writing while establishing and protecting a realm of intellectual interests that often had little to do with such instruction. But the many recent proposals to reform English studies, I believe, serve as a powerful indicator that the time has come for a more radical transformation in the discipline.

3. In recent years, a type of writing I call "craft criticism" has emerged in the discourses surrounding academic creative writing. Craft criticism, I argue, can and should serve as a bridge between creative writing and composition studies. In order to make such a case, I define craft criticism as a type of critical prose written by (institutionally defined) creative writers that seeks mostly to subvert—or at least account for—some of the persistent problems in what I call "the institutional-conventional wisdom" of creative writing. As such, it exists as a nascent kind of scholarly or professional "work" that is similar to much of the work that goes on in composition studies and suggests previously unexplored points of overlap between creative writing and composition studies that might help to form the beginnings of a productive alliance between the two fields. By expanding the concept of craft beyond its prevailing sense as mere technique, craft criticism harbors the promise of bringing sociopolitical understandings of literacy into the discourse of creative writing, where such concerns have often been absent. This expanded concept of craft also harbors the promise of returning aesthetic concerns to the discourse of composition studies, where they have sometimes been eclipsed. In other words, a "rewritten" notion of craft might provide common ground for composition and creative writing together to forge an academic disciplinary area in which writing (understood as the production of printed and electronic textual discourse) is of primary concern.

4. Even the most carefully considered and well-designed plans for refiguring English studies—particularly those that outline, in Stephen North's terms, a "fusion-based" approach to the discipline's constituent strands—tend to

underestimate the lingering institutional effects of well over half a century of dominance by the notion that literary study is the intellectual center of English studies. Even though the landscape of literary studies has changed dramatically over the past several decades, particularly as a result of the so-called theory wars and canon wars, the activity of *interpretation* still reigns supreme in the vast majority of English departments. Likewise, many of the institutional apparatuses spawned by literary study—such as the allotment of faculty lines primarily on the basis of national literatures, particular time frames or eras, and "major authors"—continue to thrive. Because of these lingering institutional effects, I argue, reforms that attempt to "unite" literary study with the other strands of English studies may be bound for failure because they offer no real means to address the massive power imbalance that exists in most English departments between the interpretive study of literature (or "texts") and the study/practice of textual production. I contend that creative writers and compositionists together should strive to invert the traditional hierarchy of English studies, which privileges interpretation over production. Such an inversion at this particular moment in the history of English studies, I argue, offers the only hope of ever crafting a discipline in which textual production and interpretation may be treated equally. I do not go so far as to contend that literary study, traditionally understood, should be completely banished from the universe of English studies. But I do believe that it should be, at best, a peripheral part of the discipline, important only insofar as it helps students and teachers understand more about *writing*.

Acknowledgments

A book of this sort is always the result of years of labor and years of collaboration. Without the help of many others—only a few named here—I would never have been able to produce the book you now hold in your hands. During my undergraduate days at the University of Scranton, John Meredith Hill spent many more hours than I deserved working painstakingly, line by line, with me on my writing. Also at Scranton, Timothy Casey patiently guided me through my first attempts to read and understand the work of Martin Heidegger. At SUNY Binghamton, Liz Rosenberg and Milton Kessler made me believe I should keep writing when I was tempted to quit. At the University of Rhode Island, Robert Schwegler saw what I did not—that my intellectual interests should draw me toward rhetoric and composition. Thanks, Bob, for the "conversion." Also at URI, Nedra Reynolds was the kindest, most rigorous, most helpful academic mentor one could imagine.

Immeasurable support for this project also came from Paul Kameen. That he would take an interest in and, via e-mail, support and nurture my work—even though we have never met—speaks volumes about his intellect and heart. Thanks also are in order for the editors at the University of Pittsburgh Press, who have provided enormous help in moving this manuscript toward completion. I especially want to thank Kendra Stokes, whose extraordinary editorial skills helped me make the final version of this manuscript more cohesive. Carol Sickman-Garner's razor-sharp copy editing added the finishing touches to this project; she has made this a better book than it once was.

At Millersville University, many of my colleagues have supported my work and taught me much about what it means to be an academic professional. Worth specific mention here are Steve Centola, Judy Halden-Sullivan, Steve Miller, and Beverly Skinner, all of whom have supported and encouraged me to complete this work while dealing with the daily rigors of life at a teaching-intensive institution. Thanks to all of you.

My parents, Bernard and Paulette Mayers, taught me by example the importance and value of learning. It was a joy to grow up in a house full of books.

My wife, Sandra, has long been an attentive reader and an enormously helpful critic of my work. She deserves much of the credit for this book. Finally,
my children, Connor and Anna, deserve my heartfelt thanks for teaching me
every day the importance of looking with new eyes not only at my profession
but also at the world.

(Re)Writing Craft

Composition, Creative Writing, and the Shifting Boundaries of English Studies

> English studies is in crisis. Indeed, virtually no feature of the discipline can be considered beyond dispute. At issue are the very elements that constitute the categories of poetic and rhetoric, the activities involved in their production and interpretation, their relationship to each other, and their relative place in graduate and undergraduate work.
>
> James A. Berlin, *Rhetorics, Poetics, and Cultures:*
> *Refiguring College English Studies*

ASPIRING PROFESSIONALS IN ANY academic discipline must learn that discipline's boundaries; they must work toward a clear understanding of the discipline's object or objects of study, its accepted research methods, its guiding questions and modes of inquiry. In many cases also, newcomers to an academic discipline need to learn the history of their chosen discipline—the trajectory the discipline's inquiry has followed; the theories that have been developed and then either kept or discarded; and the current methodological, ideological, or interpretive disputes (if any) in the discipline. This is rarely an easy process. It is, after all, more than simply gathering and remembering information. Ultimately, it involves a reorientation of worldview; it involves allowing the discipline to shape (at least in part) the kind of person one is and the way one looks at things.

If this process of professional enculturation is challenging for aspirants in most disciplines, it can be downright maddening for those in composition or creative writing, for these are almost always (at least administratively) subsidiary pieces of a larger structure called "English." This larger structure exerts tremendous influence on composition and creative writing, sometimes in ways that compositionists and creative writers find objectionable. Newcomers and outsiders often feel that composition and creative writing ought to have a great deal in common—as, on an intuitive, "commonsense" level, they certainly should—but are puzzled and dismayed to discover just how different the two areas are. This highlights the challenges of the project in which this book engages: an argument that composition and creative writing, at this particular historical moment, have much to gain by forming an institutional alliance and perhaps much to lose if they do not. Such an argument must take into account the historical, ideological, and institutional underpinnings of the fact that composition and creative writing are now, for the most part, separate fields of activity, even though they are putatively "united" as part of English studies and even though some people are actively working to cross or blur the boundaries between them.

In the Shadows

Both composition and creative writing, in spite of their rapid institutional growth during the latter half of the twentieth century, still exist largely at the periphery of English studies, in the shadow of their dominant (and often domineering) counterpart called literary studies. Quite recently, scholars in both composition (Crowley) and creative writing (Ritter) have lamented that these fields—not to mention the work done by practitioners within them— are often "invisible" to many in the very academic departments in which they exist. Literary studies serves as an institutional wedge separating composition and creative writing, compelling most members of those disciplines to understand their own fields either in complete isolation from the rest of English studies or only in relation to the dominant presence at the center.

I recently taught, for the first time, a graduate seminar in "rhetoric and composition." During the first class meeting, before distributing the syllabus, I asked students to meet in small groups to formulate definitions of what they would be studying for the semester. Or, to put it more simply, I asked them, "What *is* 'rhetoric and composition'?" Some of the students seemed to know a bit about rhetoric—that it had to do with making speeches, with persuasion, and with argumentation. A couple even asked pertinent and interesting questions about whether or how well the principles of rhetoric as they apply to speaking could be effectively brought into the realm of writing. A number of students attempted to define composition as well, and while these definitions were sensible, they also tended to be superficial, identifying composition merely as the physical act of stringing words together on paper or perhaps typing them on a computer keyboard. What none of the students seemed to know, however, was that "rhetoric and composition" is the name (though certainly not the only name) of an academic discipline—or "subdiscipline," or "field," if those terms are preferable—that focuses on the functions and purposes of writing in schools, workplaces, and other contexts. Some readers may not find this lack of knowledge about rhetoric and composition unusual; indeed, perhaps it is fairly common. But these were all graduate students; they had all been through complete undergraduate curricula in English; they were all bright, skilled, capable people who were nonetheless unaware of the very existence of the subject they were about to study. How many graduate-level classes are there in other disciplines, I wonder, where something like that happens?

For those who professionally identify themselves with rhetoric and composition, or any of the field's subtly different names, like composition studies, the scene described above may seem all too familiar, though perhaps regrettably so. For rhetoric and composition, composition-rhetoric, composition studies, composition—whatever one chooses to call it—exists, as I have already noted, at the periphery of English studies. Or, at the very least, it exists at the periphery of most individual English departments. Perhaps this is the most important thing composition has in common with creative writing, though the two fields have arrived at and frequently dealt with their peripheral status in different ways. And while a good deal of work has been done recently—mostly by compositionists but also by creative writers—to question, cross, and redraw disciplinary boundaries, almost none has adequately accounted for the sheer dominance of literary studies over both composition and creative writing in most English departments. This is not intended primarily to criticize those who engage in such efforts; rather, I believe this absence has more to do with the very structure of English studies—its ideological structure as manifested through its administrative incarnations, which tends to install literary study so "naturally" at the center of the discipline that most professionals (and certainly most students) in English never question it, and many compositionists and creative writers (consciously or unconsciously) understand their own fields as mere branches of literary study.

Anyone who doubts the proposition that literary study is the dominant institutional core of English studies need only read a few of the histories of the discipline published within recent years, most by compositionists, but some by literary scholars. They all tell different versions of the same story: college and university English departments built themselves into large academic empires, usually much larger than those in other liberal arts disciplines, as a result of housing the first-year composition course—the course that is, in Sharon Crowley's apt term, the "universal requirement," the one course that virtually all students at virtually all American colleges and universities are compelled to take. Yet this course, the economic engine that allowed the discipline of English studies to grow and prosper, was never regarded as the intellectual center of the discipline. Far from it, in fact. Much more often, the composition course was (and in many cases still is) regarded as a necessary evil. Teaching it is something to be tolerated or endured while one struggles (often unsuccessfully) to move up the career ladder into the institutional nirvana of literary teaching and scholarship. Large doctoral programs in literature use the first-year composition course as an institutional support mechanism. Students aspiring toward careers as scholars and teachers of Shakespeare, Milton, Toni Morrison, Margaret Atwood, or contemporary horror films teach composition not because they have any interest in it but because it offers the benefit of a full tuition waiver and a modest stipend while they work toward their Ph.D.'s. The same is sometimes true, though far less often, for students working on graduate degrees in creative writing. The emergence of composition studies as a legitimate academic field has done surprisingly little to undo this institutional arrangement, in spite of scathing critiques authored by scholars like James Berlin, Sharon Crowley, Susan Miller, and Thomas Miller, to name just a few. In most English departments, the notion that literary study is the center and primary reason-for-being of the discipline has demonstrated incredible staying power.

Of course, the disciplinary centrality of literary study has not prevented signs of discord from emerging. Much of the discourse surrounding English studies is now volatile and chaotic; strands of argument that seem utterly independent and unconnected coexist within individual departments and occasionally in the same professional journals or at the same conferences; discourses steeped in a rich consciousness of history, ideology, and institutional reality stand alongside those that seem oblivious to all those things. A wonderful example of this can be found in the January 2004 issue of *College English*. Patrick Bizzaro's "Research and Reflection in English Studies: The Special Case of Creative Writing" is a groundbreaking and much-needed inquiry into the present and future disciplinary status (or potential disciplinary status) of creative writing, arguing for a critical and reflexive examination of the kinds of research and knowledge-generating activities that take place in the field and ultimately for redesigned graduate-level degree programs that specifically articulate the epistemological and methodological differences between creative writing and other branches of English studies and train students to be not only writers but also teachers, scholars, and responsible institutional citizens. The innovative nature of Bizzaro's work here cannot be overstated. His project challenges conventional wisdom both in creative writing as it currently exists and in English studies generally; it takes virtually nothing for granted and asks readers to question their founding assumptions about what they do and why they do it.

Immediately prior to Bizzaro's article in this issue of *College English* is "Who Killed Annabel Lee? Writing about Literature in the Composition Classroom," in which Mark Richardson revisits the issue of how best to incorporate literary interpretation into composition classrooms. Like all good scholars must, Richardson realizes that the debate he wishes to enter has a history, and he briefly outlines that history in order to contextualize his own argument. As most people working in English studies probably know, the debate over whether or not literary texts are appropriate material for composition classrooms is an old one, having much to do with the fact that composition teaching was often (and in some cases still is) viewed as an apprenticeship for aspiring scholars and teachers of literature. Such people, of course, are likely to bring into their classrooms that which they know best and love most. Probably the most recent full-scale flaring up of this debate occurred as a result of the widely read and much-debated exchange between Erika Lindemann and Gary Tate in the March 1993 issue of *College English*. (Sharon Crowley, in

Composition in the University, later provided incisive analysis of this debate and its significance to the institutional relationship between literary study and composition.) Richardson summarizes the debate well but argues that scholars and teachers really need to "move beyond" it, primarily because "graduate English programs aren't changing quickly enough to produce a new generation of rhetoric and composition teachers sufficient to meet the staffing needs of first-year composition at all of our colleges and universities. For the foreseeable future, many postsecondary institutions will continue to staff FYC [first-year composition] with faculty trained primarily in literary studies." Likewise, Richardson argues, "the debate prevents us from examining best practices for writing about literature in FYC" (280). I find this reasoning nothing short of stunning. In two deft moves, Richardson asserts that it is essentially useless to debate whether writing about literature is appropriate for the first-year composition classroom because the practice *will* continue; then he asserts that such debate is useless because the practice *should* continue. In other words, Richardson takes a debate that may very well illuminate one of the major structural fractures in English studies and banishes it into irrelevance so that he may move on to what seems most interesting to him, that is, the best possible *methods* for writing about literature in first-year composition classrooms.

It is difficult to imagine such debates continuing for so long in other professional contexts. What if, for instance, orthodontists were performing root canals or automobile mechanics were repairing jet engines on commercial airliners? Could these practices be justified by arguing that a continued shortage of oral surgeons and certified jet-engine mechanics makes them necessary? Would it be possible to assert that arguments about whether such situations should persist prevent us from looking at the best ways for orthodontists to perform root canals or auto mechanics to repair commercial jet engines? If some readers find these analogies overstated or exaggerated, perhaps that is because the purported "naturalness" of the relationship between literary interpretation and composition is so deeply embedded in the "institutional unconscious" of English studies that it seems strange even to question it. Still, it stuns me that Richardson can recognize that the practice of writing about literature in composition courses stems in large measure from an overproduction of literary scholars and an underproduction of compositionists without focusing on how that problem might be solved as soon as possible. Perhaps a clue, though, can be found in the biographical note accompanying Richardson's article, which reads, "Although his degrees were originally in British literature, he has since then developed into a teacher of writing concerned primarily with disciplinarity in writing programs" (278). Perhaps Richardson's project involves an attempt to reassert the putatively essential disciplinary connection between reading literary texts and learning to write at a time when the emergence of composition as a disciplinary force within English studies threatens to undermine this once-unquestioned practice.

The appearance of these articles back-to-back goes a long way toward illuminating the volatility of discourse in English studies today, where forward-looking and groundbreaking discourses challenge the "givens" of disciplinary history and practice while reactionary discourses aim to cover over the cracks emerging due to the contradictory ideologies embedded within disciplinary structures. Bizzaro, while not ignoring the roles of institutional structures, ideology, and inertia, nonetheless works actively to overcome these conditions. Richardson, on the other hand, accepts them as givens and attempts to work in spite of rather than against them. Some readers might be tempted to argue that such a contrast actually demonstrates the health of a discipline that can support such different strands of debate as scholars and teachers examine the myriad issues (pedagogical, administrative, and theoretical) facing English studies. I would counter that discourse like Richardson's cannot be considered healthy; in fact, it represents a fundamental failure on the part of many in English studies to understand their own discipline except through utterly insufficient ideological lenses. This is a prime manifestation of "the privilege of unknowing" (Schmertz 78) through which literary scholars and teachers, by virtue of their positions within the dominant strand of the discipline, can essentially get away with knowing little or nothing about composition or, for that matter, about creative writing.[1]

From Required Course to Expanding Field

For many who profess composition today, reflecting on the situation of their chosen enterprise reveals some striking ironies or paradoxes. Although the institutional inequities decried by many prominent scholars in composition have remained, there can be little doubt that scholarship in composition has become a thriving enterprise. Likewise, recipients of doctoral degrees in composition, if they find full-time academic employment in English departments, may find their work ignored or undervalued. But the graduate programs that produce such degree holders are thriving, as are the professional journals, conferences, and other forums where the fascinating "work" of composition studies proliferates. On some levels, composition studies might be called one of the most impressive academic success stories of the twentieth century, a genuinely interdisciplinary field of activity and knowledge-making. On other levels, composition remains the unwanted stepchild of English studies. How could it have come to be both of these things at the same time?

Composition's history is perhaps different from that of any other academic discipline or subdiscipline. By most accounts (e.g., North, *The Making*; Young and Goggin) composition did not exist in anything like its current form until the late 1950s or early 1960s. Some historians argue persuasively that composition's origin came even later, with the emergence of process-oriented theories and pedagogies in the late 1960s and early 1970s. Further, the theoretical explosion of the 1980s and 1990s transformed composition into an enterprise so diverse that some of its original practitioners and scholars might no longer recognize it. No matter where one stands in the debate over composition's origin, though, the fact remains that the discipline of composition came into full existence long after composition burst on the scene as a course taken by students at American colleges and universities.[2] And, in fact, it was composition-as-college-course (or, more precisely, the proliferation of real or perceived problems associated with its teaching) that at a certain historical point seemed to compel the formation of composition-as-academic-discipline. The origin of composition as a universally required course in American institutions of higher learning is probably quite familiar to those in composition studies, though inevitably surprising, and sometimes even shocking, to those encountering it for the first time. As several scholars tell the tale, the college composition course first appeared at elite Eastern American institutions late in the nineteenth century as the classical curriculum—a rigid set of requirements taken by all students—was giving way to an elective curriculum in which students chose areas or subjects to major in and as the older practice of assessing student learning through oral declamation and disputation was giving way to the practice of assessing student learning through written composition. Professors and administrators at these institutions became horrified at what they believed was the virtual illiteracy demonstrated by their students (students, ironically, who had attended the most prestigious preparatory schools and academies in the nation). In 1875, Harvard replaced its required sophomore-level course in rhetoric with a freshman-level course in written composition that, it was believed, would correct the linguistic infelicities of its entering students and prepare them to engage in college-level writing tasks. The measure was supposed to be temporary; Harvard's administrators imagined that the existence of this new course would implicitly compel preparatory schools to clean up their acts and do a better job preparing their students to write and that after some time the required composition course could be discontinued. They could not have been more wrong. By the turn of the twentieth century, virtually every college and university in America had a required first-year composition course, almost always housed within an English department—and that fact remains, with a few notable exceptions, even today. When composition emerged as an academic discipline later in the twentieth century, it was largely because a number of factors—demographic, economic, historical, and institutional—seemed to create the sense that the college composition course was not succeeding in what it was supposed to do, that is, teach students how to write at the college level. This practical concern quickly spawned widespread theoretical inquiries into the questions of just what, exactly, writing is and just how, if at all, knowledge about writing might engender better teaching of writing.

Composition studies developed quite rapidly from the late 1960s through the early 1980s, so much so that Stephen North in 1987 could publish his groundbreaking *The Making of Knowledge in Composition: Portrait of an Emerging Field*. This book is both an extensive catalog and a methodological analysis of many of the disciplinary strands compositionists had crafted by 1987; North carefully traces the development of composition scholarship with roots in history, philosophy, ethnography, cognitive psychology, and other academic fields. And it certainly would not be a stretch to argue that composition studies continued to develop and diversify with increasing rapidity after the publication of North's study. A decade later, in 1997, Victor Villanueva published the first edition of *Cross-Talk in Comp Theory*, an anthology designed primarily for people new to composition studies, especially graduate students. Composition studies has become more diverse and sophisticated, Villanueva writes, adding, "But with the greater diversity and sophistication has come greater confusion" (xiv). Naturally, the more complex and developed a field becomes, the more difficult it is for practitioners—especially new ones—to gain a broad understanding of its intellectual currents. That a second edition of *Cross-Talk* appeared in 2003 indicates that the development continues and shows no signs of slowing.

One of the most interesting debates within composition studies now—at least in terms of the argument of this book—revolves around the role of the first-year college composition course as a subject, direct or implied, of composition scholarship. Some scholars argue that the development of the discipline (i.e., the development of scholarly and theoretical treatments of writing) is hampered by the notion, sometimes called "the pedagogical imperative," that all scholarship ought to serve the cause of teaching, especially teaching in the required first-year composition course. In other academic disciplines, these scholars argue, no such arrangement exists; most scholarship is geared toward the discovery, production, or reassessment of knowledge. But in composition, the pedagogical imperative limits the available field of knowledge and therefore, in the minds of some, prevents the emergence of writing scholarship that does not have any obvious applicability to teaching. Other scholars argue that a constant and intimate relationship to teaching is precisely what makes composition different from other academic disciplines and that this relationship ought to be preserved. No matter what one's position is in this debate, it serves as evidence, I believe, that composition studies has reached an important stage in its development and is possibly ready to expand its scope to encompass territory commonly thought to belong only to creative writing.

The Privileged Marginality of Creative Writing

Creative writing, as an academic subunit of English studies, has a good deal (though not, by any means, everything) in common with composition. Like composition, creative writing has an interesting and unusual academic history. If composition is the only discipline to have been spawned by a single college-level course, perhaps creative writing is one of the few disciplines to have originated within an economic conundrum. According to D. G. Myers, author of the only book-length historical study of academic creative writing, the discipline (if one can call it that) began in the early part of the twentieth century largely because writers of fiction, poetry, and drama often could not earn enough money through writing to support themselves and therefore needed jobs.[3] College and university teaching, though not always palatable to such writers, nonetheless seemed more desirable than most other kinds of employment, since it at least offered the possibility of spending a good deal of time reading and discussing books, as well as the opportunity to use publication for career advancement.

Creative writing thus differs from composition and most other academic disciplines and subdisciplines in the kind of outside-the-classroom publication or professional work expected of its practitioners. The oft-maligned "publish or perish" dictum is perhaps even more pronounced in creative writing than in other academic disciplines—largely (and ironically) the result of a hyper-competitive market for teaching positions—yet many creative writers, not to mention academics from other fields, do not consider their work "scholarship." Indeed, creative writers most often publish, and are expected to publish, original works of poetry, fiction, and sometimes drama or so-called creative nonfiction. While most academic disciplines have engendered the development of scholarly journals where research findings can be published and shared with a national or international disciplinary community, creative writing has spawned the development of numerous journals and magazines where poets and fiction writers can publish their work. Yet many outside the discipline might be surprised to discover that creative writing has also developed or co-opted a series of other professional discourses or genres as part of its professional "work." And it is from some of these discourses that we might tease out an interesting analysis of creative writing's guiding assumptions and ideologies.

An extensive analysis of the professional discourses of creative writing (i.e., those discourses other than poetry, fiction, drama, and creative nonfiction) would be tangential here, so I will simply outline what these discourses are and mention their relative importance within the field. Book reviews are probably the most common, and though book reviews are part of the discourse of almost any academic discipline, they are perhaps even more important in creative writing as guides for interested readers about which books they might (and might not) want to read or buy. Interviews, perhaps not quite so common in other academic disciplines and fields, are very common in journals and magazines for creative writers; the *Paris Review*'s widely read interviews with writers are probably the most notable examples, but many other journals continue to publish interviews with creative writers. Perhaps the prominence of interviews as a form of discourse within creative writing indicates that many in the field do not think of creative writing as a body of knowledge enriched or moved forward by collective contributions so much as they consider it an arena for individual achievement. Textbooks, fixtures in many academic disciplines, also have their place within the professional discourses of creative writing and are important as indicators of creative writing's prevailing notions and ideologies. Finally, we might include among creative writing's professional discourses a type of writing that perhaps is just now beginning to emerge—the scholarly analysis of creative production. Though some of this scholarship is produced by people located institutionally within literary studies, it differs significantly from most literary scholarship, which focuses almost exclusively on interpretation. A few interesting examples of this kind of scholarship are Marjorie Perloff's *Radical Artifice* (an examination of poetry writing in a culture saturated by other sorts of media), Vernon Shetley's *After the Death of Poetry* (an argument that contemporary American poets need to appeal to readers of literary theory and criticism), Timothy Clark's *The Theory of Inspiration* (a fascinating attempt to explain and demystify exactly what might be happening when writers feel "inspired"), and Jane Piirto's *"My Teeming Brain": Understanding Creative Writers* (an extensive analysis of 160 contemporary creative writers that draws heavily on cognitive psychology). Though this kind of scholarship certainly harbors the potential to transform, perhaps dramatically, the field of academic creative writing, it has yet to exert much influence.

Throughout most of its history as an academic enterprise, creative writing has not been very visible to most outside its rather insulated circle of practitioners; in fact, creative writing has often remained virtually invisible to many within college and university English departments. During the 1990s, *College English* published only one article devoted entirely to creative writing—Ron McFarland's 1993 essay "An Apologia for Creative Writing." Though I do not imagine either McFarland or *College English*'s editors intended it this way, this article served as one of the primary official representations of creative writing to the rest of English studies during the last decade of the twentieth century. And tellingly, I believe, this article provides a neat and cogent summary of the often unstated assumptions that guide theory and practice in creative writing. McFarland cuts to the heart of his argument when he claims: "I once ascertained five essentials of a serious writer: desire, drive, talent, vision, and craft. . . . My point . . . is not altered whether the list is held at five, cut to three, or expanded to twenty: of the essentials, only craft can be taught" (34). A whole cluster of assumptions about writers and writing lurks beneath the surface of this statement. But four essential elements of this position might be stated as follows. First, "creative writing" as understood in academic terms is "serious writing."[4] This presumably distinguishes it from commercial or utilitarian forms of writing, though this distinction is certainly problematic. Second, most of the really important, essential elements of creative writing cannot be taught, because they are, in essence, intrinsic aspects of the writer's personality or psychological makeup. Third, only "craft," a minor though nonetheless essential aspect of writing, can be taught. Craft, in this context, refers to rules and techniques; it resides in surface or formal features of particular texts. Students, assuming they are motivated enough, can learn to master craft, but they either have or do not have the other essentials of a "serious writer," and nothing a teacher of creative writing does can change this. Finally, there is the implication of a strong connection between creative writing and literature: "What else we do, generally, in creative writing courses [besides critique student writing in a workshop setting] parallels what we do when we teach courses in literature, and most of us do teach those courses" (35).

Together, the beliefs articulated by McFarland constitute what I call the "institutional-conventional wisdom" of creative writing. Though perhaps it sounds a bit awkward, this term is intended to denote a system of belief that often appears to some creative writers to be a form of "natural" or "common-sense" knowledge. Thus, it is "conventional wisdom," believed by many to be beyond dispute. But it is also "institutional" in the sense that it has become embedded within institutional structures and therefore has helped to form the kind of academic enterprise creative writing is. And because creative writing has developed into an enterprise cut off in many ways from other academic enterprises—simultaneously a part of English studies and something apart from English studies—this institutional-conventional wisdom has not often been critiqued or challenged from within creative writing. In fact, the most notable challenges to this wisdom tend to come from outside creative writing, which means that they often rely on limited understandings of what the field is like. Theoretically minded readers will likely wonder why I have not simply named this cluster of beliefs the "dominant epistemology" of creative writing. Certainly that term would be appropriate too, but "institutional-conventional wisdom" should serve as a constant reminder that the field of academic creative writing possesses a sort of "commonsense" knowledge of its own subject, a knowledge that is reinforced and naturalized by the institutional positioning of creative writing, in relation to both English studies and the academy at large.

Briefly summarized, this institutional-conventional wisdom holds that creativity or writing ability is fundamentally "interior" or "psychological" in nature and that it is thus the province only of special or gifted individuals and is fundamentally unteachable.[5] What *is* teachable in creative writing, according to this institutional-conventional wisdom, is "craft," which is understood in this context as a collection of skills or techniques that writers can explore or use to demonstrate their creativity. Those people who possess the right kind of creative talent, if they can learn to master craft, can produce "serious writing" or works of "literature" that are aesthetically distinguishable from other kinds of texts. The institutional-conventional wisdom of creative writing also characterizes professionals in the field as writers first, teachers second. In fact, it is often argued or implied that achievement as a writer of fiction or poetry is an essential (indeed, at times the only) thing that qualifies one to teach creative writing to others.

Abundant anecdotal evidence attests to the existence of this institutional-conventional wisdom. Patrick Bizzaro offers the following story in a review essay: after presenting a paper on creative writing pedagogy at the annual convention of the Association of Writers and Writing Programs (AWP), Bizzaro was approached by "a poet acquaintance" who "explained that she was of the opinion that *real writers* spend their time writing, and that AWP's Pedagogy Forum wasn't really taken seriously by writers anyway. . . . Creative writers, she insisted, 'don't give papers at conferences'" ("Should I" 286; italics mine). In the end, though, the evidence goes far beyond anecdotes. Articulations of the institutional-conventional wisdom of creative writing appear throughout the professional discourses of the field.

Michel Foucault's idea of the "author-function" has become a commonplace concept within much of the scholarship of English studies. For the purposes of examining the institutional-conventional wisdom of creative writing, however, I find it more useful to refer to the "author-figure"—a concept also suggested by Foucault in "What Is an Author?" when he writes, "I want to deal solely with the relationship between text and author and with the manner in which the text points to this 'figure' that, at least in appearance, is outside it and antecedes it" (101). This term suggests a person—a body, a "character"— implied by a piece of discourse and also reminds us of the importance of *figurative* language as an element of academic creative writing. I do not wish to argue here that it is better, in any general sense, to think of the author as a "function" or as a "figure." I merely mean to suggest that in the discourse of creative writing, the author is virtually always treated *as* a figure. The author-figure constructed in much of the professional discourse of creative writing is a *psychologized* figure. By this I mean that all aspects of the text-generating situation are supposedly governed by the writer's "imagination"; the author's solitary mind is the source of all texts composed and even in many cases pre-determines what the purpose of the text and its audience will be. Everything about the text is purported to come from "within" the writer.

Mary Kinzie, in *The Cure of Poetry in an Age of Prose*, advances the idea that poetry is a "calling," a moral activity, and that "real" poems can only be written by a particular type of person. She asks (possibly in a challenge to Language Poets or post-structuralist literary theorists), "How can a *real poet* take the deep divination of poetry to be illusory?" (xv; italics mine). Later, she writes, "However different the religious beliefs and social ease and individual forwardness of artists in time, only one kind of individual—someone intimately possessed of personality, if not with the egoism that often comes with it—ever composes poems worth saving and rereading" (307). In other words, a real writer, a real poet, is a transhistorical and transcultural creature, a type of person who (though rare) occurs in many different time periods, cultures, and situations. From this notion proceeds the belief that it is the job of creative writing teachers to identify and encourage "real writers" when and if they show up in creative writing classrooms.

So when Mary Oliver asserts, boldly, "Everyone knows that poets are born and not made in school," apparently erasing the possibility that creative writing should even exist as a school subject, she hastens to add, "This book [*A Poetry Handbook*] is about the things that *can* be learned. It is about matters of *craft*" (1; italics mine). In this, Oliver quite neatly sums up one of the key elements of creative writing's institutional-conventional wisdom: it is not possible to teach people to *be* writers (since they either are or are not that "one kind of individual" Kinzie extols), though it is possible to impart to them certain (though quite limited) technical things *about* writing. Oliver continues, "Something that is essential cannot be taught; it can only be given, or earned, or formulated in a manner too mysterious to be picked apart and redesigned for the next person" (1). This brings to light another facet of creative writing's institutional-conventional wisdom—the notion that since creativity is individual, intrinsic, even "mysterious," it cannot really be analyzed or explained in any significant way. In many cases, this notion has been deployed to argue against the idea that creative writing courses should even exist. But Oliver insists that some aspects of poetry writing can be taught. "Still," she writes, "painters, sculptors, and musicians require a lively acquaintance with the history of their particular field and with current theories and techniques. And the same is true of poets. Whatever can't be taught, there is a great deal which can, and must, be learned." And what can be learned, as we have already seen, is craft, which is "that part of the poem that is a written document, as opposed to a mystical document, which of course the poem is also" (1). For Oliver, then, craft is that part of poetry writing that can be learned, as opposed to that part that cannot. While one cannot be a poet without being born a poet, one can learn the technical aspects of poetic composition. One can learn to employ "devices of sound," "the line," "given forms," "verse that is free," "imagery," "voice," and other such devices, devices that are the subjects of the chapters of Oliver's handbook. For Oliver, craft encompasses the technical devices—the tools—that can be learned by students. It does not encompass the "essence" of being a poet, that mysterious thing with which a precious few people are born.

The claim that "real" writers are particular kinds of people is not limited to commentary on poetry writing. Fiction writer and critic John W. Aldridge paints a bleak picture of the contemporary landscape for fiction writing and blames creative writing programs in large measure for this bleakness, noting that "the writing programs have not yet devised a way to reproduce or incorporate into their curricula the conditions that are best suited to the creation of writers." He further explains: "Part of the problem is that most *real writers* have already been formed psychologically to become writers long before they are old enough to enter a program. At some time in childhood or early adolescence they will have learned to live with the fact that somehow they are different from others, that there is a detached and perversely watchful ingredient in their natures that causes them to stand just outside those experiences to which their contemporaries so robustly and mindlessly give themselves" (28; italics mine). Aldridge's larger argument is that "real" writers cannot be cultivated in college and university creative writing programs and that such programs have (perhaps irreparably) harmed the very enterprise of fiction writing. In an ironic sense, then, Aldridge affirms the institutional-conventional wisdom of creative writing, though perhaps in a way that would make many academically employed creative writers uncomfortable.

This notion that "real" writers are particular, often rare, kinds of people is intimately linked (as we have seen in Mary Oliver's case) to the idea that the creative writing class should focus only on matters of craft—that is, matters of surface-level technique. Fiction writer Madison Smartt Bell claims: "It's not that a student's inner process can't be influenced from without. It's that it shouldn't be. Inner process is the student's business and not the teacher's. An ethical teacher may *recommend* devices to stimulate the process of imagination, but that is a different matter from *participating* in them. It's probably true that, for the individual, the practice of art is not entirely distinct from the practice of working out one's private psychological problems, but as a teacher, you don't want to go fooling around in the area where these two overlap. As a student, you really probably don't want anyone else messing around with the *inside* of your head" (15). Frank Conroy echoes these sentiments, arguing: "The [creative writing] workshop cannot tell or teach a student what his or her text should be in the service of. Such presumption would be outrageous. . . . If the text is to have pressure it must be the author's pressure, which can only come from the *inside*. . . . In the end it is the intuitive preconscious forces at work *in* the writer that matter the most" (87; italics mine).

While such theories, articulated and implied in the discourse surrounding academic creative writing, do not always entirely erase or deny the importance of social elements in the process of composition, they certainly—at the very least—make social (and political, cultural, and economic) factors far less important than an individual's psychology. As such, creative writing seems radically opposed to much of what goes on in composition studies and literary studies at both the theoretical and pedagogical levels. Therefore, creative writing cannot, in any sense, currently be considered part of either composition studies or literary studies. Nor can it be easily assimilated into either of these strands of the larger discipline of English studies, unless, of course, creative writers can successfully challenge—from within the field—this institutional-conventional wisdom.

Creative writing's major professional organization, the AWP, serves as a powerful force maintaining this institutional-conventional wisdom. In 2000, D. W. Fenza, the executive director of the AWP, published "Creative Writing and Its Discontents" in the *Writer's Chronicle*, AWP's official journal.[6] Fenza styles his essay "an apology for the profession of writers who teach," presumably made necessary by an increasing chorus of criticism about academic creative writing programs. It will be worthwhile, I believe, to engage in a rather detailed analysis of this essay here, since Fenza, even more so than McFarland, appears to articulate and defend creative writing's institutional-conventional wisdom. As executive director of creative writing's official academic professional organization, Fenza writes from a position of notable authority—the authority, that is, to define what creative writing is and what it does. In fact, Fenza has a history of trying to do just this; in 1992, he published an essay savaging "theory" for its alleged contamination of English studies and arguing that theory ought to be kept out of creative writing.[7]

The opening section of "Creative Writing and Its Discontents" is, in my estimation, a shrewd piece of rhetorical analysis—a quasi-Aristotelian tour of the topoi of criticism directed at creative writing programs. Fenza deftly sums up some of the strategies writers can use to compose effective (i.e., persuasive to a significant number of readers) cultural criticism. His point is to demonstrate how "easy" it apparently is to criticize creative writing programs—and even to provide plenty of evidence for these criticisms—without addressing the "reality" of the situation. Plus, Fenza argues, people want someone or something to blame for what they see as "bad writing," and creative writing programs are an easy target; in other words, there is a ready market for this criticism. As a result, creative writing programs are subject to "lurid misrepresentations." Although this is an important cautionary note, I think Fenza's argument takes several unfortunate turns after this. He simplistically attributes all of the criticisms of creative writing to the selfish agendas and ambitions of those doing the criticizing. Then he goes on to provide a defense of creative writing that is perhaps even more dependent on assertions and shaky evidence than any of the criticism he denounces.

Fenza stakes out creative writing as perhaps the last academic territory in which the notion of individual control over the circumstances of the world (or in his words "the efficacy of the human will") can be maintained. Creative writing is the only strand of English studies, Fenza maintains, in which it is still possible for students to feel that they can actually do something that matters. Fenza makes this claim by setting up a stark, polarized opposition between the (alleged) goals of "literary theories" and those of creative writing. He complains that "professors of literary theory often deprive writers of their humanity," making writers, in other words, "mere unwitting conduits through which society, markets, religion, politics, and prejudices of all kinds—the real authorities—manufacture literary texts." We all live, Fenza asserts, within "a culture where individual acts often seem of little consequence." Creative writing classes offer respite from such a culture: "Word by word, line by line, sentence by sentence, paragraph by paragraph, students make personal choices in a creative writing class, and each choice makes a difference. The students create worlds of their own making."

Much of Fenza's argument revolves around the notion that creative writing is a necessary complement to the study of literature. There is merit to this argument. D. G. Myers traces out in careful detail how creative writing may very well have originated as a counterpart to interpretive literary study. And there can be little doubt that one way—though certainly not the only way—to learn about certain kinds of texts is to attempt to write similar ones. So I am not disputing this aspect of Fenza's argument, but it does seem curious that he neglects or refuses to address the possible relationships between creative writing and composition. He comes closest to doing so when he draws a distinction between the goals of graduate-level creative writing programs and those of undergraduate creative writing classes. Fenza believes the goal of graduate programs, particularly MFA programs, is clear: "The goal of graduate study in creative writing is to become, first and foremost, an accomplished writer who makes significant contributions to contemporary literature. All the other goals, like becoming an academic professional, are ancillary to that artistic goal." Undergraduate creative writing courses, on the other hand, "differ from graduate workshops because their primary goal is not to educate artists but to teach students critical reading skills, the elements of fiction and verse, general persuasive writing skills, and an appreciation of literary works of the present and past." Fenza is not particularly clear about how creative writing classes teach students to read critically or write persuasively, except to note that such classes "usually include reading assignments and a critical paper or oral presentation." What I find most interesting about Fenza's series of assertions here is that they mimic many of the justifications that were offered throughout the twentieth century for the value of literary studies. Although he does not use these terms, Fenza effectively tries to characterize creative writing as an enterprise in which the "traditional" goals of English (literary) studies are preserved and protected. It is only creative writing among all the strands of English studies that remains unsullied by developments within the academy and the corrosive forces of society at large. Literary study, in Fenza's eyes, has become contaminated by theory, and composition studies does not even merit any direct consideration.

Ultimately, I believe Fenza's essay can be read as a bid to preserve and protect creative writing's isolation from the rest of English studies. He does make a number of valid and useful points, particularly with regard to how creative writing courses can, as part of a larger curriculum in English studies, provide students with opportunities for intellectual development. Even so, he appears to articulate virtually every element of creative writing's institutional-conventional wisdom as I have outlined it above, and he appears to do so quite purposefully and willingly. He proudly refers to academic creative writing as "the profession of writers who teach," elevating the former term over the latter. He also argues, in numerous ways, that creative writing is all about individuals making choices that "matter," thus making individual psychology or "the human will" the center of the field. He goes on to assert—without offering any solid evidence—that those who write well (as determined by the amount and kind of acclaim they get for their writing) make the best teachers of writing. As such, Fenza's argument, situated firmly within the institutional-conventional wisdom of creative writing, severely narrows the field of pedagogy for creative writing. In this version of creative writing pedagogy, "craft," understood as the manipulation of the surface features of language, is the only legitimate thing that can be taught, and the teacher becomes little more than a technician, albeit a highly skilled one.

Creative writing thus tends to be positioned as an anti-academic field existing within academic institutions. For some in the field—especially those whose writing is the currency that gained them good academic jobs—this arrangement has proved fortunate. They enjoy what might be called a "privileged marginality," insulated largely from the turmoil of English studies, not drawing much attention from outside their own coteries of students and like-minded colleagues. But this arrangement has never really worked for everyone in creative writing; there are never enough academic jobs for all the holders of MFAs and creative writing Ph.D.'s, and many graduate students, as well as many professors with some background or interest in creative writing who also have some connection to another part of the discipline, have begun to question and challenge this arrangement. While there may be considerable debate about where creative writing should go, and how it should get there, it is difficult to deny that, as David Radavich argues, "We stand again at a crossroads for creative writing programs" (112).

The Discourse of Change in English Studies

English studies has never been a particularly stable enterprise. Maureen Daly Goggin, while introducing her compendious bibliography of the history of the discipline, concludes, "From the beginning, English studies has been a contested site; debates over how to define it and what it is have raged on since the turn of this [the twentieth] century" (64). Delving even further into disciplinary history in *The Formation of College English*, Thomas P. Miller argues that English studies is perpetually involved in a sort of identity crisis because it originated in a moment of crisis during the eighteenth century, when cheap print technology allowed written material to be spread across England and the British cultural provinces, creating an expanded, literate reading public and necessitating (at least in the minds of some) a need for standardized rules of language use. The late nineteenth and early twentieth centuries, as Goggin and many other historians note, were times of turmoil for English studies in America, as literary studies grew out of and later supplanted the German-influenced philology that had characterized language study at the university level in prior decades. I would add, though, that once literary studies became established (although it was almost always wracked by internal disputes), it did lend at least an apparent stability to many departments of English—especially in the practices of organizing curricula according to national literatures, historical periods, and canonical authors and of hiring new faculty members on the basis of their specialized expertise in these categories. In many departments, these practices still operate.

During the last two decades of the twentieth century, the crisis in English studies intensified; or, at the very least, the amount of attention paid to it intensified. Many more scholars turned their attention to disciplinary history, and quite often the historical impulse was yoked to a reformist impulse. In other words, people began to study the history of English studies not only to understand how things came to be the way they are today but also to argue that things should change. Scholarship focused on redesigning English studies for the future has become a vibrant strand of disciplinary discourse, and although some practitioners have advocated change since the very inception of English studies, the number and type of proposals for the future undeniably increased in the 1980s and 1990s; this pattern shows no signs of slowing. The notion that English studies ought to rethink and change its practices has become so common, in fact, that in 1994 the National Council of Teachers of English (NCTE) inaugurated the "Refiguring English Studies" book series. Writing in *College English* in May 2003, Jessica Yood argues: "The rhetoric of 'crisis' about the 'fate of the field' is not some elusive idea; it is the material of a new genre of writing. . . . The genre of disciplinary discourse has created a new kind of scholar—one who searches for deep relations and connections between systematic ways of knowing and experiential realizations of knowledge" (526, 538). In other words, discourse about where English studies came from, where it is now, and where it can or should go in the future now constitutes a genuine scholarly subfield in the discipline.

This is neither the time nor the place for a detailed overview of such historically and future-oriented scholarship. However, the project of this book —examining past, present, and future relationships between composition and creative writing—needs to be contextualized within this sort of discourse, because I intend this book to be both a contribution to the discourse of disciplinary change and a critique of that discourse. For the purposes of this discussion, we might divide this discourse into two rough categories, the theoretical and the structural. By theoretical discourses, I mean those that leave departmental and institutional hierarchies intact, that do not disturb the boundaries between literature, composition, and creative writing. Scholars who propose theoretical changes usually argue for alterations in the *way* in which poems or novels are interpreted, or the *way* in which writing is taught, but do not challenge or question the institutional and curricular divisions between courses. Gerald Graff, for example, urges that competing interpretive theories should be highlighted, and thus brought into conflict, in literature classrooms. But he does not challenge the idea that the interpretation of literary works (however this term might be understood) is what should be going on in English classrooms. And thus, Graff's discourse remains at the level of theory.[8] By structural discourses, I mean those that challenge, disrupt, and perhaps even break down the boundaries within English studies. Scholars who propose structural changes often suggest that elements of *all* the existing subfields of English studies might be brought together in the process of revising the entire English curriculum. Frequently, these scholars contend that reading and writing should be given equal weight in courses across the English curriculum. James Berlin, for example, argues that student writing should become a focus of class discussion in courses where it often has not been so, such as surveys of literature from specific historical eras.

The presence and progression of theoretical proposals for change are quite visible in the history of literary studies in the twentieth century. Calls for theoretical change came in many forms, often because scholars and teachers found operative definitions of "literature" too narrow for their own purposes. There were, for instance, pointed debates at one time about whether there was such a thing as "American literature"; more conservative scholars and teachers argued that there was not, since the United States did not yet have a long and distinguished enough tradition, and that most of the works of poetry and fiction produced in America were inferior to those in the much more refined and noble tradition of British literature. Others argued, eventually with some success, that there was in fact such a thing as American literature and that it was every bit as worthy of university-level study and scholarship as British literature. This pattern tended to repeat itself again and again, with new sorts of literature, once excluded, being ushered into the expanding canon. In some ways, this process transformed the category of "literature" into the much broader category of "text," so that films, television shows, comic books, and many other types of discourse became part of the potential field of analysis. What remained remarkably unchanged, though, through much of this development, was the general method—interpretation—applied to the field's objects of study. This allowed many of the institutional structures in individual departments, like curricula and hiring practices, to remain relatively stable even while the field of scholarship was in virtual turmoil. This institutional stability, in turn, allowed the different strands of English studies to develop and exist largely in isolation from each other.

This stability, though, was not without its critics, and these critics began to offer structural discourses of change. Structural discourses seek to challenge, and often to eradicate, many of the institutional lines drawn within English studies, most notably the lines between composition and literature or between textual interpretation and textual production. Frequently, scholars working in this mode argue for some sort of unification of the disparate strands of English studies. James Berlin, for instance, provides an extensive argument in *Rhetorics, Poetics, and Cultures* for replacing the traditional dynamic of English studies, in which textual interpretation is privileged over textual production, with one in which production and interpretation are given equal weight. Stephen North, concentrating on doctoral-level graduate education, argues for the bringing together of literary study, composition, and creative writing in a "fusion" model where the concerns of each strand are continually brought into dialogue and negotiation. Other scholars propose drawing together the separate strands of English studies under some overarching umbrella concept or method that would render traditional disciplinary divisions untenable. For example, Richard E. Miller proposes rethinking the history of the discipline and reimagining its future by focusing centrally on student writing, and the various kinds of responses to student writing, in all English classes. Patricia Bizzell argues that the notion of "contact zones" is an organizing principle under which the differences between composition and literary study would be largely eradicated. And James Seitz offers metaphor (and the constant dynamic interplay between figurative and literal uses and interpretations of language) as a central concept that would unify the various strands of English studies.

I believe that the significance of these structural reform proposals cannot be overestimated; indeed, some of these proposals would move the discipline forward in dramatic and much-needed ways. Still, it seems to me that these proposals in general tend to suffer from two significant kinds of flaws. First, many of them tend to divide English studies in half—usually between literature and composition. When this happens, other areas of the discipline, usually creative writing, are either ignored or regarded as not important enough to consider. D. G. Myers offers an excellent and cogent critique of the tendency among scholars to thus divide English studies, although the division may take a number of different manifestations, such as literature versus composition, reading versus writing, or interpretation versus production. Myers finds two-part division inadequate to describe what has gone on historically within English studies: "What I am suggesting is that historically there has been a three-way split in English departments: the terrain has been carved up into sectors representing scholarship, social practices, and what I am going to refer to as constructivism" (9). Myers goes on to note: "I am going to base my own historical analysis on the premise that scholarly research in English, the teaching of practical composition, and constructivist handling of literature are three distinct 'faculties' of study, thought, and activity in English, differentiated by aim and method, by the uses to which they put their materials, at times even unrelated to each other. . . . English itself is not a consistent order; its existence is bureaucratic (or 'economic,' if you prefer), not logical. . . . It is less a name than the designation of a plurality of interests. For historical reasons, English has become home to several logically indistinguishable and perhaps even mutually incompatible modes of activity" (10).

For this line of argument alone, Myers's *The Elephants Teach* is a crucially important contribution to the history of English studies. It opens up the possibility that English studies might be analyzed not in terms of an ongoing battle between two rival camps but rather as a constantly shifting coexistence of at least three general kinds of *ideas*, each of which is bureaucratically, economically, and institutionally inscribed within a particular department and each of which occasionally overlaps with one or more of the others. But since his interests are primarily historical, Myers focuses almost exclusively on how things got to be the way they are and leaves unanswered the question of where things might go in the future.

In many cases, the tendency to view English studies as a two-part enterprise prevents scholars from considering interesting possibilities. For example, when Richard E. Miller proposes reconceptualizing English studies by focusing first and foremost on the solicitation of and response to student writing, he seems to miss a tremendous opportunity, considering how this would change the institutional relationship between literary study and composition but not how creative writing would fit into this mix. Other scholars who at least recognize the triple division of the discipline tend to be so unfamiliar with creative writing that they offer it only passing attention; perhaps the best example of this can be found in James Berlin's *Rhetorics, Poetics, and Cultures,* where creative writing is considered as a potential "player" in a reformed and unified version of English studies but only offered a few pages.

The second major problem with the vast majority of structural reform proposals for English studies is that they fail to acknowledge the significance of literary studies' dominant institutional position and its capacity to absorb and neutralize ideas that might challenge its structure. Compelling demonstrations of how this happens can be found in much of Gerald Graff's work, where he describes how the "field coverage" model in literary studies has allowed the discipline to deflect a number of oppositional discourses by institutionally transforming them into new fields that are then tacked on to the existing apparatus of the discipline. For example, many of the theories that found their way into English studies in the 1970s and 1980s—especially poststructuralism and some variants of feminism and Marxism—directly challenged some of the very assumptions upon which literary study is based, like the notion that literature encompasses a type of textuality so different from other sorts that it merits a discipline of its own, and that literature is best categorized in terms of nationalities and historical eras. But the potentially transformative power of these ideas was blunted because "theory" (at least on the institutional level) became its own field to be covered, and many English departments simply hired a "theorist" or two to cover that new area of the discipline, leaving the rest of the apparatus completely intact. Even some scholars who offer institutionally radical plans for reorganizing English studies, like James Berlin and James Seitz, do not seem to consider the possibility that their plans to make composition and creative writing equal institutional partners with literary study might likewise be severely diminished by the ability of literary scholars to preserve their institutional authority by assimilating (and effectively rendering powerless) oppositional discourses. Stephen North seems far more aware of this potential problem, as is evident when he writes that his "fusion-based" proposals for change "will present more of a challenge for some departments than for others. There are a number of institutions—including some of the most hoary—in which the field's discounting practices run so deep that no tenure-track lines whatever are devoted to scholars in . . . writing-related areas" (North et al. 259). By "discounting practices," North means those tendencies in English studies to devalue—in terms of institutional capital and monetary capital—the practice, study, and teaching of writing. He does not spend much time, however, speculating about how this problem might be overcome.

Perhaps the only recent works of reform-oriented scholarship that do adequately take into account the dominance of literary study within English departments are two edited collections, *Coming of Age: The Advanced Writing Curriculum* (Shamoon et al.) and *A Field of Dreams: Independent Writing Programs and the future of Composition Studies* (O'Neill, Crow, and Burton). In somewhat different ways, these two collections explore the provocative notion that productive advancements in the study and teaching of writing might only be realized *outside* of English departments or, at the very least, in the form of separate and autonomous curricular tracks within English departments. *Coming of Age* outlines a series of courses—some already existing, some as yet only imagined—that together might form complete undergraduate majors in writing. *A Field of Dreams* examines a number of independent writing departments (most of which "split away" at some point from the English departments at their institutions) and explores the significance of such programs to the ongoing development of composition studies. Many of the programs described, however, include areas not traditionally connected with composition studies —especially creative writing—raising the possibility that "composition studies" may be too narrow a term for the field of scholarship such independent writing departments would support.

I will return later in this book to the question of whether independent departmental status for writing, separate curricular tracks within English departments, or some form of fusion between writing and literary studies is the best option; local conditions probably make it impossible to provide a single satisfying answer to the question, though I believe the first two options are infinitely preferable to the third. First, though, I would like to explore some of the provocative questions raised by the very existence of *Coming of Age, A Field of Dreams,* and many of the other structural discourses about the future of English studies. For instance, has the institutional separation of composition and creative writing, with literary studies wedged between them, prevented or forestalled potentially productive developments in the study and teaching of writing? Have the two fields grown so far apart that fusing them now would do irreparable harm to both, or would some sort of merging of the two fields actually create a much stronger and more institutionally viable entity than composition and creative writing currently, and separately, are?

What are the theoretical, pedagogical, historical, and institutional points of overlap between composition and creative writing, and what kinds of work might be done to bring these points of overlap into sharp relief? Not all readers of this book will be inclined to answer these questions in the same way or to agree with all of the answers I will attempt to provide. These questions, however, must be asked, and the issues implied must be explored and debated, as the sprawling institutional apparatus called English studies attempts to continue its work into the future.

"Craft Criticism" and the Possibility of Theoretical Scholarship in Creative Writing

> Let's admit it: I see in a definition the critic's equivalent
> of a lyric, or of an aria in an opera. . . . In actual develop-
> ment, the definition may be the last thing a writer hits
> upon. Or it may be formulated somewhere along the line.
>
> Kenneth Burke, *A Grammar of Motives*
> *and a Rhetoric of Motives*

THE POET THEODORE WEISS, IN an interview published in 2001, says: "Language, it's true, is the closest we come to others. And closest to the self that's our own. But, beyond the personal, there's a self in language itself. It arises in those rare moments when, anonymously for us, the language utters itself. The poet, suddenly in the middle of the language, is content to be little more than its medium." Interviewer Reginald Gibbons—himself a poet, critic, and editor—marvels, "When the critics told us [things like that] . . . that was to diminish the role of the author, but when you say it, it does not sound like a diminishment." Weiss replies: "I certainly hope not. Some of the theorists have staged a conspiracy against language itself and so particularly against the professionals of language, the poets" (36). This exchange is remarkable for a number of reasons. It is simultaneously an act of theorizing and a condem- nation of "theorists." It simultaneously affirms and denies the agency of the "author" in the composition of poetry. As such, it is both an affirmation and a denial of one of the central tenets of the institutional-conventional wisdom

29

of creative writing. But what is most interesting to me about this passage is that "poets" are granted status as "the professionals of language" and "theorists" are conspirators against the professionals. In other words, the dispute here is as much about institutional turf within English studies as it is about the rightness or wrongness of any theory about language and composition.

Weiss and Gibbons seem to provide a situational answer to Michel Foucault's insistent question, "What does it matter who is speaking?" And the answer is, "It matters a great deal," especially when the person speaking (or, more often, writing) is positioned within one of the three competing strands of English studies. Within the terms of Weiss and Gibbons's discourse, Weiss is "allowed" to theorize in a certain way because his theorizing does not seem to threaten the enterprise of creative writing. Yet when institutionally identified "theorists" proffer the same ideas, they seem—again, within the terms of this particular discourse—threatening and conspiratorial. Moments like this— when creative writers theorize writing in ways that *might* bring them into dialogue with so-called critical theorists and compositionists yet remain comfortably enmeshed within their institutional identities—are becoming more and more common these days. In these moments, a genuine potential to transform English studies is simultaneously unleashed and constrained. The transformative potential is "theoretical," while the constraining factors are "structural" or "institutional" (see chapter 1). Here I will argue that something I call "craft criticism" has begun recently to emerge in the professional discourses of creative writing, and the theoretical issues it addresses may be related to theoretical issues raised in composition scholarship. Readers with a background in creative writing may already be familiar with much of what I categorize as craft criticism, though perhaps not in the context in which I present it here. Readers with a background in composition are perhaps less likely to be familiar with this work. But its importance to both audiences, I hope, will become obvious.

Criticism and the "Work" of English Studies

English studies, as we have already seen, is a divided field. Agreement about what professionals in English do, or should do, is difficult to come by. Part of this difficulty arises because several key terms that (apparently, at least) denote the fundamental concerns of English studies are themselves under dispute. *Literature* and *criticism* are two such terms, as is *writing*, which may be preceded by adjectives such as *creative, academic,* or *technical.* Difficulties in pinning down exact meanings for these terms, and others, indicate a field or discipline in "crisis," as some commentators would have it. But this crisis has not really inhibited the field's growth or development, and English studies has for some time now been an exciting, vibrant, and diverse enterprise. Definitions of and disputes over key terms have helped constitute important sites of work in the field.

Of course, the word *work* itself is one that might cover a good deal of ground, that might generate its own share of disagreement and dispute. As Evan Watkins points out, professionals in English studies engage in many different kinds of activities that might qualify as work, including classroom teaching, writing minutes for committee meetings, and writing letters of recommendation. But when English studies professionals converse with each other about their work, they most often refer to publications and presentations at professional conferences (Watkins 85). Bruce Horner, in *Terms of Work for Composition,* offers an extensive and insightful critique of the problems that arise from this narrowed conception of "work." Nonetheless, while I understand that published articles and conference presentations are only a portion of the "work" English studies professionals do,[1] I will—out of strategic necessity —employ this particular definition of work in the current discussion. Publications and conference presentations, aside from being vehicles for professional advancement, provide those in English studies with opportunities for articulating and demonstrating their own theoretical predispositions toward the material they teach. And such work remains perhaps one of the best ways in which ideas might be shared between people at different institutions. Both Watkins's and Horner's critiques, for instance, are disseminated within the very sphere of work whose definition they wish to challenge.

Even this particular sphere of work, though, is a broad and diverse one, and this diversity is complicated by the division of English studies into various subfields or strands such as literary studies, composition, and creative writing. Each strand has distinctive forms of written work that are expected by readers of journals and attendees of conferences. What "counts" as work (i.e., that for which an individual receives credit toward admission, employment, or promotion) varies from position to position and from place to place.

It is determined not only by which strand(s) within English studies a person is affiliated with but also by what kind of institution a person learns or teaches within. Even when scholars recognize and acknowledge these distinctions and complications, they often do not clarify them adequately enough. Susan Miller, for instance, places work in literary study and work in creative writing into virtually the same category in order to distinguish them from work in composition. Miller points out, for example, that authors of composition textbooks often do not enjoy the same rewards as those who produce "scholarly research or creative work" because textbooks are not considered to be "of the same order" as these other kinds of work (*Textual Carnivals* 157). Miller's observation is valid but also problematic, since it invokes an image of English studies in which creative writing and literary study entail one kind of work, while composition entails another. On the surface, Miller recognizes creative writing as a distinct division of English studies, but then she effectively falls back upon the binary distinction between literature and composition.

Miller's casting of creative writing across the border and into the realm of composition's institutional other—literature—is symptomatic of a general trend. Many scholars in composition and literature pay little attention to creative writing, even when they are engaged in broad speculations about the entire enterprise of English studies. Such scholars may quickly dismiss creative writing on the grounds that it is not really a field of scholarly inquiry. More often, though, they maintain a curious silence toward creative writing, either not mentioning it at all or mentioning it only in passing, with no attempt to describe or understand it. Some creative writers themselves are perhaps partially to blame for this, having established their courses and programs as fenced-in private preserves where they can retreat from the rest of the university and do as they please. In many institutions, though, particularly "teaching-intensive" public and private liberal arts colleges, those who teach creative writing also teach other English courses, making such a clean separation effectively impossible, making the silence even more curious and the territory, in effect, less private.

Many of those in creative writing would find Miller's characterization of their activity—as effectively "of the same order" as scholarly research in literature—highly inaccurate, I am sure (see, e.g., Kercheval). Beyond that, even, there are important differences among types of work done within creative writing, and such distinctions are not acknowledged by most scholars, who assume that the written work of creative writing professors takes place entirely within the bounds of traditional literary genres—particularly poetry and fiction. "Craft criticism," though, is something quite different.

A (Preliminary) Definition

I have some misgivings about the very act of defining, particularly as understood in the Aristotelian sense of clearing away all "accident" in order to get down to "essence." That sort of definition, whether it operates explicitly or implicitly, is often used in scholarly discourse as a weapon against adversaries. This is evident, for example, when one scholar accuses another of not being "really" or "truly" critical, or Marxist, or feminist, or whatever term is under contention. Many poets and fiction writers do this too, establishing definitions of poetry and fiction that allow them to dismiss the writing of others on the grounds that it is not really poetry or fiction.[2] In offering a reconception of the categories within which scholars tend to think about the activities of English studies, I am not suggesting that all prior scholars have gotten it wrong. I am suggesting that at least some of the available ways of categorizing work in English studies prevent us from seeing certain kinds of relationships. I am thinking specifically here of the tendency to view English departments through the binary distinction between literature and composition, which effectively eliminates creative writing from serious consideration. I am particularly interested in exploring particular kinds of relationships between creative writing and composition. And I have found it necessary to offer a "new" category— craft criticism—in order to throw these relationships into relief. I would like my definition of craft criticism, then, to be considered rhetorical rather than metaphysical.[3]

I should also note briefly here why I choose the term *craft criticism* to denote this particular type of work. I do so partly because *craft,* by virtue of its seeming ubiquity, is one of the most important words in the discourse about creative writing in America. At the same time, it is essential for me to point out that "craft criticism," as I will define it, depends on a far more capacious sense of the word *craft* than that which might most often be encountered. I first coined the term *craft criticism* during the early 1990s when, in reading through many of the professional discourses of creative writing, I began to get the sense that something new, something different, something unusual was occasionally happening. Since then, in many ways, I have been working to fine-tune a definition for craft criticism as I understand it. So while I will attempt to provide a concise definition of craft criticism, I hope readers will (in the spirit of the Burke epigraph) regard the ensuing discussion as a process of development toward a richer definition of craft criticism than I can offer in just a few sentences.

Craft criticism, then, refers to critical prose written by self- or institutionally identified "creative writers"; in craft criticism, a concern with textual production takes precedence over any concern with textual interpretation. Often, though not always, craft criticism has a pedagogical element. This is not surprising, since the vast majority of craft critics teach creative writing and struggle daily with questions about how and why they might be able to "teach" poetic or fictional text production to their students. Craft criticism also often has an evaluative element, in the sense that craft critics are frequently concerned with how they (and often their students) can write "better" poems and fiction or choose the "best" among available poetic and fictional forms. The historical and material circumstances of craft criticism are the contemporary historical and material circumstances of English studies. Craft criticism attempts to situate the writing of poetry and fiction, and the teaching of poetry and fiction writing, within institutional, political, social, and economic contexts. As such, many of the concerns of craft critics might be called rhetorical. Some craft critics are concerned, for instance, with audiences for poetry, with the ways in which these audiences might receive poems, and the ways in which these audiences might be expanded. Craft criticism operates within the same system of exchange, reward, and marginalization as all of the other professional activities of English studies. While the particulars of this system obviously vary from school to school, there are also similarities. These similarities are those that allow some cluster of activities to be recognized as "English studies" in the first place.

In presenting my definition in such terms, I am marking out particular directions this study will take. Just as important, I am marking out directions this study will not take. I will not attempt, for example, to establish a canonical tradition of "roots" for craft criticism—including Horace's "Ars Poetica," Sidney's *Defense of Poetry,* Eliot's "Tradition and the Individual Talent," Woolf's *A Room of One's Own,* and so on—and then go on to argue that craft criticism has been wrongfully ignored in the contemporary American university. It might be interesting to try to make such a case—since at least some of today's craft criticism bears similarities to, or even draws upon, these canonical texts —but I will not make it here. Instead, I will concentrate on craft criticism as an activity that takes place within the current configurations of English departments, and I will speculate about how some craft criticism might pertain to efforts to reconfigure English departments. Since craft criticism results, in large measure, from the migration of creative writing into academic institutions, it cannot be properly understood outside of this institutional context.

To review a bit, then: craft criticism is part of the work done by certain professionals in English departments. It can be distinguished, at least superficially, from realms of work like teaching and service; it falls under the realm variously referred to as research, scholarship, or publication. It is generally assumed that for creative writers, professional publication activity consists of their "creative" work, such as poems, stories, and novels. And indeed, for most creative writers, this area makes up an important part of their professional work. For some, it is the only kind of publication in which they engage. Yet many creative writers publish, and present at conferences, other kinds of work. Some—having divided professional duties—publish and present academic literary criticism or composition scholarship as well. And many produce critical prose that focuses squarely on issues of contemporary "creative" text production in academic settings. This kind of critical prose is craft criticism.

Of course, by naming something "craft criticism," I am claiming that although it has a specific character, it is nonetheless part of the broader field of "criticism." The meaning of the word *criticism* has undergone dramatic— though gradual—changes during the years in which English has been taught as a college- and university-level subject in America. In fact, as Raymond Williams notes in *Keywords*, "Criticism has become a very difficult word" because for several centuries it has been the site of multiple and occasionally incompatible meanings (84–85). In the late nineteenth century, for example, criticism would have been considered a realm entirely separate from scholarship. Today, however, some might regard the two terms as almost synonymous, at least when used to refer to the professional activities of English professors. There are, of course, many different kinds of criticism written by English professors and a number of schemes for classifying those different types of criticism. According to Thomas P. Miller, "criticism"—understood as a primarily interpretive and (allegedly) apolitical activity—became the dominant field of work in English studies when departments of English discarded their allegiance with classical rhetoric and cast their lot instead with "literature" (274–76). Thus, criticism became an activity in which interpretation prevails, in which textual production is rarely considered and, even when it is, gets put at the service of interpretation.

Craft Criticism versus Academic Literary Criticism

One of the easiest ways to point out the difference between craft criticism and what I will here call academic literary criticism is to look at the different journals in which they appear.[4] Craft criticism most often appears in journals oriented toward the publication of new poetry and fiction, journals like *Poetry*, the *American Poetry Review*, the *Georgia Review*, the *Hudson Review*, and others. Each of these journals, of course, has its own particular editorial slant, but there are noticeable similarities among the types of criticism they publish. Academic literary criticism appears most often in journals like *PMLA*, *Papers in Language and Literature*, and the countless journals devoted to specific authors and literary-historical periods. Here again, each journal has its own particular editorial preferences, but there are broad similarities among them. I would like to contrast two examples of criticism from the mid-1990s —one craft criticism, the other academic literary criticism. Obviously, no single article can serve as an adequate example of either of these categories, but the two discussed here will at least serve to highlight some of the most important features of each type of criticism.

James Berger's "Ghosts of Liberalism: Morrison's *Beloved* and the Moynihan Report," which appeared in *PMLA* in May 1996, can serve as an excellent example of academic literary criticism. I have chosen this example for several reasons. First, it is not "traditional" or "canonical" in its choice of texts to analyze. Unlike most academic literary criticism, it actually focuses on something written by a living author. In some ways, then, it pushes at the boundaries of academic literary criticism. Second, the essay does not confine its interpretation to "the text itself," as the most commonly maligned version of New Criticism did. Berger's essay, in other words, considers Morrison's text *in context*, that is, as part of a larger discursive field and not as a supposedly self-contained aesthetic artifact. But despite its apparent progressiveness, Berger's essay remains thoroughly rooted in the interpretive mode, which is the third and most important reason why I have chosen it; even though it does, at times, seem to summon forth questions about textual production, these questions are always subsumed by questions of interpretation. Berger begins his clear, thorough introduction by noting, "This essay places Toni Morrison's 1989 novel *Beloved* in particular discursive contexts of the 1980s, reading the text as an intervention in two ongoing debates about American race relations" (408). Specifically, Berger intends to argue that *Beloved* should be read as a document that accepts neither liberal nor conservative positions about race relations in America. Instead, the novel forges a third position that, while bearing some important similarities to the type of liberalism characterized by Daniel Patrick Moynihan's 1965 report on the African American family, also incorporates African American perspectives that Moynihan's report—and his particular brand of 1960s liberalism—did not (408–9).

In choosing to "read" (i.e., interpret) Morrison's novel as an intervention in political debates about race relations, Berger chooses interpretation as the primary mode in which his essay will operate. While he could, given the concerns of his essay, address questions of *how* a novelist (or, for that matter, a short-story writer or poet) might intervene in political or public debates, he does not do so. Practicing (or aspiring) novelists and poets might be more interested in such questions than they are in particular interpretations of texts. But for Berger, the conditions under which the text was written become interesting only insofar as they shed light on what the text might mean. Indeed, for Berger, meaning is such a vital concern that he even provides an interpretation of the 1980 and 1984 presidential elections (414) and, in order to clear a space for his own interpretation, discredits other interpretations: "Several influential interpretations of *Beloved* . . . neglect or misinterpret Morrison's portrayal of family violence" (409). While I might suggest that Berger "neglects" some important questions regarding how a novel like Morrison's might get written, it might be more accurate to note that for Berger, and for the kinds of readers he expects to find by publishing in *PMLA*, such questions are not very important. Interpretation is primary.

Interpretation is not necessarily primary, however, for writers like Donald Revell. His essay "Better Unsaid: On Poetic Fragments," published in the *American Poetry Review*'s July–August 1996 issue, cites a number of passages of poetry, but Revell's concern is never primarily with what these passages might mean. Instead, he focuses more sharply on how the poets in question came to write these passages. Overall, he wants to explore how certain conditions surrounding the act of writing poetry make the composition of fragments a viable (indeed, sometimes the only) option for poets. These conditions are historical rather than "eternal"; there are no stable standards that govern the production and reception of poetry for all time. Revell's essay begins in a manner somewhat similar to Berger's, that is, with a statement of intention: "Only what cannot begin cannot end. Once begun, an activity possesses trajectory, and, anticipating a form, trajectory anticipates an end. Only what cannot begin remains innocent of anticipation, retaining the necessity and thus the privilege of incompleteness. In trying to understand the fragment as a genre rather than as an abolition of poetic activity, I want to find some of the accents of such an innocence and some of the attributes of its necessity" (29). In attempting to establish the fragment as a legitimate poetic genre, Revell is engaged in a decidedly anti–New Critical (and perhaps even an anti-aesthetic) project. While not entirely discounting the value of "form" and "completeness" in poetic composition, Revell argues that under certain conditions, they are not viable options for the practicing poet:

> The occasions of a fragment—interruption of the incessant, deprivation of posterity, astonishment by awe—may be ingathered by a circumstance which is a condition also: piety. . . . In each instance, the insuperable entirety of experience-in-time insists upon the incompleteness of the written work. Otherwise, the poet would be guilty of an impious rivalry with the source of what he [*sic*] writes and is. Under such conditions, completeness is plagiarism. Under such conditions, the ambition to make something whole, to usurp the primary creativity of the real, constitutes a hubris whose tragic motions must not begin, not because they threaten reality, but because they confront the poet with only equally fatal options: impiety or self-destruction. (30)

As I have already mentioned, all of Revell's citations of other poets (e.g., Rilke, John Berryman, and Dylan Thomas) are employed not to establish the meaning of particular poetic passages but to speculate about the conditions that surrounded and shaped the composition of those passages. Revell's central concern with poetic textual production leads him to use citations in this way. Berger's central concern with textual interpretation, on the other hand, leads him to employ citations as evidence that substantiates his claims for a specific meaning of a specific text.

A Brief History of Craft Criticism

How do we account for this difference? One way might be to consider craft criticism and academic/interpretive criticism as belonging to different genres. I do not intend *genre* here to be understood in a purely formalistic sense—the sense in which, traditionally, poetry, fiction, and drama have been marked off as "the literary genres." I prefer instead Mikhail Bakhtin's concept of "speech genres," genres as phenomena that are inherently social. According to Bakhtin: "Each sphere in which language is used develops its own *relatively stable types of* . . . utterances. These we may call *speech genres*" (60). The fact that speech genres are "relatively stable" means that they have recognizable, though not entirely unchangeable, sets of rules and conventions. Any utterance a speaker or writer chooses to make must take place within an existing speech genre. Some speech genres offer far more opportunities for individual expression than do others (Bakhtin 63), and each individual utterance harbors at least the potential for slightly altering the boundaries of the speech genre in which it occurs. Speech genres, then, though relatively stable, are always also in flux, at least to some degree. As Bakhtin notes, "The wealth and diversity of speech genres are boundless because the various possibilities of human activity are inexhaustible, and because each sphere of activity contains an entire repertoire of speech genres that differentiate and grow as the particular sphere develops and becomes more complex" (60). So while it is certainly possible to discern formal differences between genres, these differences cannot be fully understood without some acknowledgment of the social, political, and institutional contexts in which the different genres have developed; for me, this is the key to Bakhtin's analysis and the reason why it is so useful here. Although I have already suggested a term, *craft criticism,* as a "new" term for an already existing field of discourse, I do not intend to employ Bakhtin's concept of speech genres in a primarily taxonomic way. Instead, I believe that Bakhtin's account of how speech genres develop and stabilize provides a useful angle from which to begin considering what craft criticism is, where it came from, and how it currently functions.

Some of the specific moments leading to the development of craft criticism might be discerned by studying the many available histories of English studies in America. Gerald Graff's *Professing Literature* (1987) drew widespread attention for its compelling account of the cyclical nature of struggle and debate within English departments and for its near-complete avoidance of writing instruction, which makes up the vast majority of the instruction conducted by English departments. Scholars in composition and rhetoric, though, have provided extensive histories of rhetoric and writing instruction. Some examples include James Berlin's *Writing Instruction in Nineteenth Century American Colleges* (1984) and *Rhetoric and Reality: Writing Instruction in American Colleges, 1900–1985* (1987) and David Russell's *Writing in the Academic Disciplines, 1870–1990: A Curricular History* (1991). Most of these histories, though, pay little or no attention to creative writing and the way it grew and developed in relation to (or in many cases separately from) the other spheres of English studies. There are, however, notable exceptions. Katharine H. Adams's *A History of Professional Writing Instruction in American Colleges: Years of Acceptance, Growth, and Doubt* (1993) includes an entire chapter on creative writing, and D. G. Myers's *The Elephants Teach: Creative Writing since 1880* (1996) is a rigorous, extensive historical treatment. Even these works, though, focus little attention on the ways creative writers *as critics* have operated within English departments. Reading between the lines of these existing histories of English studies, however, can help provide a framework for understanding what craft criticism is and how it works.

Although Gerald Graff's *Professing Literature* is often critiqued (rightfully so, I think) by composition scholars for quickly glossing over the importance of writing instruction to the history of American English studies, Graff's analysis does offer some important insights into English studies in general. Graff argues throughout his book that English studies in America has been characterized by two important tendencies. The first is an inability to come to a consensus about basic object(s) of study, basic theoretical principles of investigation, and the purpose of the discipline in general. The second is a systemic covering-over of the conflicts that would arise from such a lack of consensus. This covering-over is achieved through the field-coverage model, in which each scholar in the department is responsible for her/his own area. Emergent theoretical challenges are often defused by adding new areas to English studies, tacking them on, in effect, to the collection of areas that already exists (*Professing Literature* 7). For the purposes of this study, the most important example of such an assimilation is the following:

> After the war, the literature department seemed abruptly to have changed sides in the cultural quarrel over modern literature. An institution that had once seen itself as the bulwark of tradition against vulgar and immoral contemporaneity was now the disseminator and explainer of the most recent trends. One might imagine that such a transformation could not have taken place without open violence and confrontation. Yet the assimilation of modern literature had been accomplished so quietly and with so little open discussion of its cultural or ideological implications outside the pages of journals specializing in that sort of controversy that most students and perhaps most professors hardly noticed what had happened. (*Professing Literature* 206)

Though Graff does not make this explicit, the assimilation of contemporary literature into the university coincided with the assimilation of creative writing into the university. Many of the earliest professors of contemporary literature were themselves creative writers. Some of them may have attempted to bring contemporary writing into the university (at least partly) as a means of securing an audience for their own writing. Craft criticism—as I define it here—became one of the dialects or speech genres in which creative writers could communicate with each other. It came to be one type of criticism among many within English departments, although it remained invisible to many professors and students because it was (and is) outside their chosen areas.

D. G. Myers considers the relationship between creative writing and criticism in much more detail than Graff does. Myers locates the "beginning" of creative writing quite some time before the advent of the New Criticism. In Myers's account, "creative writing" is at heart an idea, an idea that originates within the objections to the kind of philological scholarship that characterized the offerings of U.S. university English departments in the late nineteenth century. As an idea, creative writing is related to, though not identical with, criticism. Myers writes, "From the late 1920s to the early 1940s . . . most English departments were split between a right wing that stood for philology and a left wing that stood for anything but" (128). So when criticism, "the sworn enemy of philology" (Myers 27), made its way into the American university as an acceptable—and later the dominant—mode of work in English studies, it brought creative writing along with it. Many of the university-sanctioned critics were also poets, and "their criticism grew out of their practical interest in writing poetry" (Myers 131). Just as literature came to be taught in a radically new way thanks to the perspectives of these new critics, since "the new criticism was first of all a pedagogy" (Myers 130), courses in "creative writing" began to appear at colleges and universities as well. Both criticism and creative writing, in Myers's account, proceeded from the notion that literature is best taught as literature, not as raw material for history, sociology, psychology, or anything else.

This notion, of course, gave rise to its own share of problems. Foremost among these was a lack of consensus about what "literature" might be and who might be able or qualified to produce it. Perhaps the most stubbornly recurring idea in the professional and cultural conversation about creative writing has been the idea that true literature can be produced only by those who possess individual genius, an undefinable quality that no type or amount of schooling can provide. Or, as James Berlin notes, "The attempt to teach creative writing in the academy is regarded as an effort to produce 'pseudo-literature,' the product of attempting to teach what cannot be taught" ("Rhetoric, Poetic, and Culture" 32). Basic questions like whether and/or how creative writing should be taught in academic settings (along with other questions) are those that gave rise to craft criticism. These questions became particularly important, at least for some people, during the time *after* Myers ends his history of creative writing—that is, after creative writing had acquired some of the trappings of a traditional academic discipline, like conferences, textbooks, and graduate programs.

Following Myers's account, one might be tempted to believe that academic literary criticism and what I have called craft criticism are the same thing. But they are not. Had criticism not become institutionalized as an almost exclusively interpretive enterprise, there might be no need today to distinguish between craft criticism and academic literary criticism. Clearly, the interpretive and productive emphases in criticism became separated somewhere. A hint about when and where this parting took place might be found in David Richter's account of the history of criticism. In the introduction to *The Crit-*

ical Tradition: Classic Texts and Contemporary Trends, Richter presents several "maps" designed to provide readers with a historical and theoretical perspective on criticism and critical theory. The first of these maps follows a scheme drawn up in 1953 by M. H. Abrams. In this scheme, literary criticism is divided into four basic types—mimetic, rhetorical, expressive, and formal. According to Richter, the first three types enjoyed periods of proliferation in the past, and although they have not disappeared, they are no longer dominant. Particularly interesting here is the distinction between rhetorical and formal theories. Rhetorical theories address questions about "how the literary work should be formed to please and instruct its audience," while formal theories are concerned with "the purely aesthetic relationship between the parts of a work of literature, analyzing its 'themes' or 'motifs' as if a literary text were a form of classical music or abstract painting" (Richter 2–3). Clearly, what Abrams and Richter designate as formal criticism is nearly identical to the "New Criticism," which gained an institutional foothold in the 1930s. Despite the fact that many of the New Critics were poets, their primary concerns (or, more precisely, the way those concerns manifested themselves pedagogically) were formal and not rhetorical. New Criticism rapidly became a way to teach students how to interpret poetry by searching for the poems' own internal structures and rules. Rather than becoming institutionalized as a focus on writing poetry in general, New Criticism became institutionalized as a focus on reading, interpreting, and appreciating particular kinds of poems. Although the work produced by English professors underwent radical changes as the New Criticism was challenged (e.g., attention turned to kinds of texts the New Critics designated as "lower," and texts came to be read from a position that challenged, rather than honored, the literary text's internal schemes of organization), the focus on close reading and textual interpretation remained strong.

Abrams's four-part map of criticism, at least as Richter presents it, seems largely inadequate to address some of the relationships between the types of criticism produced by those working in English studies. Perhaps this is because it does not take into account the ways in which criticism is tied to the professional identities and functions of the critics who produce it. Simply placing craft criticism into the "rhetorical" category and academic literary criticism into the "formal" category is tempting, but this would cover over some important factors. Craft critics sometimes do focus on formal aspects of texts. And academic literary critics often address issues that might be called rhetorical—issues, that is, relating to the production of texts. The difference between craft criticism and academic literary criticism, then, cannot be reduced to a simple distinction between rhetoric and formalism, between production and interpretation. But the distinction between craft criticism and academic literary criticism has at least *something* to do with the difference between rhetorical and formal approaches to texts. For it might be noted that craft criticism and academic literary criticism operate according to different fundamental dynamics. Specifically, these dynamics involve not only the choice to focus on textual interpretation or textual production but also the choice about how to relate them to each other—to consider textual production only insofar as it sheds light on textual interpretation, or vice versa. The institutional position of the critic often, at least to a degree, determines the way in which rhetorical and formal emphases, along with other emphases, might be mixed in a particular piece of criticism. The institutional position of the critic may also determine which forum (i.e., through which journal or which conference) s/he attempts to distribute work.

What all of this history might indicate is that the affiliation of creative writing and criticism to the university changed both activities, as well as their relationships to each other. Eve Shelnutt claims that as more creative writers attempted to become affiliated with colleges and universities, and thus needed to publish their work as a matter of professional necessity, "what happened in many journals was a splitting off of creative writing from intellectual discourse" (6). I do not think this is an entirely accurate observation. In order to make it, Shelnutt must ignore those journals where creative writing coexists with intellectual discourse, for example, the *American Poetry Review* and the *Minnesota Review*. Perhaps a better way to look at the situation would be to note that New Criticism, the very movement that helped bring creative writing into the university, also effectively worked to disenfranchise many creative writers from the act of criticism. Creative writers continued to write criticism, of course, but increasingly they wrote it (as they still do) for an audience consisting largely of themselves. Over time, the number of journals in which English professors might publish multiplied—a sure sign, in Bakhtinian terms, that the sphere of activity known as English studies was (and is) differentiating and growing. As this happened, "poets" developed their own journals, "critics" developed theirs, and rarely if ever were these the *same* journals. Over time, the word *criticism* came to acquire divergent meanings for the two camps. This may explain, at least in part, the obvious differences between the two articles outlined above and the apparent territorial dispute between "authors" and "theorists" to which Theodore Weiss and Reginald Gibbons refer in their exchange.

The Contemporary Landscape of Creative Writing

English studies, as a discipline (if it can even be called "a" discipline any longer), has grown and multiplied dramatically in America since the turn of the twentieth century. This growth has been so pronounced that craft criticism, which might at the outset seem a minor subcategory of a much larger enterprise, itself covers a tremendous deal of ground. I will attempt to offer some idea of just how diverse and extensive a category craft criticism is by cataloging numerous examples of it as it appears within the professional discourses of creative writing. Through this process, I hope to establish a clearer understanding of craft criticism and its most immediate contexts. But before outlining some examples of craft criticism, I should note that these discourses are properly understood only within the context of the contemporary landscape of creative writing. The terrains of both poetry and fiction writing today are marked by discussions (and at times disputes) about the distinctions between the "traditional" incarnations of these genres as opposed to "experimental," "innovative," or "avant-garde" incarnations.

Observers of the American poetic landscape, writing early in the 1990s, noted the increasing division and fragmentation of poetic practice at the time. Both Vernon Shetley and Jonathan Holden argue that there were three major "camps": the "mainstream," consisting primarily of poets who write self-expressive free-verse lyric poetry and tend to be affiliated with college or university creative writing programs; the "New Formalists," consisting primarily of cultural conservatives who believe poets need to regain a lost rigor and status for poetry by returning to traditional metric and rhythmic forms of writing; and the "Language Poets," consisting primarily of social and political radicals who believe that poetry should be revolutionary, part of a project to shatter Modernist and bourgeois notions about selfhood and politics. Writing in 1996, Jed Rasula argues for the existence of a fourth camp (or "zone," in his words) consisting of "various coalitions of interest-oriented or community-based poets" (440). By 1999, Christopher Beach could claim that even Rasula's complication of the earlier map was inadequate to capture the fullness of the American poetic landscape, which also includes numerous "nonacademic" poetic practices, such as "slam" poetry, "cowboy" poetry, and various experimental combinations of poetry with other media (171–73). While Beach offers an important caution against oversimplifying the poetic landscape, I would argue that it is still possible to address the central tension between "mainstream" poetic practices and various "alternative" poetic practices and that understanding this tension is important to understanding the professional discourses of creative writing, particularly craft criticism.

The contemporary fictional landscape is perhaps not as fragmented as the poetic landscape. But in fiction, a distinction is still commonly drawn between "realistic" writing, which is believed to constitute "the tradition," and various nonrealistic kinds of fiction writing. The realistic and allegedly traditional modes of fiction writing are favored in articulations of creative writing's institutional-conventional wisdom, especially in textbooks. Though there may be no fictional equivalent of Language Poetry, there is the interesting phenomenon of hypertext fiction, which in many cases (at least apparently) undermines traditional concepts of narrative and authorship by breaking stories down into "bits" or "links" and transferring a substantial amount of power from the writer to the reader. The contemporary fictional landscape, then, like the poetic landscape, is marked by a tension between "mainstream" practice and other sorts of practice. Within the realm of fiction writing, however, the "mainstream" is somewhat more allied with the "traditional" than it is in poetry writing. And across the entire landscape of creative writing, this tension provides an important impetus for many of the arguments and discussions that take place within craft criticism.

Examples of Craft Criticism

Craft criticism is engaged theorizing about creative production—theorizing that arises from and is responsive to the social, political, economic, and institutional contexts for creative writing. Because of its inevitable entanglement in these contexts, craft criticism can only be understood adequately if these contexts are also understood. In effect, craft criticism is a practice that takes place largely within the professional discourses of creative writing. The questions that give rise to craft criticism inevitably arise in discussions about what creative writing—particularly within the institutional structure of English studies—is and should be.

Craft criticism is held together in the loosest sense by the tendency to challenge or question the institutional-conventional wisdom of creative writing; this tendency, in effect, is the ideological "glue" that holds all craft criticism together. But this is certainly not to say that craft criticism is completely unified in its ideological concerns. Craft criticism, like other sorts of criticism, is a ground upon which ideological battles are often fought. Craft critics—despite whatever ideological differences they have—tend to focus on particular types of questions. Though the specific forms of these questions vary from writer to writer, and from situation to situation, they tend to fall into four basic categories—process, genre, authorship, and institutionality.

Questions of *process* focus on the act of composing. Craft critics exploring questions of process might ask, for example, whether it is possible for the poet or fiction writer to determine in advance what the particular piece of writing might look like, sound like, or mean. They might also analyze their own processes of composition, or those of others, in order to draw conclusions about the quality or effectiveness of certain methods of composing. Critics exploring questions of process are often motivated by pedagogical concerns, since most craft critics are also teachers of creative writing. Questions of *genre* most often concern definitions and boundaries. The most basic questions of genre simply ask: What is poetry? What is fiction? About these questions, fierce ideological battles may be fought, as critics seek to establish boundaries for poetry and fiction by arguing what should or should not "count" as "serious writing" and distinguishing "real" writers from mere pretenders. Questions of *authorship* focus on writers themselves. Most often, critics pursuing questions of authorship debate whether or not the ability to write poetry or fiction is confined only to innately talented, gifted, "special" kinds of people. Critics exploring these questions may be motivated by pedagogical concerns, such as how to identify genuine creative ability in students and how to cultivate it once it is recognized. Or, more important in the context of this study, they may challenge the notion that writing ability is inherently personal or psychological and question instead why so many people seem to believe it is so. Questions of *institutionality* focus on how the teaching of writing (and reading) is institutionalized within creative writing programs at colleges and universities. Usually, critics addressing questions of institutionality examine the effects of the academy on the general enterprises of poetry and fiction writing. Often, they debate whether or not creative writing belongs in the university, with some critics vigorously defending creative writing's place in the curriculum and others arguing that the enterprise of creative writing is dramatically harmed when it becomes institutionalized.

In the following, I will examine pieces of criticism written by New Formalists, Language Poets, mainstream poets, and fiction writers. In other words, I will demonstrate how craft criticism exists across the entire range of the contemporary landscape of creative writing. In so doing, I hope to provide readers a clearer understanding of what I mean by "craft criticism" and also to delineate some of the ways in which writers from different "camps" tend to approach craft criticism's key questions. Often, more than one of the major questions of craft criticism (i.e., process, genre, authorship, institutionality) is addressed in any specific work of criticism; many critics regard these questions as essentially interrelated, so it is common to find their analyses of them interwoven.

As I mention earlier, craft criticism arises from and responds to historical and material contexts. Perhaps one structural feature all pieces of craft criticism share is that they must work to situate themselves within those contexts, often by providing analyses of the conditions surrounding creative production at a particular time. Dana Gioia—whose *Can Poetry Matter?* is an example of craft criticism by a New Formalist poet—is no exception to this rule. The first essay of his book—and the one that provides its title—is an extensive analysis of the current conditions surrounding poetry production. Before this essay, though, Gioia includes a preface in which he identifies the kind of reader for which his collection was written:

> I wrote these essays with the conviction that poetry appeals to a broader audience than is usually acknowledged. I tried to find a style that satisfied the demands of my fellow writers and critics but was also accessible to the common reader. By the common reader, however, I did not imagine an uninformed or unreflective individual. Nor did I assume the incurious mass audience of the popular media. I kept before me the idea of the general reader on whom both Samuel Johnson and Virginia Woolf felt the

vitality of literature depended—the intelligent, engaged non-specialist. Whether such individuals ever read most of the essays was immaterial. What mattered was keeping my responsibilities to them in mind as I explored each issue. (xii)

Although Gioia seems to have a keen sense of some of the historical and cultural conditions surrounding the production and reception of contemporary American poetry, he also seems to regard "the general reader" as a curiously transhistorical creature.[5] In any event, he backs off from his pronouncements somewhat at the end of his preface: "Perhaps when I claimed to have written these pieces for a mixed audience of writers, critics, and readers, I meant I wrote them largely for myself. I enjoyed the intensity of attention they required. I hope other readers will share that pleasure" (xiii).

Gioia begins the title essay of the book by considering what he calls "a paradox, a Zen riddle of cultural sociology" (2), regarding the situation of contemporary poetry. Specifically, the production of poetry, from a purely numerical standpoint—that is, the numbers of new poems published in books and journals each year—is at an all-time high. Yet the audience for poetry has become an increasingly isolated (and even isolationist) "subculture" centering almost exclusively around university creative writing programs. Attempting "to look at the issue in strictly economic terms," Gioia writes: "Most contemporary poets have been alienated from their original cultural function. As Marx maintained and few economists have disputed, changes in a class's economic function eventually transform its values and behavior. In poetry's case, the socioeconomic changes have led to a divided literary culture: the superabundance of poetry within a small class and the impoverishment outside it. One might even say that outside the classroom—where society demands that the two groups interact—poets and the common reader are no longer on speaking terms" (10). This subcultural nature of current American poetry, in Gioia's view, has disastrous effects: "To maintain their activities, subcultures usually require institutions, since the general society does not share their interests" (12). All of this is dramatically different from "fifty years ago," when poets found various ways of making a living and were thus obliged to become involved in "the artistic and intellectual life of their time" (14–15). Today, by contrast, "Poets . . . occupy niches at every level of academia, from a few sumptuously endowed chairs with six-figure salaries to the more numerous part-time stints that pay roughly the same as Burger King. But even at minimum wage, teaching poetry earns more than writing it ever did. Before the creative-writing boom, being a poet usually meant living in genteel poverty or worse. While the sacrifices poetry demanded caused much individual suffering, the rigors of serving Milton's 'thankless muse' also delivered the collective cultural benefit of frightening away all but committed artists" (13). And so, though he has some difficulty placing himself in the category of "New Formalism," Gioia here works from many of the general assumptions that characterize New Formalism as a movement. These include the notions that poetry is an "art"; that too much poetry is being published today; that an association with academia is generally bad for poets; and that the failure of the capitalist or "free-market" economy to deliver any material rewards to poets is actually good for poetry itself, since it scares away pretenders.

Gioia concludes this essay with a series of prescriptions for how poetry can once again "matter" in American culture. These include casting aside personal ego and professional friendships when poets perform public readings or write reviews of other poets' work, emphasizing performance over analysis of poetry in high-school and undergraduate education, and using radio to expand poetry's audience (22–24).

The other essay from this book that deserves attention here is "Notes on the New Formalism." Gioia is often identified as a New Formalist, but in this essay he distances himself from those who would argue that received form, and received form alone, is what poets should be writing in. Gioia claims there is no inherent value in form: "Formal verse, like free verse, is neither intrinsically bad nor good" (32). Gioia associates formal verse primarily with meter, which he claims is a "primitive . . . aural technique." Free verse, on the other hand, is "a much more modern technique that presupposes the existence of written texts" (32–33). Gioia offers a sort of pluralistic approach, arguing that poets should learn to write both formal and free verse—like he does—in order to take advantage of "the full resources the English language offers" (45). Yet while Gioia claims not to place any intrinsic value in any particular form, he offers a curious idea about what might be called metrical purity, especially when he engages in a harsh critique of "pseudo-formal verse." Pseudo-formal verse, Gioia suggests, arose in the 1980s as a result of poets in creative writing programs "grow[ing] up in a literary culture so removed from the predominantly oral traditions of metrical verse that they can no longer hear it accurately" (44). Pseudo-formal verse is either verse that contains some metrical lines, although the poem "never sustains a consistent rhythm long enough to establish a metrical base" (42), or verse that merely looks metrical, with lines on the page that are all roughly the same length (42–44). Altogether, Gioia seems to me to be arguing that, while forms do not have intrinsic value, they do have essences that are incompatible with each other and therefore cannot —or should not—be mixed.

Though he does not explicitly claim himself to be a member of the New Formalist camp, Gioia clearly qualifies as a New Formalist as Vernon Shetley and Jonathan Holden describe the term. In other words, Gioia seeks to get poetry out of the dangerous rut of the free-verse personal lyric by returning to historically available poetic (i.e., metrical and rhythmic) forms. While Gioia laments the supposed sequestration of poetry within the university, and urges the "restoration" of "a vulgar vitality to poetry" (24), he also distances himself —and "poetry"—from "the incurious mass audience of the popular media" (xii). This leaves him with a rather narrow definition of poetry. But perhaps this is the only definition he can maintain if he wishes for a poetry that can command and maintain a popular or common audience.

In one sense, then, Language Poet Charles Bernstein's collection entitled *A Poetics,* published the same year as *Can Poetry Matter?,* seems almost a direct response to Gioia and the New Formalists (among others). Bernstein begins by considering the fragmented nature of poetry's audience in contemporary America: "The state of American poetry can be characterized by the sharp ideological disagreements that lacerate our communal field of vision, making it volatile, dynamic, engaging" (1). For Bernstein, the apparent lack of any single, unifying American poetic consensus, the fact that there is little if any common ground among all those who profess an interest in something called "poetry," is a sign of health rather than weakness. He knows, though, that this position puts him sharply at odds with some other commentators on poetry. He writes: "One response to this new proliferation of audiences is to lament the lack of a common readership. I'm not talking about those who want to resurrect a single canon of western literary values. . . . What I take more seriously are pluralist ideas supporting an idealized multiculturalism: the image of poets from different communities reading each other's works and working to keep aware of developments in every part of the poetic spectrum" (4). Such an approach, claims Bernstein, runs the risk of transforming minority writers into tokens valued only as representatives of their specific identity groups. Bernstein seems to me to be taking aim here at both New Formalists and "mainstream" poets—who often disagree sharply with each other about the course of American poetry—because they both hanker after a common readership. The very notion that there can *be* a common readership troubles Bernstein, because it proceeds from "a highly idealized conception of American culture that effectively quiets dissent" (4–5). Bernstein puts his own take on the matter quite bluntly: "We have to get over, as in getting over a disease, the idea that we can 'all' speak to one another in the universal voice of poetry. . . . For as long as social relations are skewed, who speaks in poetry can never be a neutral matter" (5).

It should be clear that Bernstein's account of the current poetic situation is far different from Gioia's. But like Gioia, Bernstein argues in favor of a particular kind of poetic production. Where Gioia urges poets to become more structurally and historically aware of poetic forms in order to avoid what might be called formal confusion (exemplified by what Gioia calls "pseudo-formal verse"), Bernstein argues that "*poetry is aversion of conformity* in pursuit of new forms, or can be. By form I mean ways of putting things together, or stripping them apart, I mean ways of accounting for what weighs upon any one of us. . . . By form I mean how any one of us interprets what's swirling so often incomprehensibly about us" (1). Bernstein does not argue that traditional poetic forms are inherently flawed or bankrupt, but he does reject the notion that these are the only (or even the "best") forms available to poets now. He yearns "for poetry that insists on running its own course, finding its own measures, charting worlds otherwise hidden or denied or, perhaps best of all, never before existing" (1). What is most interesting and promising for Bernstein about poetry is its potential to be a space in which dominant or widely accepted ideologies (and this includes ideologies about poetic form and tradition) can be questioned, challenged, and sometimes subverted.

Bernstein attempts to practice what he preaches, so to speak, in an eighty-page text entitled "Artifice of Absorption," which might be called a scholarly essay in verse form, or a poem-essay. In any case, the piece seems designed to call forward questions about such forms as the "poem" and the "scholarly essay" by providing readers with typographical and conceptual elements commonly associated with both forms and combining them in such a way that readers might be drawn constantly to question what the piece "is" or might be. Bernstein invites this sort of questioning when he writes, "If there's a temptation to read the long essay-in-verse ["Artifice of Absorption"] which follows these opening notes, as prose, I hope there will be an equally strong temptation to read the succeeding prose as if it were poetry" (3). Such potentially subversive modes of reading, Bernstein suggests, might allow readers to move beyond the "frustratingly superficial or partial" readings characteristic of current critical-interpretive practice (9). Throughout the rest of "Artifice of Absorption," Bernstein returns in numerous ways to a fascinating point: that writing and reading constitute a constant dialectic between "absorptive" and "anti-absorptive" practices. In other words, writers and readers are drawn, on one hand, to absorb themselves in texts, to acquiesce to those texts' ideologies and assumptions, and on the other hand to resist those very same ideologies and assumptions.

It is also worth noting that Bernstein's book exhibits other traits associated (by Shetley and Holden) with the Language Poets. For example, while Bernstein rejects the (apparently) antitheoretical posturings of New Critical humanism, he does not exactly embrace postmodern theories simply because they call New Critical humanism into question. In fact, Bernstein rejects radical postmodernism's denial of the possibility for textual meaning (92–93). He also seeks to rescue Modernism from its "gutted" form, its common academic representation as a culturally conservative project. Such a representation is only possible, Bernstein claims, if Modernism's "more formally radical and avant-garde directions not only among excluded poets but, significantly, within the poets canonized" are "purged" (94). Bernstein locates the roots of his own poetic practice—and the practice of other poets he admires—in the Modernist experiments of writers like Gertrude Stein. He seeks a relationship between poetry and its readers similar to that which some of the early Modernists maintained.[6]

As I mention earlier, both the New Formalists and the Language Poets define themselves in opposition to so-called mainstream poets. The mainstream poetic sensibility, as characterized by New Formalists and Language Poets, values personal insight revealed in free-verse lyric poems. The value of a mainstream poem, in this scheme, largely rests upon the likability and believability of the poem's central speaking persona—its "I"—and the extent to which this "I" can make observations based on personal experience. The Language Poets are suspicious of this mainstream "I" because it tends to position itself outside of society and politics, to create an observation point supposedly exempt from forces outside of itself. In other words, Language Poets reject the notion of a unified, coherent "self," upon which mainstream poetics is supposedly based. The New Formalists, on the other hand, oppose the mainstream because they do not believe this "I," by itself, can be the basis of a good poem if the poet is not also skilled at employing traditional poetic devices and working in traditional poetic forms. This characterization of the poetic mainstream (against which Language Poets and New Formalists define themselves) may be somewhat reductive. But there are some poet-critics willing to defend a notion of poetry based upon the personality of the poem's speaking subject; most often, these poet-critics embrace the institutional-conventional wisdom of creative writing.

Certainly, though, there are many poets in the mainstream—that is, those who publish in journals not identified with the New Formalist or Language Poetry movements—who challenge the notion that poetic value is determined by the genuineness of the poem's speaking subject and, in so doing, challenge the institutional-conventional wisdom of creative writing. In an essay entitled "Obscenery," Joe Wenderoth distances himself from arguments that valorize the unity and personality of the speaking poetic subject. Wenderoth scrutinizes a television commercial for Jockey underwear, a commercial that employs the term "genuine people": "The ad is not so much asserting that the product is magical, or that simply wearing Jockey underwear will bring about this kind of joyful security—no, there is a much more important and subtle assertion here, and that is *that there is a realm of genuine being, there is a genuine State,* and that not everyone is capable of maintaining a self in that realm, that State. . . . The ad is not much different—not different in essence—than most of the 'poems' written by Americans in the last thirty years" (32).[7] Wenderoth then provides detailed analyses of poems by William Stafford and Robert Hass, demonstrating how these poems, in effect, operate in a fashion similar to the Jockey ad. The poems differ from the ad only insofar as they cast the *poet* as the privileged keeper of the genuine realm, a figure who sees the danger of the genuine realm's dissolution (and the disintegration of the "I" who dwells there) and who ushers the poem's readers back into the safety of the genuine realm. The underwear ad, on the other hand, merely asserts the existence of the genuine realm and those who live within it (Wenderoth 33–35).[8]

"Poetic knowledge," as Wenderoth moves on to define it, stands in opposition to this assertion of the genuine State and the genuine personality. Poetic knowledge is articulated through what Wenderoth calls "obscenery." Here is his definition of the term and explanation of its significance: "Obscenery is a *view* on to the place of places, a view on to the emergence and standing of the fundamental—unownable—energies that both compose and make temporary our being. Obscenery is, then, necessarily ambiguous. But as Heidegger has put it: 'The ambiguity of poetic saying is not lax imprecision, but rather, the rigor of him who leaves what is . . . as it is.' . . . The *will* to poetic knowledge is not the will of an intact subject, but rather, is a violence toward the unity of that subject'" (Wenderoth 33). Poets who attempt to establish—or to protect—a "genuine" subjectivity in a "genuine" realm of being, according to Wenderoth, are actually *fleeing* from poetic knowledge. As such, these poets are engaged in the same sort of project as the makers of the Jockey underwear ad—a project that continually reinforces and re-creates the values of a materialist, consumer-centered culture.

Wenderoth ends his essay by challenging another commonplace position found in the discourse about creative writing—the position that institutionalization within creative writing programs is harmful to the enterprise of poetry writing. Perhaps this position is linked to the belief in a genuine, unified subjectivity as exemplified by some poets' assertions about what the "real" poet is; perhaps those who believe in such a subjectivity also believe it is necessarily harmed by exposure to institutions, since it operates best in the genuine realm, in direct experience of the "real world." In fact, most articulators and defenders of creative writing's institutional-conventional wisdom are cautious about, if not downright dismissive of, the placement of creative writing in institutions of higher education. But Wenderoth believes poetry-writing *belongs* in the university: "What is necessary now is not the poets' exodus from the university, but the renewed power of poetic speech—a revolutionary power, to be sure—*within* the university, which is to say, 'within the position' out of which social and historical activity unfolds" (35). For Wenderoth, poets' positions within the university are an advantage rather than a drawback, particularly at this historical and cultural moment.

Perhaps one of the most intriguing and unusual treatments of questions about the institutional position of poetry writing can be found in John Koethe's *Poetry at One Remove*. Koethe, like the vast majority of craft critics, is a "creative writer" employed as a college professor. Unlike most other craft critics, however, Koethe is not employed in an English department or a creative writing program; he is a professor of philosophy. Most of the essays in *Poetry at One Remove* explore both the tensions and the "kinship" between the enterprises of philosophy and poetry writing (1, 9) and attempt, tentatively at times, to explore how the two enterprises can be mutually enriching. Koethe claims (justifiably, I believe) that his particular convergence of identities—poet, philosopher, professional academic—affords him an unusual and valuable vantage point from which to address key questions about creative textual production and its relationship to academic institutions.

Two essays in the book merit specific attention here. The first is "Contrary Impulses: The Tension between Poetry and Theory." This tension should be obvious to anyone familiar with the professional discourses of creative writing, as many creative writers—most notably D. W. Fenza, the executive director of AWP—have argued strenuously that theory is harmful to the enterprise of creative writing. Other creative writers, as the exchange at the beginning of this chapter indicates, are not exactly hostile to theory but raise questions about who ought to be authorized to "do" theory, under what circumstances, and according to what motivations. As a philosopher, Koethe is clearly not averse to theory, but he does recognize the (at least *apparent*) division that seems to exist between poetry and theory:

> A striking fact of our current literary culture is the estrangement between poets and critics and reviewers of contemporary poetry, on the one hand, and proponents of that loosely defined set of doctrines, methodologies, and interests that goes by the name of "theory," on the other. There are individual exceptions to this on both sides, and one can find counterexamples to every generalization I shall suggest here. Nevertheless, anyone familiar with the climates of opinion to be found in English and philosophy departments, poetry workshops and critical symposia, creative writing and cultural studies programs . . . has to acknowledge the lack of acquaintance and interest—and often even the disdain and contempt—that characterizes the relations between poets and those engaged in the kind of high-level, quasi-philosophical reflective activity that literature, and poetry in particular, used to occasion. (37)

Koethe is quite wise, I believe, to warn about the dangers of generalization, but I think he also quite subtly suggests that counterexamples to general trends are often proffered to prevent dialogue and debate about these issues from actually happening.

Koethe draws a distinction—one that he admits is perhaps too simple, but nonetheless useful—between "'institutional' and 'intrinsic' explanations" for the tension between poetry and theory (38). The former, of course, arise from the ways in which poetry and theory have been incorporated in academic structures like departments and course offerings, while the latter arise from the natures of the activities themselves. Although Koethe believes institutional tensions probably account for most of the apparent divide between poetry and theory, he is more interested (at least in the context of this essay) in intrinsic tensions between the two enterprises. Much of the tension stems, he believes, from "a difference in their attitudes toward the fact of the contingent basis of human communicative practices" (46), since, in Koethe's estimation, theory—at least in its common "deconstructive" form—tends to regard this contingency as a reason to disavow or invalidate communicative practices, while poetry—except in its retrograde "instrumental" form—attempts to accommodate the contingency and establish some sort of communicative possibility in spite of the obstacles. Koethe does believe it is possible to develop a poetics in which the two impulses are more cleanly integrated: "Such a poetics would neither reject the domain of subjectivity, as deconstruction does, nor try to incorporate it into the domain of the objective, as the poetics of authenticity tries to do. Unfortunately, this kind of poetics remains largely unformulated, and, given the institutional factors I described earlier, I am not terribly optimistic about its prospects" (49). Perhaps this pessimism is justified, but Koethe never explores the possibility that interested people might work to change these institutional factors and thereby open the possibility that a closer relationship between poetry and theory might come into being.

In the title essay of the collection, "Poetry at One Remove," Koethe continues his effort to establish a possible philosophical (or theoretical) basis for the act of poetic composition, and he addresses his own situation much more specifically. He writes, "The conception of poetry that animates my work is based on what I take to be the fundamental impulse underlying romanticism: the enactment and affirmation of subjectivity and the contestation of its inert, objective setting in a world that is emblematic of its annihilation" (111). Yet—and this is an extremely important caveat—Koethe does not take this form of romanticism literally, defining it instead as "a necessary illusion or fiction, a fiction to be affirmed and enacted in spite of the knowledge that it *is* a fiction" (111). In other words, he rationally accepts "theory's" critique of the poetic impulse but does not, as many theorists do, take the next step of fully disavowing that impulse. Regarding his own position as a creative writer operating within the academy but outside of an English department or creative writing program, Koethe believes he is at an advantage: "Central to my conception of poetry . . . is the notion of a freely assumed poetic identity as a subject of self-reflective consciousness, an authorial self that attempts to enact and portray that subjectivity in one's work. . . . But if one's poetic identity is in part a matter of an institutional role one occupies, there is always a danger that one will come to see it as externally imposed—in which case the relation between the authorial self and the work that flows from it will be altered" (113). I find this argument problematic, and perhaps even a bit disingenuous, since one might argue that Koethe's institutional role as an academic philosopher clearly has some kind of influence on his role as a poet. Further, it might also be argued that Koethe's sense of having "freely chosen" to be a poet is just as much an illusion as the romantic subjectivity whose illusoriness he acknowledges and celebrates. But this is neither the time nor the place to quibble with Koethe's argument. I contend instead that *Poetry at One Remove* is an important work because of the questions it asks and the way in which it grapples with those questions. Koethe is clearly a "craft critic"—a fine example of the term I have been trying to define throughout this chapter.

Up until this point, I have focused on craft criticism written by poets, but fiction writers too have engaged in this type of discourse. Perhaps most notable among these is Katharine Haake, whose *What Our Speech Disrupts: Feminism and Creative Writing Studies* stands as probably the most extensive attempt yet to infuse creative writing (and, perhaps more specifically, fiction writing) with the various discourses of "theory" that have exerted so much influence elsewhere in English studies. Haake challenges the rejection of theory that has so long characterized the institutional-conventional wisdom of creative writing, a rejection that has transformed "creativity" into an (anti)theory of its own, a notion that, for so-called real writers, writing happens naturally in a way that defies or eludes any kind of explanation: "Creativity is a dangerous theory because it is exclusive, because it sets the value we place on who is speaking, because it masks itself as natural, without a theory, and because it marks the manner by which texts move through the world. Having no theory is a dangerous theory because it reinscribes the structures we can't see that nonetheless contain us" (240). As the title of Haake's book suggests, her argument is motivated largely by feminist concerns, especially insofar as the anti-theory stance common to creative writing has almost always reinscribed a highly romanticized, and highly masculinized, concept of "the writer," even when women have attempted to use it to explain (or not explain) their own writing.

Haake's book is remarkable too for its deft combination of the "theoretical" and the "practical." In addition to theoretical speculation about writing —both Haake's and her students'—*What Our Speech Disrupts* includes classroom writing exercises derived from various theoretical principles. For instance, in a section of the book entitled "Self-Reflections and the Scene of Writing," Haake describes a two-part writing exercise, occasioned by her own experiences as a writer and a teacher and also by Linda Brodkey's essay "Modernism and the Scene(s) of Writing" and "by Foucault's questions about the modes of existence of a discourse, where and how it has been used, and who can use it" (192). In the first part of the assignment, students are asked to compose brief autobiographies of themselves as writers—to think back, in essence, to their own arrivals at the scene of writing. The second part of the assignment challenges student writers to place their experiences within historical, ideological, and cultural contexts: "Now, think about the garret where the genius (male) writer sits, authoring great literary works by the light of his thin gray candle. Where are you in this picture? What do you have to do to make yourself fit in at all? . . . What matters [in this exercise] is the dissonance created between your ideal image of a writer writing and you fumbling for words. What matters is how this dissonance makes obstacles to writing" (Haake 196–97). According to Haake, many of her students have first rebelled against this exercise but later come to appreciate the ways in which it brings them to a fuller and more productive self-consciousness of the ways in which their own writing experiences have moved within and against discursive constraints (192). And, like the vast majority of exercises and assignments in the book, this one, according to Haake, can "work" whether or not teachers and students want to delve into its theoretical background in feminist and postmodernist texts.

What Our Speech Disrupts also includes outlines for entire creative writing courses enlivened by theory. Most interesting among these is "Creative

Writing Studies . . . a graduate seminar in the theoretical, institutional, and poetic concerns of creative writers, especially (but not exclusively) as they may be experienced in academic settings" (225). This course represents the realization of what only a handful of academically employed creative writers (e.g., Patrick Bizzaro) have been arguing for recently: a greater willingness on the part of those institutionally defined as creative writers to acknowledge the crucial role that institutions have played in shaping who they are and what they do. If it seems unusual to append the word "studies" to "creative writing," that is only because creative writers have so frequently resisted such acknowledgment, preferring instead to regard their institutional position as purely incidental to what and who they are. But such a stance is becoming more and more untenable now, as Haake and the other craft critics I have considered here would probably all agree. Ultimately, what Haake's book does is radically challenge the notion of "craft" that operates within the institutional-conventional wisdom of creative writing.

Another good example of craft criticism by a fiction writer is novelist Charles Baxter's *Burning Down the House*—a collection of essays exploring the intersections between contemporary culture and the production of fiction. In the preface, Baxter writes, "Looking them over, I find that the essays [in this book] have a quality of slightly comic desperation, as if the house of the imagination had to be burned down in order for its contents to be revealed and its foundations made visible" (xi). This might be an apt metaphor for the philosophical approaches of thinkers like Heidegger, Foucault, Derrida, and many others. Indeed, though Baxter's essays are not steeped in the language of postmodern theory (they would probably strike most readers as more "familiar" than "academic"), they do attempt to dismantle many operative assumptions about fiction writing, and in so doing they challenge much of the institutional-conventional wisdom about creative writing. "In almost every essay in this book," Baxter writes, "I have tried to set forth a widespread belief or practice—the belief in Hell, for example, or the recent mania for happy endings and insight—as a precondition to the way in which storytellers . . . come up with narratives and then tell them" (xi). So while some influential figures in creative writing seem to recoil at the thought that some or many aspects of fictional or poetic composition may not fall within the realm of conscious choice by the writer (recall, e.g., D. W. Fenza's protestations that literary theory tends to make writers into mere conduits for outside forces),

Baxter thoughtfully examines the ways in which elements of culture inevitably color the choices writers make, often in ways writers may not be consciously aware of.

A couple of examples should suffice to illustrate Baxter's approach. In "Dysfunctional Narratives, or: 'Mistakes Were Made,'" he asks: "What difference does it make to writers of stories if public figures are denying their responsibility for their own actions? So what if they are, in effect, refusing to tell their own stories accurately? So what if the President of the United States is making himself out to be, of all things, a *victim*? Well, to make an obvious point, they create a climate in which social narratives are designed to be deliberately incoherent and misleading. Such narratives humiliate the act of storytelling" (5). Baxter goes on to argue that the conditions of people's everyday lives, both public and private, have made it increasingly difficult to employ a traditional narrative model in the telling of stories. Narratives become "dysfunctional" when their protagonists cannot be blamed in any satisfying sense for their wrongdoings or when their wrongdoings can be attributed to some other force or figure. Baxter sees this current running throughout contemporary American culture, not only in politicians' evasive explanations of their actions but also in the public representations of private lives, especially on daytime talk shows like those hosted by Oprah Winfrey and Montel Williams (12). But Baxter's is not a run-of-the-mill conservative lament about the coarseness of popular culture; indeed, he admits to watching daytime talk shows himself. Rather, he is attempting to explore conditions that frame the contexts in which fiction is written today, and he refuses to retreat into the safety of the notion that "real writers" are psychologically special, gifted individuals who are immune to the effects of the culture around them.

A second interesting speculation about the intersections of contemporary culture and fiction writing can be found in Baxter's essay entitled "Stillness." There, he asks the provocative question, "What conceivable relation is there between narrative violence and data processing?" (223). His answer, essentially, is that in a culture where information, especially through the medium of language, moves at an ever-increasing rate of speed, people find it easier to be "in touch" with violence than with stillness: "People who work all day at computers often get keyed up, tense, and anxious because of the speed of the information flow" (224). And this, he believes, has an inevitable effect on the way people are able to read (and, perhaps more important, to write) stories:

"It's just possible that benign stillness has become a condition in our time that everyone feels now and then but which almost no one can describe with much accuracy. This has everything to do with what adult readers will believe and accept about their own past experiences. My sense of these matters is that we have become remarkably fluent in our narratives in describing violence and complaint but timid and insecure in describing moments of repose. In the nineteenth century, the reverse was true" (231). What is most significant again here, I believe, is that Baxter implicitly rejects the idea that writers are, or can be, somehow separate or apart from the cultures and times in which they live. There is, in other words, no transhistorical writerly subjectivity shared by all writers of literary fiction. Subtly but deftly, then, Baxter suggests that "craft" in fiction writing is much more than most of the textbooks make it out to be.

Novelist Samuel R. Delany's "Remarks on Narrative and Technology, or Poetry and Truth" pursues some of these same issues, though often in more self-consciously "theoretical" language than Baxter's; Delany's is less a thesis-driven essay than a collection of observations whose interconnections readers are left to consider. Many of these observations deal with issues of creative production—both of fiction and of poetry—in a world dominated by science and technology. Most pertinent to the current context are Delany's remarks on the ways in which people form "expectations" for fiction—that is, how they learn to read it and write it. "Rarely," writes Delany, "have I been in a creative writing class that even mentioned them, much less talked about them at any length" (274). But it is crucial, Delany implies, that writers of fiction consider the way fictional expectations are formed, even though these expectations are complex and always changing and even though the writing of the past can only go so far in guiding the writing of the present: "While it is always good to know the history of the language you are speaking, and while that history will often tell you the reason why certain expectations are (or are not) still in place today . . . the great stories of the past hold the key to writing the great stories of today no more than an oration by Cicero will tell a modern politician the specifics of what to mention in his next sound-bite, even when Cicero and the modern politician can be seen as having similar problems" (274–75).

In other words, Delany (like Baxter) argues that knowing the tradition is important, but that tradition alone can never be a complete guide for contemporary writing practice because contemporary practice is always, whether the writer wills it or not, departing from tradition at the same time it is operating within tradition. Again, this is an implicit challenge to the notion, so central to the institutional-conventional wisdom of creative writing, that "the writer" of today is a subjectivity fundamentally the same as "the writer" of the past—a notion that perhaps explains why so many creative writing textbooks contain an apparently haphazard collection of "model" texts, often from different cultures, time periods, and contexts, without any apparent sense that those contexts need to be accounted for in order for the models to make any sort of sense to the aspiring writer of today.

The preceding examples should make clear that craft criticism is a site of both consensus and conflict, loosely united nonetheless in a challenge to the institutional-conventional wisdom of creative writing. All craft critics value the enterprise of creative writing. For one reason or another, all craft critics believe creative writing plays (or can play) a vital cultural role. And all craft critics are interested in determining and preserving creative writing's possible future(s).

Craft Criticism in Context

Craft criticism is part of a larger field of discourse about creative writing. Craft criticism emerges as an attempt to address some of the fundamental questions about poetry (and occasionally fiction) writing in a fashion that is consciously situated within historical, political, economic, and institutional realities. In craft criticism, dominant notions about creative writing are brought forth, sometimes to be discredited, but always to be questioned. One of the key words in almost any discussion of creative writing during the twentieth century has been *craft*. Exactly what this word means is a matter of contention, though a dominant (and, I contend, reductive) notion about craft does prevail in much of the discourse about creative writing, and this reductive notion is, in fact, central to the institutional-conventional wisdom of creative writing. Of course, this dominant notion is also challenged by many critics. Some of these challenges are noteworthy insofar as they do not pursue the "radical" (but ultimately easy) avenue of discarding the word *craft* entirely. Instead, they seek to redefine, expand, and enrich the possible meanings of the term.

Craft criticism, I believe, should be regarded as an emergent theoretical scholarship of creative writing—though I am aware some readers may find that assertion bold. One might argue, for instance, that what I am calling craft criticism is really just the latest in a long line of discourses about the production of poetry and literature, a line of succession that would include such landmarks as Poe's "The Philosophy of Composition," Shelley's "Defense of Poetry," the Preface to *Lyrical Ballads*, Aristotle's *Poetics*, and so on. Certainly craft criticism owes something to these works and others like them, but to regard craft criticism as simply a continuation of these works is, I believe, a mistake. Craft criticism is occasioned primarily by the migration in the twentieth century of fictional and poetic production into university settings; in other words, craft criticism is fundamentally rooted in academic, institutional conditions. I accept the argument that composition studies, rather than being a simple continuation of the ancient tradition of rhetoric, is a product largely of twentieth-century institutional conditions in America, and I am making the same claim for craft criticism. Insofar as they share a type of origin in common, then, craft criticism and composition studies might have something to say to each other if brought forth out of their institutional isolation.

Writing, Reading, Thinking and the Question Concerning Craft

> The Utopian writing program will be broad-based . . .
> abolishing the distinction between creative writing and
> composition. . . . Words such as *imagination* and *creativity*
> would be . . . replaced by *craft*.
>
> W. Ross Winterowd, *The English Department:*
> *A Personal and Institutional History*

"CRAFT" IS PROBABLY ONE OF THE central concepts—if not *the* central concept—within the professional discourses of creative writing. Yet "craft" is rarely ever explicitly defined and probably serves to connote a broad realm or, to borrow a phrase from Raymond Williams, a "structure of feeling." Much of what enables and drives craft criticism is the sense that the available and commonplace uses of the word *craft* are inadequate. In other words, craft criticism is based upon not only a concept of craft but also an interrogation of the prevailing definitions of craft. And perhaps no thinker offers stronger possibilities for opening up, questioning, and expanding the definition of craft than does Martin Heidegger—a figure widely cited by craft critics.

How, though, has the concept of craft become so problematic? The short answer to this question would be that the term *craft* has deteriorated, through its use in discourses about writing and art, into a rather reductive definition. Craft is an essential concept within the discourse about creative writing, but its meaning has usually been assumed or implied, rather than defined or articulated; in the process, its meaning has gradually eroded. It would be fascinating to analyze extensively the changing senses of the word *craft* in the discourse of creative writing, especially since the institution of creative writing programs in American universities early in the twentieth century, but that is not my project here. A brief overview should suffice.

Although the reductive sense of craft-as-technique is primarily an aspect of the institutional-conventional wisdom of creative writing, and thus largely a product of the twentieth century, it certainly has roots in earlier trends. The earliest fiction writers and poets who took academic jobs more out of economic necessity than out of any affinity for the academy were able to look to the past and find ideas that supported their developing sense of creative writing as an anti-academic enterprise existing in the academy only because the debased society outside the academy failed to allow poetry or fiction writing (except for a select few) to be a financially viable activity. Those who believed that being a "real writer" depends on a distinctive kind of natural talent, probably present at birth, certainly formed in its entirety long before one might become an academic, sought aesthetic theories compatible with such an ideological framework. And such theories were certainly available for those who might seek them.

The brief but helpful history of the concept of "craft" found in Carl Fehrman's *Poetic Creation: Inspiration or Craft* illustrates where the reductive sense of craft may have originated. After pointing out that the Romantic era, especially in Europe, marks the first time writers began to "manifest a significant interest in the genesis of individual works of art," Fehrman notes: "When writers, artists and musicians wish to indicate how a work of art is created, they often have recourse to images. It is possible to identify two recurrent types of image. One, prevalent in the aesthetics of romanticism, consists of images taken from the world of growth, from organic life. The other belongs to the world of craftsmanship, industry, and artifacts, and became common during the second half of the nineteenth century" (4). In other words, theories about poetic composition can be roughly divided into an "aesthetics of inspiration" and an "aesthetics of work." Fehrman's ambitious book, which examines the process of poetic creation from a number of theoretical and disciplinary standpoints, concludes that neither of these metaphors, by itself, suffices to explain the creation of poetry. But the "aesthetics of work" (i.e., the focus on the techniques employed by writers in their processes of composition) was to become the concept of craft as *nothing but* technique—as the technical or mechanical aspects of composition completely severed from invention, which remained in the realm of "inspiration," completely mysterious and entirely resistant to explanation.

Clearly then, the notion of poetry and fiction writing as "craft" belongs, at least originally, to Fehrman's second cluster of images. D. G. Myers suggests that the notion of writing as a craft became widespread in America some time around the beginning of the twentieth century, as publishers became more and more commercially oriented and writing, as a result, developed affiliations with business. In 1897, Myers notes, Katharine Lee Bates claimed that literature had become "a craft rather than a calling" (57). The profit motive had transformed writing into a type of work. The idea of the writing "workshop" also arose from this circumstance. The term *workshop* was first used in the late nineteenth century to describe drama classes at Harvard designed to "shorten a little the time of [the writer's] apprenticeship" (Myers 69). Because so many people clung to the notion that writers are born, not made, craft became virtually synonymous with the one small aspect of creative composition—technique—that these writers believed could be taught. In this way, the realm of craft, which may once have been conceived in a much more expansive sense, was dramatically narrowed. And as we have seen, the conceptual reduction of craft to technique establishes craft as a realm separate from that of talent; as the institutional-conventional wisdom of creative writing goes, writing talent is something pedagogy cannot confer, but craft can be productively taught to those who already have talent. This does not mean, however, that everyone who uses the term *craft* does so in a purely mechanistic or technical sense. Indeed, I hope to show that for some current poet-critics, the question of what constitutes poetic craft is very much an open one, and exploring it is taken to be one of the central intellectual tasks of the poet-critic. To make a very broad generalization: some creative writers are currently pursuing a notion of craft that includes but is by no means restricted to technique.

In chapter 2, I cite Joe Wenderoth's essay "Obscenery" as an example of craft criticism by a "mainstream" poet. In that essay, Wenderoth quotes Martin Heidegger on the topic of "poetic saying." In one regard, then, Wenderoth joins a number of contemporary poet-critics who invoke Heidegger as they explore the conditions surrounding contemporary poetic production. In fact,

Heidegger has been one of the theorists cited most frequently by American poet-critics during the last decade or so. This is not to say that Heidegger's work is relevant only to those interested in the composition of poetry, as the composition theorists discussed later will amply illustrate. Still, Heidegger has not yet seemed to draw as much interest from fiction writers as from poets. This may change in the future, and I believe the issues raised by the poet-critics in this chapter, especially in light of their similarities to the issues raised by composition theorists, are quite relevant to the entire enterprise of creative writing. Because Heidegger is becoming such an important figure for craft critics such as Wenderoth, and for some composition theorists, it will be helpful to provide a brief outline of Heidegger's work and to speculate about why it might be particularly appealing to certain poet-critics in contemporary America.

Heideggerian Thinking and the Problem of Writing

The work of Martin Heidegger is difficult to categorize. This is partly because his work radically challenges many received systems of categorization. Perhaps this challenging of categories helps explain why some contemporary poets, who for various reasons are wary of or hostile to received systems of categorization, find Heidegger's work amenable to their own projects. As I demonstrate in chapter 2, some poets feel that the situation of poetry in contemporary America has reached a crisis point in which poetry has no audience outside a narrowly cultivated academic/professional splinter group. Even if this perception is not entirely accurate, it remains, specterlike, haunting those who might wish to write poetry. "What are poets for in a destitute time?" (Heidegger, *PLT* 91) becomes a vital question.[1] Some poets choose to point the finger of blame at potential audiences for poetry (who presumably lack the aesthetic cultivation necessary to appreciate contemporary poetry), at "bad" poets (who produce so much incompetent verse that potentially receptive readers are turned off), or at the educational institutions that presumably produce both incompetent audiences and incompetent poets. Though I don't presume to speak for any of them, I suspect that those poet-critics who draw upon the work of Martin Heidegger find such positions more than a little off target.

It might be said that Martin Heidegger came to poetry by way of metaphysics, although the case could also be made for the opposite trajectory. As a young man, Heidegger published poems in Catholic journals in Germany (Ott 88–89) and later in his career produced "The Thinker as Poet," a philosophical meditation in verse form (*PLT* 1–14). Nonetheless, Heidegger is best known as a philosopher. The first work for which he received major attention, *Being and Time,* appeared in 1927. In this work, Heidegger sought to rescue the inaugural question of Western metaphysics—the question of Being—from the sediment that over two thousand years of metaphysical speculation had deposited upon it (*BT* 1–12). To do so, he began an analysis of the only "being" (or entity) capable of raising the question of "Being" or of interrogating its own existence. By this entity, Heidegger meant the *human* being, proposing the term *Da-sein* (which literally translates as "being-there") to denote this entity (*BT* 5–6). Through a phenomenological investigation of human consciousness—the manner in which human beings apprehend "the world" in which they live—Heidegger sought to rekindle the question of Being.

Being and Time was initially published as two thirds of a "Part 1," with the promise of a third section of Part 1 and a Part 2 (*BT* 35). These promised additions never appeared. Instead, Heidegger's thinking, and his method, underwent what many commentators call "the turn"—a shift in primary focus from *Da-sein* to *Sein,* or from the human being to Being itself. I would contend, though, that this idea of a "turn" is misleading,[2] since in one important regard, Heidegger's methodology remains the same throughout *Being and Time* and all of his later work. Specifically, what Heidegger does is to look to the "correct" (the everyday, commonsense, dominant conceptions about things) in order to find pathways to the "true" (the ontologically "primordial" essences of things). As Heidegger puts it himself: "All ontological inquiries into phenomena . . . must start from what everyday Da-sein 'says' about them. . . . Whenever we see something wrongly, a directive as to the primordial 'idea' of the phenomenon is also revealed" (*BT* 259). For Heidegger, the everyday, commonsense notions about things, while correct, tend to conceal far more than they reveal. And in many cases, what gets concealed is far more important, and far more essential, than what gets revealed.

In Heidegger's writings after *Being and Time,* poetry and poets often assume a vital role. In Heidegger's view, poetry (or at least a certain kind of poetry) stands in opposition to a disastrous tendency at the heart of Western metaphysics. Heidegger addresses this tendency from a number of perspectives and perhaps names it most clearly as "the essence of technology." In his 1955 essay "The Question Concerning Technology," Heidegger states flatly, "The essence of technology is by no means anything technological" (*QCT* 4). By this, he explains in his essay—and in many of his other late works—he means that the pervasive conception of "technology" as a collection of material artifacts (airplanes, automobiles, power plants, atomic bombs, etc.) produced as a result of scientific progress is fundamentally misleading. This "instrumental" view of technology grasps technology as a tool, as a means to an end. And while this view is undoubtedly "correct," it is by no means "true" (*QCT* 5). Here, then, we have a clear example of how Heidegger tends to make such distinctions. The instrumental view of technology blocks off the potential for human beings to grasp their own actual relationships to technology, because it leads them to confuse the *products* of technology with the *essence* of technology. This essence of technology is, in Heidegger's terms, "a mode of revealing" that , when it "holds sway . . . drives out every other possibility of revealing" (*QCT* 27).

To this essence of technology, this mode of revealing, Heidegger applies the name "Enframing." Enframing sets things "in order," so to speak, so that "everywhere everything is ordered to stand by, to be immediately at hand, indeed to stand there just so that it may be called for further ordering. Whatever is ordered about in this way has its own standing. We call it the standing-reserve" (*QCT* 17). As an example of this concept, Heidegger considers a hydroelectric power plant on the Rhine River. In response to the demand for electricity along the network of cables supplied by this power plant, the river itself becomes standing-reserve. It is ordered to stand on call, to become a supplier of electric power that is dispensed on demand. In response to the anticipated objection that the river nonetheless "is still a river in the landscape," Heidegger writes: "Perhaps. But how? In no other way than as an object on call for inspection by a tour group ordered there by the vacation industry" (*QCT* 16). The ultimate danger in this, according to Heidegger, is that eventually human beings will come to conceive of everything, including themselves, *only* as standing-reserve (*QCT* 27).

What does this have to do with poetry? Heidegger most likely would have answered this question by saying technology has everything to do with poetry. According to him, one of the dangerous strands running through

Western metaphysics is the notion of truth understood in a representational sense, that is, as an accurate representation (in language) of that which is outside language. Heidegger believed truth should be more properly understood in the sense of the Greek word *aletheia*, or, as he translates it, "unconcealment." The essence of technology acts to bring things out of concealment, to set them in order for future use, to reveal them as standing-reserve. But this is not the only possibility for revealing. In the sense of the Greek word *poiesis*, things may be brought out of concealment to stand "as they are," or in their own Being. This is the goal of poetry and, by extension, of all art. As such, poetry shares something in common with technology (because both are modes of revealing Being), but it also stands sharply in contrast to technology (because poetry and technology reveal Being in radically different ways). Poetry and technology, then, are crucial concerns for metaphysics, since any attempt to think the question of Being involves thinking it in some particular mode(s).

In essays such as "What Are Poets For?" (*PLT* 89–142) and "The Origin of the Work of Art" (*PLT* 15–87), Heidegger outlines various ways in which poetry (and certain poems) works to reveal Being, and he compares and contrasts these ways of revealing with those typified by modern technology and modern science. In a course of lectures delivered in 1951 and 1952, later published as *What Is Called Thinking?*, Heidegger further pursues the questions of poetry and technology, looking specifically at their relationships to thinking and language. Here he takes up the question of craft: "The cabinetmaker's craft was proposed as an example for our thinking because the common usage of the word 'craft' is restricted to human activities of that sort. However—it was specifically noted that what maintains and sustains even this handicraft is not the mere manipulation of tools, but the relatedness to wood" (*WCT* 23). Both poetry and thinking, for Heidegger, fall into the realm of craft. The poet's craft, from this perspective, not only entails the manipulation of linguistic "tools" like meter and rhyme but extends also into the poet's relationship to language. And this sort of definition of craft—expansive rather than reductive—is perhaps one reason why some contemporary poet-critics find Heidegger so appealing. For Heidegger's concept of craft eradicates the problematic and artificial distinction between craft and talent (and it may, in fact, eliminate the category of talent altogether or at least make it secondary rather than primary to craft).

The relationship between poetry and language is, in this scheme, a complex one, but Heidegger probably comes closest to explaining it succinctly as follows:

> According to the common view, both thought and poesy use language merely as their medium and means of expression, just as sculpture, painting, and music operate and express themselves in the medium of stone and wood and color and tone. . . . Thought and poesy never just use language to express themselves with its help; rather, thought and poesy are in themselves the originary, the essential, and therefore also the final speech that language speaks through the mouth of man [*sic*]. To speak language is totally different from employing language. Common speech merely employs language. This relation to language is just what constitutes its commonness. But because thought and, in a different way poesy, do not employ terms but speak words, therefore we are compelled, as soon as we set out on a way of thought, to give specific attention to what the word says. (*WCT* 128)

"Common speech," then (which would include virtually all scientific and philosophical discourse), operates in a realm where "the essence of technology" reigns. In this sort of discourse, language is viewed as a means to an end, an instrument with which to communicate or express meaning. The poet, though, actually attempts to allow language (an ontological category that encompasses all particular languages) to speak—or to be written—*through* her/him. Language is not a medium for the poet; the poet is a medium for language. This does not necessarily mean that the poet is a mere mouthpiece in the service of language; the poet is one who has done the hard work of breaking free from technological, instrumental thinking *in order to be able* to listen to language. While Heidegger's critique of technology and science, and his valorization of poets, might at first seem suspiciously akin to Romanticism, his version of the "poet" is not—at least as I read it—anything like that of the Romantics. For Heidegger, the poet is not an autonomous genius, a dispenser of wisdom and insight. Instead, the poet is a craftsperson, one who has learned the difficult art of listening to language and not forcing language to submit to intention.

Heidegger does not entirely discredit "scientific" ways of examining language, such as linguistics and philology, but he does warn that these types of inquiry are limited and that they cannot be taken as the only ways to examine language. Those interested in language must, according to Heidegger, pay attention to the ways in which poets explore language. While engaged in a close reading of a poem by Stefan George, Heidegger writes, "In a poem of such rank thinking is going on, and indeed thinking without science, without philosophy" (*OWL* 61). In poetry, we have access to realms of thinking that are not available in science and philosophy. In poetry, we can explore the possibility that "no thing *is* where the word is lacking. The word alone gives being to the thing. . . . The being of anything that is resides in the word. Therefore this statement holds true: Language is the house of Being" (*OWL* 62–63). Heidegger's theory of language is far more complex than my summary here can suggest, but I believe I have treated it in enough detail to suggest why it might catch the interest of contemporary poet-critics.

Despite the usefulness of Heidegger's work for those interested in theorizing about poetry, technology, language, and thinking, Heidegger himself is an extraordinarily problematic figure. In some circles, he is regarded as the greatest thinker of the twentieth century. In others, he rates as nothing more than a well-educated snake-oil salesman. Also, his personal political involvements cast long shadows across his work. In 1933, as a card-carrying member of Hitler's National Socialist Party, he delivered a rectoral address at the University of Freiburg that might be read as a ringing endorsement of Nazi policies. Though his relationship with the party soured soon after this, and he was later harshly critical of many of the Nazis' actions, he never publicly retreated from his statement that National Socialism had possessed an "inner greatness" that had been thoroughly perverted by "racial-biological ideologues" (Wolin 5).[3]

Heidegger's theories about poetry are also regarded by some commentators as problematic. Veronique Foti's *Heidegger and the Poets* outlines some of the potential problems with the ways in which Heidegger employs the work of certain poets, and the term *poetry,* to illustrate his ideas. Yet Foti's treatment of Heidegger is not dismissive. It is, rather, an attempt to work through some problems in order to arrive at a clearer understanding of the value of Heidegger's thinking. Despite any problems that might arise from this thinking, the fact remains that Heidegger has become an important theorist for a number of craft critics over the past decade or so. And his work has also drawn the attention of several composition theorists over the past two decades. So it is through this collection of writers—craft critics and composition theorists who draw upon the writings of Martin Heidegger—that I wish to begin exploring the possibility that creative writing and composition, despite being segregated from each other in many English departments, actually share a number of theoretical and pedagogical concerns.

Reading Heidegger, Writing Poetry, Theorizing Composition

There are a number of reasons why Heidegger might be an attractive theorist for craft critics. Foremost among these reasons, probably, is that Heidegger saw poetry as culturally and ontologically valuable—even more valuable than science, since poetry's realm is less limited than that of science. In an institutional setting where science virtually always garners more respect and prestige than poetry, a theorist like Heidegger offers craft critics a positive angle from which to examine the place of poetry writing within the university and within the larger culture the university serves. But Heidegger's high regard for poetry is not the only reason why craft critics might find his writings useful. Heidegger also enables broad-based inquiries into the relationship between poetry and technology, and these inquiries seem particularly urgent as technological developments such as the Internet transform, day by day, the conditions of language use.

To frame this issue in a slightly different way, I might note that Heidegger's writings allow craft critics to respond in unique ways to all of the basic questions of craft criticism. Regarding the question of process, Heidegger enables craft critics to explore the possibility that poems—as many poets claim —sometimes seem to "write themselves" rather than emerging as pure products of the poet's intention. Regarding the question of genre, Heidegger enables craft critics to pursue definitions of poetry that are not rooted entirely in formal phenomena like line breaks, rhyme, meter, or the poem's appearance on the printed page. Regarding the question of authorship, Heidegger enables craft critics to formulate a definition of "the poet" that is rooted neither in the individualistic, apolitical stances of Romanticism nor in the deterministic extremes of some literary theories. And finally, regarding the question of institutionality, Heidegger enables craft critics to think and write not only about how poetry has come to attain an almost irrelevant position in contemporary American intellectual (and general) culture but also about how poetry might regain some cultural importance and what role university creative writing programs might play in the process.

These broad questions—process, genre, authorship, institutionality—are also of interest to scholars in rhetoric and composition, although the focus of their investigations, and the ways in which the questions are framed, may at first glance look quite different from those of craft critics. Of course, this is due in part to the different institutional histories and trajectories of composition and creative writing. And the effective segregation of these two areas within many English departments cannot simply be ignored. It would be as large a mistake, though, to ignore potential similarities and points of overlap, points at which craft critics and composition theorists may be addressing the same problems, albeit from their own particular disciplinary perspectives. While I will consider the questions of process, genre, authorship, and institutionality, it is important to note that this way of dividing up the key concerns of craft criticism is one that I have devised for the sake of descriptive convenience. These questions, as I indicate earlier, are broad and interrelated. The boundaries between them are fuzzy, and each question can, and often does, bleed over into the others. The investigations of the craft critics and composition theorists I will consider are not beholden to the "integrity" of these questions; they do, however, touch upon these questions in the process of broader investigations, so the questions do serve as one possible way to organize an initial exploration of the similarities between craft criticism and composition theory.

On the Question of Process

Sherod Santos begins a 1993 *American Poetry Review* essay by invoking Heidegger's *What Is Called Thinking?*[4] Santos writes, "And if, indeed, it's true that thinking lies closer to poetry than to science—by an 'abyss of essence,' as [Heidegger's] lectures conclude—then perhaps there's something to be learned about thinking, about which we presumably know little, by asking some questions about poetry, of which we presumably know a lot" (9). Santos's interest is that of the practicing, publishing poet and teacher of creative writing. He wants to describe, as effectively as possible, how poems come to get written; he is engaged, in other words, in a response to the question of process. He writes:

Since some form of thinking inevitably precedes the physical act of writing out a line of poetry, however automatic or spontaneous it seems, then our questions should probably begin with that period before the words are scratched to life. That is, what do we know beforehand when we sit down to write a poem? At what level is it consciously determined what our poem will think about? And when, in advance, we do already have a "subject" in mind, what does it mean, as so often happens, when the poem decides to pursue some wholly different inclination? Those questions all point to an ongoing problem poets face, the problem of choosing a subject: do we choose it, or does it choose us? (9)

Throughout his essay, Santos pursues the second alternative, the possibility that the poem writes the poet, not vice versa.

Santos knows that to pursue the issue in these terms seems both "rash" and "odd" (9, 11). He also knows that the view of poetry he is pursuing here stands "in apparent contradiction to that age-old advice handed out like gospel in our writing schools—'Write about what you know the best'" (9). This received bit of "common sense" in creative writing instruction assumes that the writer is a knowing subject *before* the composition of a poem and that the poem issues from this prior knowledge. Santos, though, relying on his own experience and the accounts of numerous other poets, reports, "We're most engaged . . . in those very moments when we're only discovering *as we write* what we're actually writing about" (9). This perspective renders the write-about-what-you-know commonplace virtually useless. In its place, the person who wishes to teach creative writing needs to figure out "how . . . one go[es] about putting oneself 'in the pull' of thinking" (10). Santos does not provide definitive answers for these questions. Perhaps he has taken to heart the Heideggerian notion, raised first in *Being and Time* and echoed throughout his later works, that asking questions is far more important than finding answers. Too quickly rushing toward answers, in this view, is the surest way to overlook the importance of questions.

This essay does contain, though, the seed of another potentially fascinating idea. Santos reports both Elizabeth Bishop and Richard Wilbur as having said, "It's impossible not to tell the truth in poetry" (11). This truth-telling is intimately related to the way subjects choose poets. According to Santos, poetry must tell the truth, "however incongruous, however insufferable the telling may be. Poetry, like dreaming, seems most intent on saying those very things we're most determined to hide—even from ourselves. Or, to put it more directly: The poem revises the poet, not the other way around" (11). But what kind of truth-telling is this, which poetry, *by itself*, seems compelled toward and which gives poets the sense that they are being written and revised by their poems? I would like to suggest that it is not truth understood in the sense of correspondence but rather truth understood, following Heidegger, as bringing something out of concealment, bringing it into the open. This truth is, in many cases, the truth of memory or, more precisely, of forgotten or unrecoverable memory. Santos compares the act of writing to the act of searching through memories of the past only to realize that "who we are is composed of what . . . we can never reclaim from the rubble. It may be that *that's* the thing which poets know, the presence of that marked, presiding loss, the thought beyond the reach of thought, the thought toward which our thoughts all turn when we're in the draught of thinking" (13). To cast this in a different set of terms, we might note that for Santos, poetry is that type of discourse in which a "self" attempts to think back to its own construction, or its own "birth," in the complex web of language, experience, and ideology. But this origin can never be thought exactly, since it always recedes from the poet who pursues it, and poems wind up serving as artifacts of these attempts at thinking.

Santos's account of the process of poetry seems to run remarkably parallel to Heidegger's accounts of thinking. In direct opposition to Hegel, Heidegger regards Western philosophy as a regression from the originary question of Being rather than a progression toward absolute truth. Philosophy and science, locked into a single mode of thinking, move toward truths that, though useful at times, close out other possibilities. Thinking in the "poetic" sense, on the other hand, is allowed to follow paths that are not modally predetermined. Poetic thinking works toward truths that have been forgotten or toward those that have not yet been imagined. Writing about what one "already knows" effectively locks the poet into a predetermined mode and tends to close off the possibility that the poet may discover something new during the process of writing. Santos's brief essay, then, raises some fascinating points that might be explored in more detail. Other craft critics, and some composition scholars, have already begun this work.

Perhaps the earliest attempt to explore the relevance of Heideggerian language theory to questions about the writing process (or processes) can be found in Paul Kameen's 1980 *Pre/Text* essay entitled "Rewording the Rhetoric of Composition." In 1980, college composition textbooks were probably still the richest available source of composition theory, and Kameen thus performs a rigorous analysis of many available textbooks in order to uncover the epistemological roots of the composition theories these textbooks espoused. Kameen finds three basic approaches, formalistic, self-based, and audience based (73), and argues that they all share a basic flaw: "In each of these approaches, radically different, contradictory even, as they might at first seem, the same end has been reached: the subordination of language to the service of something that supersedes it, whether that be our own thoughts, our own feelings, or the thoughts and feelings of others. These retreats to representational notions of language, for which words are harnessed to report, record or present some other, more important and distinctly separate reality, are not only unacceptable but unnecessary. For discourse is not grounded in forms or experience or audience; it engages all of these elements simultaneously" (81–82). Kameen goes on to argue that Heidegger's theories of language, as articulated in "Building Dwelling Thinking" (*PLT* 143–61), offer a possible alternative to composition process theories that subordinate language to some supposedly "higher" category (82–85). Though he relies more on Coleridge than Heidegger to make his case, Kameen clearly recognizes the potential of Heideggerian language theory to offer a way out of restrictive and reductive notions about how texts get written. And subsequent to Kameen's effort, several composition theorists have pursued the relevance of Heidegger to composition theory in more detail.

James L. Kinneavy's attempt to explore the relevance of Heidegger's thinking to the question of process in composition, for example, is similar in some basic ways to Sherod Santos's attempt to use the writings of Martin Heidegger as a means to explore the question of process in creative writing. Both Santos and Kinneavy exhibit dissatisfaction with "commonsense" notions about the writing process that proliferate in discussions about writing pedagogy. Santos wants to move beyond the common notion that poets and fiction writers should be taught to write about what they know, while Kinneavy wishes to move beyond the idea that the writing process begins when a writer begins the physical act of composing. Kinneavy's 1987 essay "The Process of Writing: A Philosophical Base in Hermeneutics" employs a single concept from Heidegger's *Being and Time* to address what Kinneavy perceives (at least in 1987) as a significant weakness within composition studies. Specifically, he notes that the "process movement," despite having provided significant pedagogical advantages, has taken concern with process to an extreme and has lost sight of the importance of the product that comes at the "end" of the process (1–2). Also, Kinneavy claims, composition scholars have never adequately theorized the process(es) of writing. Work by process theorists like Macrorie, Elbow, and Flower and Hayes all labors under the assumption that the writing process begins when the writer sets pencil to paper or fingers to keyboard. This, Kinneavy asserts, is "entirely too narrow a view of the process of writing" (2). So, in order to provide "a much more comprehensive notion of process" (2), Kinneavy turns to Heidegger's theory of interpretation in general and specifically to the concept of "forestructure," as outlined in *Being and Time*.

Kinneavy begins by addressing what might seem problematic to some readers; that is, he might seem to be subsuming production to interpretation (and, though he does not specifically make this point, he seems to be concerned not to put textual production at the service of textual interpretation, as literary studies often does). Kinneavy explains that for Heidegger, human understanding is always intimately bound up with interpretation in every realm of discourse and activity. Thus, Kinneavy claims, "I am not enlarging the area of interpretation or applying a reading theory to writing; rather, I am applying a general theory of interpretation to one kind of interpretation" (3). The "one kind of interpretation" to which Kinneavy refers is not the act of writing itself but rather that type of interpretation that is a necessary precondition for writing. It is also an inevitable precondition, as it is an integral part of our being as humans. And even calling it a *pre*condition might be somewhat misleading, because—as Kinneavy points out—interpretation-in-general and text production are related in a richly dialectical, rather than a strictly linear, fashion.

The name of this interpretation that is a precondition for writing (and for other things) is, in Heidegger's words, "the forestructure." Kinneavy notes that this word, along with those designating the forestructure's constituent parts—forehaving, foresight, and foreconception—loses something in the translation from German to English (3). Nonetheless, Kinneavy provides a concise, straightforward explanation of Heidegger's concept: "All interpretation must begin with the mental structure which the interpreter brings to the object being interpreted. Indeed, the interpreter has no other alternative but to interpret everything with the knowledge that he or she has" (3). The forestructure is simultaneously individual, cultural, and temporal. Each human being has her/his own forestructure. But the individual does not come to it alone; the forestructure is shaped both by the person's past and by the culture(s) in which s/he lives and has lived. As such, the forestructure is rooted *in* time, and it changes, sometimes dramatically, *over* time.

Kinneavy believes that Heidegger's concept of the forestructure is particularly applicable to composition theory (2, 3, 7). Specifically, it helps composition theorists understand that the writing process cannot be reduced to a sequence of strategies or techniques that can be applied by any writer in any composing situation. "In particular," Kinneavy writes, "it would militate against an almost monolithic notion floating in the journals that there is a single process underlying all invention, prewriting, and editing stages" (8). Ironically, Kinneavy himself attempts to provide a general(izable) description of the writing process, though he does not make this description into a prescription. He writes: "When an author wishes to write about something, to interpret that something to future readers, he or she brings to the act of writing a forestructure. This forestructure is constituted by the entire history of the author, including complex cultural conventions which have been assimilated. Against this background, the something which is to be written about is interpreted" (6). Although this scheme can be divided into the categories of the writer and the object written about, Kinneavy is quick to point out that neither he nor Heidegger wishes to divide the phenomenon and process of writing so simply. The interplay between writer and object is "dynamic" (6) and "circular" (7). The metaphor of "the hermeneutical circle" aids us in visualizing the dynamic nature of the process: "The metaphor should not at all suggest the closed system or internal heuristic methodologies which are sometimes read into the work of Emig, Elbow, Flower and Hayes, and others" (7). In other words, Kinneavy has invoked Heidegger's concept of the forestructure not so that he may provide a better *prescription* for the writing process than other scholars have but rather in order to arrive at a much richer *understanding* of the writing process. Kinneavy seeks to arrive at an understanding that "opposes a linear view of process that takes into account only the time a person sits down and turns out sequential prose, even if in different drafts. Egressions from the hermeneutic circle—or apparent egressions—may sometimes take hours or weeks or months, even years. They may entail reading entire books, lengthy laboratory experiments, interviews, and so on. The extemporaneous freshman theme, written to no one in particular, about nothing in particular, with no publishing medium considered, and in an information vacuum, cannot continue to be the assumed model for process or product" (9). It is fairly obvious, I think, that Kinneavy is not attempting to eliminate the freshman writing classroom as an arena for a consideration of process but rather to widen that arena considerably, to bring the concept of process outside the particular limitations of the first-year writing classroom. Like Sherod Santos, Kinneavy pursues a more capacious definition of process than the "common sense" of writing pedagogy seems to allow. This pedagogical common sense is manifested somewhat differently in composition than in creative writing, but I find the similarities between the projects of Santos and Kinneavy very striking.

On the Questions of Genre and Authorship

The questions of genre and authorship are perhaps the most likely ones to be bound together in craft criticism, since to ask *What is poetry?* or *What is fiction writing?* or *What is creative writing?* inevitably has some bearing on the questions *What is a poet?* and *What is a fiction writer?* and *What is a creative writer?* Within composition theory, likewise, *What is writing?* is integrally related to *What is a writer?* Several craft critics explore definitions of poetry and the poet by working through some of Heidegger's writings on these subjects. Wayne Dodd—poet, editor, and critic—cites Heidegger frequently in his collection entitled *Toward the End of the Century: Essays into Poetry.* Although Dodd's interests in this collection are many, his main purpose seems to be defining and defending "free verse." In one sense, Dodd's work might be considered a fresh perspective in the debate between the Language Poets and the New Formalists; that is, Dodd provides a spirited defense of the so-called mainstream that both the Language Poets and New Formalists demonize. Dodd's writing in this volume is often aphoristic and fragmentary. Though the parts of the book are called "essays," they often (at least to me) seem to lack—or perhaps resist—the type of thesis-driven coherence often associated with the essay. Instead, a number of arguments seem to swirl throughout the book—appearing, disappearing, and reappearing in the various different essays. Instead of concentrating on individual essays, then, I will attempt to provide an overview of how Dodd addresses several important points, particularly definitions of poetry and the poet.

Dodd, like Santos, advances the notion that poetry is characterized by truth-telling. He notes, for example, that poetry is a way, in a world enamored with lying, to attempt to tell the truth (5). What is the particular nature of this truth, though? On the very next page, Dodd writes that poetry is a way "to accept uncertainty" (6). Truth, for Dodd, entails just such an acceptance. The striving toward certainty, which characterizes such enterprises as philosophy and science, is actually—in Dodd's view—an attempt to escape from truth. But for Dodd, this striving toward certainty inheres not only in philosophy and science but also in received poetic forms, presumably metrical and rhythmic forms: "Western literature, like Western philosophy . . . has been obsessed with endings, giving ontological priority to form over process, the whole over its parts. In short, obsessed with metaphysics. Free verse, it seems to me, has been an attempt, at the level of the line, to break free from that obsession" (44). This is a point Dodd returns to again and again—that ideas, worldviews, and essences are inherent in generic forms. So to move from one particular type of "form," such as traditional metrical and rhyming poetry, to another, such as free verse, is to undergo a transformation in both epistemology and ontology.

Another of Dodd's major points is the relation of poetry (and poets) to language: "Poetry, it seems to me, is always, in its very essence, an exploration of language: I mean an engagement of its very nature, a venture into the very depths of its being" (70). He opposes poetry, then, to other types of "thinking about language" (presumably scientific and philosophical) that ignore language's role as "a creator of our humanness" (70). Language makes us inhabitants of a "double" world; we are both created by it and we create with it (70–71). This position is compatible with Bakhtin's theory of speech genres, and it is also compatible with Heidegger's theories on language and poetry. In other words, the poet (writer) is not an autonomous, self-determining subject, a subject entirely in control of language; neither is the poet entirely determined by language. Like Heidegger, Dodd argues for a notion of poetry as "an enactment of thinking itself: the mind in motion" (23). Dodd also rejects the "technological" mode of thinking that would reduce all things, including language, to their use-value. For him, poetry is "not so much a defining as a revealing" (24) and "more than mere meaning, more than mere use" (25).

Like Santos, Dodd seems to want to reclaim the word *craft* from the purely technical sense into which it has fallen. Perhaps he is most specific about this when he writes, in the midst of analyzing a poem: "We were not talking about clever poetic tricks, not about a mere crafty deftness by the poet. Of course by saying that I did not mean to suggest such matters should not be considered. Rather, I was reminding us that the subject was/is something more important than that, something that eludes, finally, all attempts to codify and define. My purpose was to insist that all systems (of scansion, for instance) must be judged against the living complexity of poems, not the other way around. We need a more flexible, a more subtle body of critical tools to talk about poetry with" (32–33).

While Dodd here seems wary of the received sense of the word *craft,* he is careful not to reject the word entirely. This suggests, I think, an attempt to expand and enrich the notion of "craft," an attempt that is obviously indebted to Heidegger; Dodd notes, for instance (using an unmistakably Heideggerian phrase), that a "successful" poem can be seen as an instance of "world worlding" (30). Poetry is that genre of writing, then, in which the being of the world is revealed rather than manipulated. The poet is the kind of writer who learns to listen to language and its rhythms instead of attempting to master and manipulate language in order to fulfill a predetermined purpose. For Dodd, then, the true nature of poetry and poets is to be found in free verse, which is a far more expansive and fluid realm than traditional fixed-form poetry.

The craft critic Joe Wenderoth, author of "Obscenery," is similar to Dodd in his resistance to defining poetry in easy formal terms. He differs from Dodd, though, insofar as he does not seek to replace a supposedly limited notion of poetic form with a more expansive one. To put this another way, Dodd and Wenderoth both might note that just because a piece of writing looks like a poem does not necessarily mean it is a poem. But the two critics would differ in precisely how they define what poetry really is. For Wenderoth, poetic thinking, enacted as it is in particular pieces of writing, entails stepping outside of comfortable notions about ourselves and our world, facing the possibility of our own dissolution. This dissolution may take many forms, one of which is death, but most often it involves the shattering of a stable sense of self-identity.

Wenderoth begins to dismantle the simplistic formal definition of poetry by looking at some of what gets published as poetry: "Many writers are called poets nowadays. If you are a famous fiction writer, for instance, *The New Yorker* will most likely be happy to publish your briefer more sentimental prose musings and call them, at your request, poems" (32).[5] Also, many writers who are nominally poets publish pieces that, for Wenderoth, look like poems on the page but have no real relationship to the power of poetic speech. Instead, they merely reaffirm commonplace and comfortable notions about ourselves and our world and function largely in the same fashion as many television commercials—asserting the existence of "genuine" human subjectivities within a "genuine State." To Wenderoth's way of thinking, poetry has an even more ambiguous relationship to traditional generic form than Wayne Dodd allows for. This is why Wenderoth can claim that certain passages from William Faulkner's novel *As I Lay Dying* are more "poetic" than "poems" by William Stafford and Robert Hass (33–34). And while many other critics might ascribe poetic qualities to Faulkner's novel because of the tonal modulations of its language or the occasional deviation from standard prose typography, Wenderoth locates the "poetic" instead in the kinds of possibilities entertained in Faulkner's writing.

Another contemporary American craft critic who utilizes the work of Martin Heidegger to explore the questions of genre and authorship is Heather McHugh, who has published a collection of critical essays entitled *Broken English: Poetry and Partiality*. As that title might suggest, one of the arguments McHugh pursues throughout her collection is that poems are fragmentary, not unified, as much traditional poetic theory might suggest. This idea is perhaps expressed most succinctly in the following passage: "All poetry is fragment: it is shaped by its breakages, at every turn. . . . A composed verse is the meeting of line and sentence, the advertent and the inadvertent: a succession of good turns done. The poem is not only a piece, like other pieces of art; it is a piece full of pieces" (75).

At those points when McHugh raises the question of where poetic fragments come from and how poets fashion them into poems, Heidegger's work becomes especially relevant to her. At the outset of an essay entitled "A Stranger's Way of Looking," she writes: "It is apparent that, while the seer may be solitary, the sayer requires an audience. This double impulse, both to and from others, drives—and divides—writing as it does writers. Not only do we have the feeling that every man [*sic*] is an island. But also, since Heidegger, an extra loneliness arises: even when we find conversant company, we come to entertain a modern suspicion: that language is the only one doing the talking" (41–42). For McHugh, the poet is both a seer and a sayer, "a combination of the watchman and Cassandra, the trained and the inspired, the social and the alien, the wished for and the rebuffed" (43–44). Torn between these apparently incompatible identities, the poet is explicitly *not* a unified self: "'The Self' as constituted begins to fall apart. . . . It turns into only *a* self, no longer definite in its article; no longer one's own or only, but one among many, some born, some made. And how is a self made? Like other entities (all entities are suspected of being verbal, after Heidegger) it is marked out, first; it is a matter of drawing the lines" (56). McHugh allows Heidegger's work to inform her own poetic theory, a theory that takes both "the poem" and "the self" to be *dis*unified entities. In this sense, McHugh's poetic theory is distinctively postmodern. It departs radically from other poetic theories that find unity in both the poem and the poet.

Like all of the other craft critics I have mentioned here, McHugh sees poetry as a realm marked by uncertainty, a realm in which intention and expectation are frequently subverted by language. As Santos also argues, poems and poets tend to drift toward—or get drawn toward—previously unthought possibilities. McHugh writes:

> The unsaid shapes itself in our imagination only at its boundary, where the said reaches its limits. To us the unsaid seems to surround the said and to extend endlessly outward from it. We feel that the said explies the unsaid, rather than implies it. Any poem, any work of art, negotiates this dubious relation. For part of the unsaid (that endless extent) is the world of non-words referred to by the said, a corresponding world, a matching world (just as for the extent of space there is thought to be a space of anti-matter, exactly matter's match). But we think of what surrounds as being bigger, by nature, than what it encloses; so intuitively we feel the unsaid is bigger than the said, and must contain not only the world to which the said refers, but more. (62)

Where Santos believes poems tend toward the unthinkable, McHugh believes they tend toward the unsaid. In both cases, language and thinking are not exactly the same thing, but they are related. And the work of the poet is to establish and delineate that relationship, but since that relationship itself belongs at least partly to the realm of the unthinkable/unsayable, poems (and poets) never exactly achieve the unity toward which they (seem to) strive. "Poetic thinking" plays across the boundaries of language and thus, in a Heideggerian sense, across the boundaries of metaphysics.

However abstract these notions may seem, it is important to note that they are rooted in the experience of writing poetry and of reading poetry as a writer. At one point, McHugh claims that she reads "as a grammatical crafter" (55). She rejects "the paint-by-numbers sense of craft, a craft of ease and foregone conclusions" (101). And elsewhere, in the preface to *Hinge and Sign: Poems, 1968–1993,* she describes her compositional habits this way: "I suppose I have a gift for listening to language before I make it listen to me: it's a habit of resisting habit, and keeps me (as I grow older and more patient) from some of the more presumptuous familiarities. As a daily aesthetic, it goes beyond rhetorical exercise: the main discipline is to keep finding life strange" (xiv–xv). For McHugh, then, the craft of writing is not merely mechanistic, not merely technical, though it certainly encompasses such apparently mundane things as grammar. Craft actually runs from the mundane to the metaphysical . . . and beyond.

These investigations of the questions of genre and authorship undertaken by Dodd, Wenderoth, and McHugh bear striking similarities to a 1993 essay—"The Phenomenology of Process"—by composition scholar Judith Halden-Sullivan. Halden-Sullivan claims that the following questions represent vital concerns for composition studies and that Heidegger's philosophy can help compositionists develop rich responses to these questions: "What is language? What is a human being's relation to language? How does thinking make this relation apparent? How do writing and its interpretation help characterize human beings as both historical and temporal?" (44). Scholars in composition have already come up with a diverse array of answers to these questions, yet they leave something to be desired: "Coming to prominence in a technological age, the field persists in imposing on an entity a scientific interpretive design: making the thing under discussion controllable for the human interpreter" (44). So while the craft critics discussed above fault other poets and poetic theorists for attempting (through the use of traditional forms or commonplace notions) to control the uncontrollable and thereby keep the realm of poetry stable, Halden-Sullivan levels a similar criticism at composition theorists who have sought to control and stabilize the realm of "writing" by devising rigid theories about writers and the writing process.

Halden-Sullivan pays close attention to Heidegger's analytic of Da-sein from *Being and Time* because this analytic provides a much-needed perspective on what happens in the writing classroom, especially from the perspectives of students. Noting that for students, the most obviously direct encounter with language occurs in the composition classroom, Halden-Sullivan writes: "Their thinking reverberates with their attachment to objects, family, friends, community, ethnicity, gender, race, tradition—their involvement with the totality of the world in which they find themselves. Revealing their engagement with the world and, in turn, with Being, their language should make them realize the extent to which they can participate and belong" (54). All of this is particularly important for Halden-Sullivan, who teaches "nontraditional" students, students whose families have low incomes, who may not speak English as a first language, and who have little if any experience writing "standard" English. Of such students, Halden-Sullivan writes: "These students lack a close association with *any* language that would help them reveal their own insights; hence, their repertoire of responses seems limited. Teachers inculcated in standard English usage and rhetorical traditions of development and organization sometimes judge these students as remedial—substandard learners whose expression needs 'fixing.' What they need, however, is experience: to be addressed by language in rich and complex ways and respond to it" (55). Heidegger's examinations of human consciousness, and his theories of language, provide for Halden-Sullivan a means both for understanding the situations of her students and for developing a pedagogy that will give these students meaningful experiences with language. Such meaningful experiences do not involve the attempt to control language by whittling reality down into term-paper-sized bits that can be definitively explicated in academic essays; this is particularly important for Halden-Sullivan's students, for whom "academic language" seems alien and coercive.

Halden-Sullivan reports that she organizes her first-year writing courses around the theme of "right action," having students read a wide variety of texts—from canonical to contemporary—and then asking them to "respond by making it clear who they are and how they stand in relation to the measures of right action these intricate texts support" (55–56). This approach is designed, Halden-Sullivan claims, to facilitate students' experiences with language and to allow them to reflect on those experiences. An important feature of this pedagogy is a relinquishing—by the teacher—of the will to control students' textual experiences and the various forms these may take: "In recognizing that uncovering and saying are fluid—indeed, slippery and elusive—modes of being, composition studies invites what was once left suppressed: mystery. For students, teachers, and scholars, standing open to the world and listening intently to the 'songs' it reveals are risky interpretive practices" (58). Such a view of writing, it seems to me, is one in which writing is allowed to find its own forms (i.e., to be what it "really" is) rather than having forms imposed on it. It is remarkably similar to the view of writing espoused by the craft critics discussed above.

On the Question of Institutionality

The question of institutionality—that is, of what happens to writing instruction (and writing itself) as it becomes woven into the fabric of institutions like colleges and universities—is, as I have already argued, one of the key questions of craft criticism. This question is addressed by craft critic Ann Lauterbach in a series of "columns" published in the *American Poetry Review*. Entitled "The Night Sky," these columns flout the generic conventions of columns, opinion pieces, or essays. This becomes evident at the beginning of the very first "Night Sky" piece, which begins with the following section heading, in bold print: "1. There is no Topic Sentence" ("Night Sky" 9). This clause bleeds into the first sentence of the section: "but perhaps one could be borrowed, like a pretty dress for a party which, once worn, changes the life of the one who borrowed it." This gives a small hint of what all "The Night Sky" pieces are like—evocative, metaphorical, typographically adventurous, and moving associatively from topic to topic. Lauterbach mentions Heidegger only once in these four pieces, and even then she does so only in passing. But interestingly enough, this occurs under the section heading "4. re: Topic Sentence": "The question Heidegger asked comes like a searchlight on a foggy shore: *what are poets for in a destitute time?* We seem to live within the parameters of a jaded and cowardly pragmatism, whose use-value equations have stripped our capacity to recognize persons not driven exclusively by market goals and their attendant signs of success. Poets are a special case within this generalization, since there still attaches to the *idea* of the poet a belief that poetry should be, is, exempt from market forces, from brute commerce and commodification" ("Night Sky IV" 36). Since, in effect, "there is no topic sentence," this is an ideal place—from the standpoint of my own investigation here—to begin looking at Lauterbach's columns. This is, as I have already mentioned, her only reference to Heidegger. But as a reader familiar with Heidegger, I find throughout Lauterbach's columns a remarkable evocation of many of Heidegger's concerns—with what happens to words and language over time; with the way "technology" mediates our relationship to language; and with the steady devaluation of poetry in an increasingly ordered, administered, hurried, technological world. This last concern is, of course, a larger version of the question of institutionality. In other words, the question about what happens to poetry production as a result of its institutionalization in creative writing programs, if explored in enough detail, eventually leads to speculation about how and why poetry production wound up in creative writing programs in the first place. In the passage quoted above, and in others throughout "The Night Sky" columns, Lauterbach suggests that poetry writing wound up a part of university creative writing programs because of the prevalent (though implicit) notion that that is where it belongs.

In the first "Night Sky" column, Lauterbach explores the economics of poetry production: "The economy of being a poet subverts the received relationship between ambition, money, and success. . . . People are disturbed when poets make a decent living as professors; they think it is some sort of bad joke (but of course newsworthy) when Allen Ginsberg sells his archive to a major university for big bucks, as if some breach of decorum had been committed. They are not equally bemused when movie stars, baseball players or television news commentators get millions upon millions for acting a part, playing ball, or reading the news" ("Night Sky" 13–14). In isolation, this passage may seem like little more than a complaint that poets are not made into celebrities as ballplayers and actors are. But Lauterbach notes elsewhere that poets can occasionally become celebrities, just not the kinds of celebrities who are showered with material riches. Her aim is not to bemoan the fact that poets rarely earn money writing poems but to explore why there is such a pervasive idea in this culture that poetry somehow exists outside the economic realities that envelop virtually everything else. On the surface, this idea may seem to reflect a deep and abiding respect for poetry. Its real effect, though, is to consign poetry to cultural irrelevance. Later in this same column, Lauterbach addresses poets directly: "You will annoy persons in the Real World.... They will find it utterly inscrutable that you wish to spend all your time puttering with the most ubiquitous, the least rare, and therefore least inherently valuable of all substances, *language*" (15).

The institutional consequences of this devaluation of language are explored in "The Night Sky II." Technological developments within an Americanized global society have contributed to the problem: "Television as an instrument of communication has virtually erased language not in the service of information or opinion (often a hybrid of the two). Literal language is language which flattens understanding and comprehension into subjects and categories, a rigid relation between sign and image, rendering imaginative interpretation something like obsolete" (13–14). Heidegger would have recognized this as a consequence of the spreading dominion of the essence of technology—the reduction of writing to the status of the standing-reserve. On an institutional level, Lauterbach points out, the teaching of writing is thus understood in a very narrow sense: "Many if not most of our students at City are first or second generation immigrants who speak one or more languages —Chinese, Spanish, French, Arabic, Korean, Japanese—and the view is they need to learn to read and write English as a special skill to help them get jobs; a young Afro-American woman who is teaching Composition calls this 'cash English'" ("Night Sky II" 14).[6] But composition teaching is not the only endeavor that suffers the burden of restrictive notions about writing. In her own creative writing classes, Lauterbach notes, she sees an increasing tendency for students, particularly those who are minorities, to feel obligated to write as representatives of their groups, to adopt a "rhetoric of racial identity.... This is a paradox, of course, where on the one hand you have an institutionalized approach to writing as self expression/reflection, and on the other you have a numbing reiteration of status quo assumptions about identity, in which true individual experience in and of language is somehow foresworn, lest it lead to independence of mind and spirit, a separation from the group" ("Night Sky II" 14).

Unwilling to accept status quo assumptions about language and identity, Lauterbach returns again and again to the question of what poets are for: "Is it one of our *jobs* to try to span, or notice, or illuminate, or articulate, the gap between private and public discourse and the activities associated with each?"

("Night Sky III" 20). This speculation about what the poet's "job" might be echoes Heidegger's question of what poets are for in a destitute time, and it also touches upon the complex web of relations between writing and economics. Perhaps the "answer" to this question, sought after but not reached, is the "topic sentence" after which Lauterbach also strives. But it is a sentence as yet unthought and unwritten.

The issue of how reductive but prevalent notions about writing become institutionalized, and how this in turn limits the possibility of "teaching writing," is an essential one in composition theorist Lynn Worsham's "The Question Concerning Invention: Hermeneutics and the Genesis of Writing." Worsham's article is a rich, extensive, and complex exploration of the relevance of Heidegger to composition theory. Unlike James Kinneavy, who takes a single concept from a single work by Heidegger and attempts to shed light on a particular problem in composition studies, Worsham considers Heidegger's entire collection of works and levels a critique of the very enterprise of composition studies. Loosely speaking, she argues that composition studies, in its attempts to explain the writing process systematically and provide efficient means of managing the writing process, betrays itself as a distinctively scientific and technological enterprise rooted firmly within the assumptions and methodologies of Western science and philosophy. The writings of Martin Heidegger, particularly those from later in his career, provide for Worsham a viable means of critiquing this tendency in composition studies and for envisioning alternative structures for composition studies.

Worsham situates her critique within the context of one of the most vexing questions of composition studies: the question concerning invention. Stemming from ancient rhetorical theory, the question concerning invention asks how the rhetor devises, finds, or "invents" topics to address. This question, Worsham contends, "is an expansive one, opening onto further questions concerning the nature of thinking, the nature of creativity, and the meaning and uses of writing. But in the way that the field of composition studies formulates its answers, which are really one answer with different verses, different versions, it effectively forecloses any genuine questioning of its most intimate concerns" (198). Typically, Worsham notes, the question concerning invention can be approached from at least four perspectives. These perspectives are, first, "philosophical: *What* is it? What is its *essence?*" (199); second, "pedagogical: Can it be systematized and taught? How is it to be learned?" (200); third, "historical: How did it come to mean what it means? How did it come to be what it is?" (201); and fourth, "political: How has it been used to promote the interests of the discipline, or one particular sector within the discipline? How will it be used?" (201).

According to Worsham, "The question concerning invention has [already] been answered in the ['neoromantic'] distinction between the two senses of art" (201). The two senses of art (in this part of the discussion, Worsham draws heavily upon the works of Richard Young) seem at first to contradict one another. On one hand, art is conceived as an individual, mystical/magical, and unteachable process. On the other hand, it is conceived as a logical, systematizable, and teachable process. This apparent conflict is reconciled when art is divided into genesis and technique in a "neo-romantic view . . . [in which] only the skill or craft of writing, which devolves into 'mechanics,' can be taught, but never the process of genesis, which must remain free of any attempt to manage it" (199). This neoromantic answer to the question concerning invention, Worsham claims, "forecloses the question, takes us out of the question precisely when we need to be *in* the question in order to understand what it is asking" (201). Here, Worsham clearly echoes Heidegger's sense that the Western obsession with answers often leads us to abandon questions too quickly and therefore boxes us in to restrictive modes of thinking.

The consequences of this view for composition, as Worsham suggests, are predictable. The teachable part of writing, the "skill" or "craft," is reduced to mechanical elements like grammar and punctuation or, on somewhat larger levels, paragraphs and schemes of organization for argumentative essays. In creative writing, as I illustrate elsewhere, the teachable part is also reduced to technique, which becomes synonymous with craft. Worsham claims that such distinctions are "made available to us by a technological mode of thinking" (201). Just as Heidegger suggests that the question concerning Being needs to be reopened, Worsham claims that "it is necessary to again open up the question concerning invention, but in a more radical way, to the question of thinking and being human" (202). Without reopening the question concerning invention, we will be locked inside what Worsham calls "the technical interpretation of writing" (210). This technical interpretation reveals writing primarily as a type of "problem solving" (210) and closely aligns rhetoric with the "will to mastery" (211). In other words, the goal of writing instruction is seen as teaching students to master those processes that ensure effective communication. Or, put yet another way, students are urged to get language under control, to make it behave.

Worsham argues for an escape from the narrow technical view of writing. As a means for imagining a possible alternative, she turns to Heidegger's notion of a "Topology of Being" (218). Because this alternative is so far outside the customary ways of thinking about writing, Worsham can only outline it in vague terms.[7] She hopes, though, that "this approach may lead someday to a future for composition in a hermeneutical understanding of writing, one in which no method will guarantee that process yields product, one that will recognize neither truth nor knowledge apart from an endless process of concealing and revealing" (218). Because it occurs outside the bounds of technological thinking, such an approach to writing (and invention) cannot be judged on customary terms: "Heidegger's topology . . . [only] provides hints, clues, indications of the places where the event of meaning localizes itself" (219). These places correspond roughly to Heidegger's "existentalia" from *Being and Time,* which—designated here first by their German terms and followed by the loose translations Worsham provides—are *Befindlichkeit* (mood), *Verstehen* (understanding), and *Rede* (speech or language) (220). Probably the most important things to know about these three places on the topology are that no one is primary to, or derivable from, any other and that there is no way to get "outside" of them, so to speak. By working through this topology, Worsham attempts to remain within the question concerning invention long enough to (at least begin to) understand it in a way past writing theory has not done. She writes, "Once we enter the question that brings writing into being as *writing,* and not as a means to solve a problem or create or discover knowledge or express the self, we leave behind any adherence to system and technique, and we risk the on-going transformation of ourselves and our world" (235).

Worsham concludes her article by restating how the field of composition, deeply rooted within the technological mode of thinking, has strayed away from important questions by too quickly grasping after answers. This is evident, she claims, in the various ways through which composition teachers and scholars have addressed the so-called literacy crisis. Once considered "a crisis of skills," the literacy crisis has become, for some, a "crisis of content." Worsham sees the crisis as, at heart, a crisis neither of skills nor of content but rather a "crisis of involvement" (237). By involvement, she means a type of reflective care that allows us to question our world. Her concerns, then, are similar to those of Halden-Sullivan and other composition theorists who have resisted the notion that "at-risk" students or "basic writers" need to be ushered into the world of literacy via extensive drilling in the simple mechanics of language.

Lauterbach's and Worsham's investigations are more complex and far-reaching than these summaries may have suggested, but some striking similarities have nonetheless emerged. Their perspectives—derived at least in part from their institutional positions as poet-critic and composition theorist, respectively—differ in certain ways, but I see them as engaged in explorations of the same fundamental problems. Lauterbach is concerned with the way poetry and poets effectively exist at the margins of a technological society that takes language to be a tool employed toward various ends. Worsham is concerned with the way in which the "poetic" tendency of all writing (i.e., its potential to lead to discovery, to reveal previously unthought possibilities) is likewise marginalized, or placed beyond the realm of legitimate investigation, within the theory and practice of composition studies, which is largely driven by the institutional reality of skills-oriented required writing courses. Both Lauterbach and Worsham seek to reopen the question of what writing is (a question that has apparently already been answered, albeit in a very narrow and restrictive sense) in order to effect social, political, and institutional transformation.

Theorizing the Present, Practicing the Future . . . and Vice Versa

Though the creative writers and compositionists considered in this chapter begin from several different perspectives, and arrive at positions that are sometimes in conflict, they are all united insofar as they use Martin Heidegger's writings as a springboard for their own investigations. They all challenge commonsense views about writing—unarticulated and unquestioned assumptions that are inscribed within institutionalized forms of writing instruction. Like Heidegger, they actively question and challenge received boundaries, whether those boundaries are metaphysical or institutional. As such, these craft critics and composition theorists highlight a series of questions that are of equal interest to creative writers and compositionists alike. Some of these questions include: What is the writer's relationship to language? What is the relationship between writing and technology? What is the relationship between planning and discovery within any given act of writing? How have received ideas about writing, and the institutional structures in which these ideas are embodied, prevented us from discovering previously unthought possibilities? These questions and others mark out a territory of shared concern between creative writers and compositionists. And while it is not necessary to consult Heidegger in order to explore these questions, all of the writers considered in this chapter have found Heidegger's work useful, as a means either to begin or to extend their own investigations.

Heidegger is, of course, a problematic thinker for many of the reasons outlined above. Further, his thinking is often difficult to understand and follow, which makes it even more difficult to "apply" to (apparently) everyday, nuts-and-bolts problems regarding the teaching or practice of writing. Yet his thinking may very well enable writing theorists to address a problem that vexed English studies throughout the twentieth century and continues to do so. That is, Heidegger's thinking—precisely because of its "destructive" orientation—allows both creative writers and compositionists to confront and challenge the horribly limiting and counterproductive definitions of writing that have held sway both inside and outside the academy for so long. Many composition theorists have long argued against the notion that writing can be reduced to a set of "skills" that, once learned, can free people to move on to allegedly more complex forms of intellectual work. Nonetheless, a reductive, mechanistic, skills-based theory of writing still prevails in many quarters both inside and outside academia. Academic creative writers—or at least those who wittingly or unwittingly abide by the field's institutional-conventional wisdom—have perhaps been more complicit in backing themselves into an intellectual corner. By insisting that the origin of the creative work is beyond the realm of analysis, and by reducing "craft" to mere surface matters of technique, they have (often inadvertently, sometimes not) closed off the possibility that creative writing can be a field of intellectual inquiry rather than simply an activity or trade propped up by an institutional (and therefore economic) apparatus. Ultimately, then, the value of Martin Heidegger's theories about language, poetry, and technology—for creative writing and composition —may be that they open up a space where at least some creative writers and some compositionists can realize that despite their institutional segregation,

they both have faced their own version of the same basic problem: entrap-
ment within a large academic discipline that, because it is geared primarily
toward textual interpretation, has tended most often only to allow room for
theories of textual production that are reductive, misleading, and detrimental to pedagogy.

While I am suggesting that Heideggerian language theories already serve
as a site of confluence between craft criticism and composition theory, the
larger and more important point is that the connections outlined here should
open up the possibility that creative writers and compositionists might be
able to exploit such a confluence in the future if they are willing to continue
these kinds of investigations and explicitly link the fields of composition and
creative writing together. Though the compositionists cited here published
their work during the 1980s and 1990s, readers of more recent issues of *JAC*
have no doubt noticed that Heidegger seems to be garnering renewed attention
as a theorist. Graduate students and new professionals seeking to build theoretical bridges between composition and creative writing may find promising
avenues of research here. For example, reading Heidegger's work alongside
Walter Ong's "Writing Is a Technology That Restructures Thought" might
provide a fresh perspective on some of the central problems of Heidegger's
thinking. Perhaps Heidegger never fully understood the importance of the
fact that writing is a technology and therefore never pursued the possibility
that the spread of the essence of technology is largely enabled by the operation
of writing in literate societies. At the same time, however, Heidegger's so-
called poetic thinking (a kind of thinking perhaps characteristic of all "creative writing") might, in its own essence, be an attempt to recapture, through
writing, modes of thought obscured by the changes print literacy effects in
the human mind. Heidegger's fascination with the notion that "the danger"
and "the saving power" dwell together in the essence of technology may, in
other words, be continually enacted and animated through the very act of
writing. The sense that writing is an attempt to "get at" something that perpetually recedes from us may become most evident when writers practice
modes of thinking not compatible with a hyperliterate mindset.

To put this in a slightly different perspective, even if Heidegger's writings
are worth little in and of themselves for writing teachers and theorists, their
enduring value may well be that they lead people to a place where they can
begin to imagine a different future for English studies.

Terms of an Alliance

An entirely new conception of undergraduate literacy education, one based on the centrality of writing rather than literature, . . . will be, in fact, the alternative English major for the twenty-first century.

Robert J. Connors, "Afterword: 'Advanced Composition' and Advanced Writing"

CLEARLY, THERE ARE THEORETICAL concerns that might bring compositionists and creative writers together. Such theoretical concerns, however, are often not enough (at least by themselves) to effect widespread change within institutional structures. More specifically, the convergence between composition and creative writing may turn out to matter little if composition and creative writing continue to be marked off as separate territories within most English departments. At the end of chapter 1, I ask if an alliance between composition and creative writing might be possible and if it might be desirable. I think the answer to both questions is yes. However, I do not claim, nor do I believe, that such an alliance will be easy to bring about. For while there are certainly factors working in favor of such an alliance, there are also factors working against it.

Historical Entanglements

D. G. Myers, in the second chapter of *The Elephants Teach,* makes the provocative claim that what we now know as "creative writing" was initially called "English Composition." While this may seem to suggest an originary unity (subsequently lost) between composition and creative writing, it is important to note that Myers uses the term *composition* primarily to describe a type of course taught in English departments, not the field of scholarly inquiry that later arose in relation to this course. Indeed, Myers's history of creative writing ends at just around the time composition studies, as readers today would know it, was entering its infancy. Nonetheless, Myers's claim does highlight an important point: that creative writing and composition, having both developed under the umbrella of English studies, have from time to time been in close proximity, occasionally to the point of being almost indistinguishable from each other. These moments have tended to be fleeting, but those interested in the potential for an alliance between composition and creative writing might do well to revisit them for hints about the promises and potential pitfalls of seeking an alliance between the two fields.

The scholarly and administrative career of Norman Foerster marks perhaps one of the most significant and interesting moments in the history of the relationship between composition and creative writing. Foerster has the unusual distinction of being mentioned prominently by historians of all three of the major strands in English studies—Gerald Graff in literary studies, Sharon Crowley in composition studies, and Stephen Wilbers and D. G. Myers in creative writing. This is not surprising, since Foerster undeniably exercised an influence on all of these strands—though, ironically, almost never in quite the way he desired. Foerster's most commonly noted claim to fame is that he was the architect of the University of Iowa's creative writing program, although to call him that is probably misleading. He did, in fact, make it possible for graduate students to write "creative" theses for academic credit, but a close look at his career, as Crowley and Myers both point out, indicates that Foerster never intended for creative writing to be separated from other activities, such as criticism, with which he believed it was inextricably bound. Nor did he ever intend those activities to be separated from creative writing.

Probably the most cogent and concise exploration of Foerster's influence on the development of English studies can be found in R. M. Berry's "Theory,

Creative Writing, and the Impertinence of History." As Berry points out, Foerster was a key figure in the bitter struggle to define literary studies during the first several decades of the twentieth century. Foerster was a vocal partisan of "scholarship" and an enemy of "research."[1] As director of the University of Iowa's School of Letters during the 1930s, Foerster brought creative writing into the fold of English studies as part of a larger plan (never realized) to make English studies a potent and powerful force not only inside the academy but also outside the academy. Disdaining the practice of philology that had been imported from German research universities and had characterized literary studies in the United States during the late nineteenth century, Foerster attempted to develop a "letters curriculum" that would train aspiring English professors to be practicing creative writers, critics, and public intellectuals, though not necessarily "researchers."

Foerster's plan for curricular reform sprang from his "new humanist" cultural and political ideology. He believed that the "German doctorate," which stood at the institutional pinnacle of graduate school achievement, had served an important purpose in the nineteenth century but was becoming more and more dangerous in the twentieth. Specifically, Foerster feared that the tendency toward hyperspecialization fostered by graduate education did not help to produce the kinds of public intellectuals he thought the United States so desperately needed. In 1929, he wrote:

> At present the liberal college is being ground between the nether millstone of the secondary school and the upper millstone of the graduate school, the first two years being devoted largely to elementary studies and the last two to specialization looking toward graduate studies. If the nether millstone can be removed only very slowly, the upper can and should be removed at once. That is, instruction permeated with the current graduate aims and methods should be abandoned, along with the practice of specialization without sufficient cultural background in such fields as history, philosophy, science, and language and literature. (*American Scholar* 58)

Foerster thought graduate education in the German model drew students away from a direct engagement and experience with literature and, perhaps more important, prevented such an engagement from being disseminated throughout the culture at large. Foerster seems to have had a quasi-religious faith in the power of the "great books" to effect social change, if only they had the proper institutional framework from which to do so. He steadfastly maintained that public universities played a vital role in a democratic society, an argument he outlined in great detail in his 1937 book *The American State University: Its Relation to Democracy*. He argued that the "German doctorate," if it could not be entirely abandoned, should at least be supplemented by one more in keeping with the French model, which he believed was more genuinely "literary" (*American Scholar* 60–63). This, he believed, would foster a much deeper and broader base of knowledge for students, who might at some point become specialized, but never at the expense of extensive exposure to and practice in writing, both "critical" and "creative."

In retrospect, it can be argued that Foerster's victories were also his defeats. While he succeeded at making creative writing an institutionally acceptable mode of English studies, and also at helping "criticism" become the prevailing institutional form of literary studies, he failed miserably at holding the strands of the developing discipline together under his "new humanist" ideology—or any other ideology, for that matter. When Foerster resigned his position at the University of Iowa in 1944, finally tired of trying to implement his ambitious humanist core curriculum in the face of administrative and faculty opposition, the creative writing program he had helped to create moved quickly on in its own direction (Berry 67). Literary studies eventually moved in its own direction as well, away from creative writing and toward its own "theory wars" later in the century. We can only wonder how different these theory wars might have looked had Foerster's integrationist impulses taken firm root within the discipline during the early twentieth century.

From today's vantage point, Foerster seems an odd mixture of attributes. He was a cultural conservative like Lynne Cheney or William Bennett and an institutional radical something like James Berlin or Stephen North. For those interested at the present moment in a potential alliance between composition and creative writing, Foerster's institutional vision might, at least in part, be worthy of recuperation. At the same time, his career might also serve as a powerful lesson about the incredible inertial force of institutions. Foerster's work was successful only insofar as it was co-opted by institutional forces and changed into something Foerster himself would probably have never approved of, let alone recognized. His work occurred at a time when it may have been possible to bring "composition" and "creative writing" and "literature" together into some kind of cohesive whole. Current attempts by scholars and teachers to refigure English studies are in many ways an attempt to do the same thing —to move beyond some of the narrow concerns of literary studies without casting them aside completely. But any attempt to reconsider and reconfigure the operations of English departments now moves within the shadow of literary studies. The institutional structures of English studies, particularly as represented by undergraduate and graduate curricula, still most often reflect the notion that the primary intellectual activity of English studies is the interpretive study of literature from various time periods, eras, and (at least recently) parts of the world. Even though the idea that literary study should remain at the heart of English studies has been challenged by many scholars, reform plans are often hampered by or easily assimilated within the dominant structures of the discipline. Thus, it may be that genuine reform in English studies today can occur only if composition and creative writing band together to challenge the institutional dominance of literary study—just as creative writing and literary study, according to Myers, and at least partially at the behest of Foerster, banded together in the late nineteenth and early twentieth centuries to challenge the institutional dominance of philology.

Yet another interesting historical moment occurred later in the twentieth century, during the early stages of composition studies' development into a full-fledged field of academic inquiry. Composition studies, in its early incarnation as writing-process theory, may have harbored more potential for an alliance with creative writing than many historians have realized. Consider, for example, some of the early work of Janet Emig. In her *Composition in the University* chapter on process theory, Sharon Crowley notes in passing that an early Emig essay on unconscious dimensions of composing "appeared in an issue of [*College Composition and Communication*] sandwiched between pieces by poets Marvin Bell and William Stafford" (201). Crowley does not elaborate much on the possible significance of this fact, except perhaps to note that humanism (which Crowley, following D. G. Myers, takes to be an originating ideological element of creative writing) was among the "odd conflation of sources" from which Emig's process theory was derived (203). A closer look at the *College Composition and Communication* (*CCC*) issue in question, though, may be in order here. The theme of the February 1964 issue is "Composition as Art"; the issue purports to explore "the relationship of literature and film to written composition and the teaching of composition." The lead essay (just prior to Emig's "The Uses of the Unconscious in Composing") is Marvin

Bell's "Poetry and Freshman Composition." Perhaps more interesting today than Bell's vague but sensible discussion of the potential value of poetry in the composition classroom is the anecdote with which Bell begins his essay. Recalling his own experience as a student in first-year college composition, Bell describes his instructor as "uninspiring . . . and apparently concerned with lessons so fundamental and mechanical as to seem without significance." First-year composition, writes Bell, was boring, and so was his teacher. Toward the end of the semester, however, Bell discovered, to his surprise, that "my composition instructor was, in fact, a practicing, published novelist. Still, that realization seemed to make little difference. Composition was one thing; creative writing was another" (1). Bell's essay challenges this notion, but not very vigorously—which is to say that he does not seem as interested in examining the institutional structures that support such a conceptual division of writing as in offering a few suggestions about how poetry might make the college composition class a little less boring. In the Emig essay, which follows Bell's, many of the citations are to fiction writers and poets; these kinds of writers (creative writers) seem to be those to whom Emig turns to help develop a theory of the writing process—a theory that is aimed, in part, at remedying the dull, mechanical focus into which so many composition courses had lapsed. Given the fact that literary study was well established by 1964 as the conceptual center of English studies, it makes sense that a pioneering theorist like Emig might turn to "literary" writers to help develop a theory of composition. But since literary studies was (as it still is) firmly rooted within an interpretive methodology, Emig's concern with the writing, as opposed to merely the reading, of literary texts marked a significant departure from business as usual in English departments. It might be argued that Emig's early process theory was actually a theory of creative writing developed outside the institutional parameters of creative writing, where the institutional ethos then (as now) was resistant to theory. In other words, creative writing could have latched on to process theories like Emig's in the 1960s and 1970s, but it did not. Composition did, though it obviously moved in other directions in subsequent years.

A similar point about Emig and process theory can be found in Stephen Schreiner's 1997 essay "A Portrait of the Student as a Young Writer." Schreiner writes: "Emig tried to earn respect for the creative talents of the student of writing but did so by likening the writing process of the student to that of an established literary author. This view of composing would shape her famous monograph on *The Composing Processes of Twelfth Graders*" (87). Schreiner goes on to argue that Emig's influential notions about authorship limited composition scholarship and pedagogy because such notions apply well only to a limited number of students (100). As a field, composition largely moved away from such notions in the 1980s and 1990s, focusing more sharply on differences between writers, on rhetorical contexts for discourse production, and on the cultural and material dimensions of language use. For the most part, this movement has been beneficial for composition scholars and teachers of writing, as well as for students of composition. Unfortunately, though, this movement has pushed composition and creative writing away from each other, covering over the possibility that, at least in some cases, compositionists and creative writers might productively work together and masking the fact that there have been moments in the history of English studies where such collaborations could have taken place. Schreiner's and Crowley's accounts, because they are primarily concerned with the relationship between composition studies and literary studies, tend to obscure the possible connections between composition studies and creative writing.

Perhaps we are now in the midst of, or at least at the beginning of, another historical moment in which composition and creative writing are passing through each other's orbits yet again. A few scholars' exploratory investigations of the institutional history and structures of creative writing, along with an increase in "crossover" scholarship and the likelihood that a fair number of graduate students are moving (due to exigencies of the job market as well as intellectual curiosity) into composition studies from creative writing backgrounds, all suggest a potentially fertile historical moment. Whether the power of this moment can be harnessed to initiate genuine reform remains to be seen, of course, but for those persuaded by the general arguments of this book, I maintain that this is a moment that certainly should not be wasted.

Contemporary Territorialisms

On one level, academic disciplines are territories: bounded spaces where rules and customs operate and where dwellers (or at least some of them) guard against incursions by those from other territories. This territorial aspect of academic disciplines is perhaps the greatest barrier to reform in English studies and the greatest obstacle to a potential alliance between composition and creative writing. Within English studies, the issue of territorialism is more vexing and problematic than it might be in disciplines with more clearly defined objects of study and greater methodological uniformity. Here, the issue of whether English is a single discipline with a number of subdisciplines, or perhaps simply a number of different disciplines operating within the same academic department, becomes particularly relevant—at least insofar as it highlights the disputed nature of the territory, the ongoing disagreement about where the lines are (or ought to be) drawn. It is difficult to imagine such disputes taking place within, say, a chemistry department.

While I argue that territorialism poses a problem for those who might want to forge alliances between creative writing and composition, I do not believe that territorialism should be abandoned or overcome, at least not completely. Territorialism is part of the academic enterprise, without which certain kinds of academic work could not take place. In fact, an alliance between composition and creative writing will require a specific sort of strategic territorial thinking. It is probably useful, then, to draw a distinction between unconscious and conscious territorialisms. Unconscious territorialisms are those embedded so deeply within the structures of English studies that many are not even aware of their existence. That the debate over whether or not literary texts should be studied in first-year composition continues even today (or, more specifically, that some people still argue so passionately that literary texts should be studied in first-year composition, as if this were a self-evident truth) is compelling evidence of unconscious territorialism in English studies. There are, however, more subtle ways in which unconscious territorialism manifests itself, especially through what might be called "the interpretive bias" in English studies.

The fate of cultural studies in U.S. English departments provides an interesting example of what I mean. Earlier versions of cultural studies, particularly the version associated with Stuart Hall and the Birmingham Centre, while including a strong tendency toward the interpretive analysis of cultural artifacts, were also heavily infused with a spirit of extra-academic activism and an unashamed involvement in partisan politics. As such, cultural studies involved writing for, and involvement with, both academic and nonacademic audiences and thus required a high degree of rhetorical sophistication. In the United States, however, cultural studies was (for the most part) gobbled up quite easily by English departments deeply enmeshed in literary studies' unwavering commitment to interpretation. Thus, many professionals in English studies were easily able to claim—though not without some controversy—that what they had been doing all along was, in fact, cultural studies. Compositionists too saw radical potential in cultural studies, though the result, at least at the pedagogical level, was rather predictable. Popular composition texts like *Rereading America, Signs of Life in the U.S.A.,* and *Seeing and Writing,* while commendable insofar as they dramatically open up the category of "texts" available for analysis, are also very conservative, figuring students only as interpreters, and not as potential producers, of these texts.[2] To put this more bluntly, a number of popular composition pedagogies, as illustrated in the textbooks that support them, have been territorialized by the interpretive bias of literary studies. They are, in effect, occupied spaces.

In illustrating this unconscious territorialism and its attendant interpretive bias, I should make clear that I am *not* setting the stage for a banishment of interpretation from English studies. In practice, textual interpretation and production are deeply intermingled activities, such that it is virtually impossible to "do" one without also "doing" the other. All of the most visionary and far-reaching proposals to refigure English studies have recognized this reality. It is, however, possible to tilt the scales far too heavily in one direction, and it is my contention—a contention explored in detail at various points throughout this book—that the scales in English studies have been tilted far too much toward textual interpretation, even at those times when the texts in question are not "literary" in the traditional sense and even when they are not "texts" in the traditional sense. So although textual interpretation and textual production are always to some extent intermingled in English studies, most often they are not on equal footing. Production is figured as serving its institutional superior, interpretation. Daniel Mahala and Jody Swilky, who have written extensively about curricular and programmatic reform in English studies, note this trend when they point out that even though "new texts have been introduced" into English departments, "the focus has largely remained on interpretation in American literary and cultural studies" ("Geographical" 98). It is quite possible for reformist impulses to be contained within the discipline's existing boundaries, Mahala and Swilky warn: "The new progressive specialisms in English provide a rich intersection of concerns potentially capable of disrupting or renegotiating established geographies of service. However, no curricular 'content' provides a sure-fire transformation. Even 'radical' new curricula can end up marking class, gender, or racial boundaries in much the same ways as in the past, doing the work of the old genteel specialisms, albeit in a new, more fashionable guise. If curricula merely substitute Madonna for *Middlemarch* as an occasion for students to prove interpretive rigor or sophistication, reform is more apparent than real" ("Remapping" 643). In other words —using terminology invoked earlier—those who would reform English studies must think in both theoretical and structural terms. Theoretical change may look radical on the surface, but if it leaves existing structures untouched, it has been effectively neutralized.

The unconscious bias toward interpretation has so embedded itself in the fabric of English studies that even some scholars interested in the future of the discipline cannot see, or refuse to see, any other possible focus. Consider, for example, Eugene Goodheart's book *Does Literary Studies Have a Future?*, published in 1999. Despite its insightful and far-reaching discussion of the role of politics in literary studies, and its sensible critiques of extremists on both the "left" and the "right" in recent literary debates, this book makes no mention whatsoever of literary studies' institutional entanglement with the other strands of English studies. In fact, Goodheart's entire discussion proceeds as if it were possible to consider literary studies in an economic and institutional vacuum—as if, in fact, literary studies could even exist as it now does without its institutional and economic reliance on mandatory composition courses. On one level, the fact that a major university press would even consent to publish a book despite such a shortcoming should serve as evidence enough that powerful people in English studies still participate in the fantasy that the interpretive study of literature (or even the broader domain of "culture") can, by itself, justify the size of any given English department. If "fusion"- or "integration"-minded reformers believe they can overcome this brute fact merely by declaring all of English studies' constituent strands "equal," then they have a far more optimistic (or perhaps naive) view of the situation than I do.

Not all territorialisms are unconscious, however. Some are employed quite willingly and explicitly. Recall, for instance, the interview at the beginning of chapter 2, in which Reginald Gibbons and Theodore Weiss agree that a certain kind of theorizing should be acceptable for "creative writers" but not for "critics." The issue is territory: who is authorized to say what and under what conditions. Most often (unlike in the case of Gibbons and Weiss), these territorialisms are employed to maintain the dominant order in English studies, with literary study and/or interpretation at the top of the pecking order. Many of those scholars in literary studies who have (very wisely, in my estimation) begun seriously to investigate the institutional dimensions of literature still fail dramatically to account for literature's institutional entanglements with composition and creative writing. Two recently published collections of essays —*Day Late, Dollar Short* and *The Institution of Literature*—illustrate this trend. *Day Late, Dollar Short,* edited by Peter C. Herman, "seeks to explore the ways in which recent shifts in the material conditions affecting the academy have influenced the theory and praxis of the Next Generation of literary critics" (1). This is a laudable goal, and one might expect that among these material conditions would be the emergence of composition studies as a viable academic discipline and the growth of creative writing programs within the very departments of English that house literary studies. And one essay in the collection purports to examine exactly these things. David Galef's "Words, Words, Words" is a sort of "report" to literary scholars about what has been going on in the hinterlands of composition and creative writing. Comparing English studies to the stock market (with an appropriate touch of humor), Galef notes that composition and creative writing are on the rise. He even notes that the two fields may be headed for a "merger" (161)—as I have been arguing in this book that they should. For Galef, though, this is not exactly a positive development, since it poses a threat to the dominance of literary studies within English departments. Though he is not harshly critical, Galef seems to have his doubts about the validity of these two ascendant subfields within English studies. "Comp/rhet," he intimates, is more a "marketing" success (presumably by scholars) than it is a legitimate response to English departments' responsibilities for teaching writing (162). Creative writing, for its part, has cashed in on a retrograde cultural fascination with "narcissism" masquerading as "self expression" (170–71). Though Galef grudgingly acknowledges that composition and creative writing may have done a better job than literary studies of adapting themselves to the changing material conditions of the academy, he also seems to believe that their success damages literary studies irreparably. In short, Galef's vision of a future version of English studies where composition and creative writing have joined forces is dark and ambivalent.

And that, apparently, is as good as it gets in *Day Late, Dollar Short.* None of the other representatives of the so-called next generation of literary critics even mentions creative writing, and those who mention composition, or acknowledge those who work in it, do so in contemptuous and dismissive tones. Barbara Riebling, for example, excoriates Sharon Crowley for advocating (in her 1991 response essay in *Contending with Words*) what Riebling deems "coercive pedagogy" (181). One might reasonably wonder if Riebling's choice of Crowley as a target is a backhanded attempt to discredit Crowley, who perhaps as much as any other scholar has exposed the ways in which literary studies attained its institutional status in the twentieth century by building the size of English departments economically (though certainly not intellectually) around required first-year composition courses and propping the status of literary scholars on the backs of countless underpaid and underappreciated composition instructors. And while my interpretation of Riebling's argument may be a stretch, there can be little doubt about how another contributor to *Day Late, Dollar Short,* Sharon O'Dair, feels about the ascension of composition studies as a viable force within English departments. O'Dair bemoans the "star system" that has allowed a few literary scholars to achieve celebrity while most of the promising younger ones either cannot find jobs or must settle for dreary positions at "East Podunk" or "West Jesus State" ("Stars" 55). Composition, in O'Dair's universe, is a large part of the problem, since an increasing number of the tenure-track jobs in English are going to compositionists. Further, O'Dair claims, because the prospect of teaching composition, even occasionally, is "horrifying," most graduate students in English would rather take the risk of choosing a specialty that would qualify them for only one or two jobs in the entire country than specialize in composition. The reason? Because "teaching composition isn't fun or challenging" since—in dramatic departure from the allegedly idyllic days of the 1950s and 1960s—college students "cannot construct a coherent sentence" and therefore the teaching of composition "is—or should be—a matter of rudimentary drill, dull and dulling, although necessary and important" ("Stars" 50–51). Aside from demonstrating a troublesome contempt for students, O'Dair's account here indicates an appalling level of ignorance about the history of U.S. higher education in the twentieth century and the arrogance of believing that "rudimentary drill," despite all the evidence to the contrary, is the answer to the "literacy crisis," which is now allegedly worse than ever. Many of my own composition students, who have read and admired Mike Rose's accounts of these very issues in *Lives on the Boundary,* could easily dismantle O'Dair's argument. But my overall point here is not to dismiss O'Dair entirely (she does, after all, offer some cogent critiques of the star system and of tenure as an institution) but to suggest that she represents the continued and probably willful refusal on the part of many literary scholars even to recognize composition as anything other than dreary, deadening classroom experience with allegedly "inferior" students. If a diatribe like O'Dair's can be said to represent—in any way—the relationship of the "next generation" of literary scholars to their colleagues in composition studies, then I fear that the next generation of literary scholars is very much like the generations that preceded it.[3]

A similar lack of knowledge about (or at least acknowledgment of) composition and creative writing suffuses *The Institution of Literature,* another interesting essay collection about the material conditions facing present (and aspiring) literary scholars and theorists. Based on the idea that such scholars need to begin considering literature as an institution, rather than merely an extrainstitutional collection of texts, this book, in the words of editor Jeffrey J. Williams, "aims to demarcate salient pieces of the academic puzzle—the function of theory, professionalization, the job market—but one could also imagine companion volumes devoted to rhetoric and composition and the apportionment of labor it marks, or to creative writing and its growing place in English departments" (4). One could also imagine that a scholar making such a claim might actually wander out of the literature stacks in the library long enough to discover that such volumes—certainly with regard to composition and arguably with regard to creative writing—already exist! Yet again, it seems that the twentieth-century dominance of literary-styled interpretation over all other possible aspects of English studies can assert itself even when people are genuinely trying to find fresh and useful perspectives on the discipline at large. *The Institution of Literature,* like *Day Late, Dollar Short,* largely ignores creative writing while mentioning composition only in negative terms. Terry Caesar's thought-provoking essay on the hiring process in English studies, for instance, contains an anecdote about a failed search Caesar participated in as a committee member. The key villain in this melodrama, the committee's "most vexatious member," is described as "smitten at the time by composition theory" and as insisting on "ask[ing] every candidate about one particular theorist," about whom, apparently, none of the job candidates know anything (252). Subtly, then, composition theory is figured as an alien presence, inserting itself like a virus into proceedings that presumably would be better off without it. It is certainly not unreasonable to infer that most of the contributors to *Day Late, Dollar Short* and *The Institution of Literature* regard composition studies and creative writing similarly—as upstart intruders without which the formerly pure enterprise of literary studies would be better off.

Certainly, as I have already acknowledged, not everyone who might be called a "literature specialist" is blind to or ignorant of or alarmed by the importance of composition studies and creative writing. But the notion that literary studies is the rightful center of English studies clearly persists and seems quite difficult to challenge directly from within the discourses of literary studies. Thus, what is needed at this moment in English studies' institutional history, I believe, is not a "peace treaty" among literary studies, composition studies, and creative writing, but rather a concerted effort to alter one of the fundamental dynamics of the discipline at large. In other words, the goal must be to move English studies away from a structural model in which textual production tends to be valued primarily as a vehicle for textual interpretation and toward a structural model in which exactly the opposite is true. I must emphasize again, though, that my proposal would not involve the banishment of interpretation from English studies, nor would it involve the banishment of literature. It *would* involve a fundamental shift in the *reasons why* and the *ways in which* texts are interpreted and literature is studied. Teachers and scholars with backgrounds in literary studies could certainly participate in this reform movement, since at least a few of them might find it interesting to shift the disciplinary scales from interpretation to production. But since literary studies as an institution has shown no tendency to move in this direction, the project to refigure the discipline would almost certainly have to be led by compositionists and creative writers. At the very least, compositionists and creative writers will have to put aside their very significant professional differences long enough to realize that working together—toward a disciplinary reconfiguration of the relationship between textual production and textual interpretation—they can accomplish far more than they can by working separately.

In no way do I believe that this will be easy for everyone involved. Some compositionists and creative writers guard their territories assiduously not only against incursions by literary studies but also against incursions by other forms of writing studies. D. W. Fenza has for years, as executive director of the AWP, argued forcefully against the incursion of theory—certainly the kind associated with literary studies, but presumably also the kind associated with composition studies—into creative writing. Fenza prefers to regard programs in creative writing only as technique-oriented apprenticeships for writers aspiring toward the literary marketplace—not as explicit preparation for teaching careers and certainly not as proper places for systematic investigation of the social and institutional significance of creative text production. Some compositionists have displayed a parallel aversion to crossover work between composition and creative writing. Exploring these difficulties in a 1997 Conference on College Composition and Communication (CCCC) presentation entitled "Getting Past 'Killer Dichotomies': Reinscribing the Institutional Relationship of Composition and Creative Writing," George Kalamaras pointed out how the different institutional histories of composition and creative writing have led to the formation of stereotypes that hinder—though they do not prohibit—the possibility of any alliance between the two fields. These stereotypes lead compositionists to a narrow and reductive view of creative writing; likewise, they lead creative writers to a narrow and reductive view of composition. Many compositionists view creative writers as naive, anti-intellectual romanticists who flee from the rigors of academia into enclaves of like-minded colleagues and students. Many creative writers view compositionists as dull academic drones obsessed with rules and classifications for expository writing. For someone like Kalamaras, who is both a creative writer and a compositionist, these stereotypes are especially troubling, not only because they are reductive and misleading but also because they lead his colleagues who are more firmly "in" one area or the other to regard him with suspicion. Anyone attempting to build bridges between creative writing and composition, Kalamaras pointed out, must take these stereotypes into account and attempt both to work through them and to discredit them.

The continued operation (and perhaps the strategic, territorialistic use) of these stereotypes can be observed in attempts by some compositionists to defend their discipline's borders against any incursion by creative writers. Gary A. Olson, for instance, uses an "in memoriam" essay about James Kinneavy in the fall 1999 issue of *JAC* as an opportunity to launch an attack on the notion that writing might be taught "creatively." He writes:

> One might read the recent special issue of *College Composition and Communication* (51.1, 1999) as an opening salvo in what undoubtedly will come to be known as "the new theory wars." The attempt to drag composition

back to its expressivist roots constitutes a direct assault not only on a two-decade long tradition of substantive theoretical scholarship but also on a particular *kind* of work: that which attempts to lead the field *away* from a debilitating preoccupation with individual psychology, "genius," "talent," and "creativity" and *toward* a recognition of how and why dominant discourse enacts a kind of violence on people . . . who do not share fully in all of the privileges that society reserves for the few. ("James Kinneavy" 538)

I was particularly disturbed by this passage when I first read it because a brief article of mine, about craft criticism and its potential relationship to composition theory, is part of an "Interchange" in that *CCC* issue about composition studies and creative writing. And while I found myself agreeing with Olson that certain concepts found in the discourse of creative writing are "debilitating," I felt that his critique was directed at the wrong target. So I sent an e-mail message to Olson in which I objected to his characterization of the *CCC* issue. He responded almost immediately, noting that he had not intended for his criticism to apply to my article and suggesting that perhaps I should write a response essay to be considered for publication in *JAC*. I did so, arguing that my article and several others in the *CCC* issue in question actually aimed to do exactly the opposite of what Olson claimed. Olson's brief published response to me, along with a more fully developed version of his original argument (in the form of a CCCC Research Network Forum plenary address, later published as an article in *Composition Studies*), clarify his position somewhat. His main disagreement is apparently with Wendy Bishop's article in the *CCC* issue in question; if I read his argument charitably, he seems concerned that Bishop's article sets the tone for the entire issue, even if other authors do not share her argument.

In retrospect, I am disappointed by two aspects of this exchange. First, I am disappointed by Olson's inability or refusal to consider the institutional structure of English studies as a key element in any "theoretical" dispute. It is possible, for example, that his employment in a major doctoral degree–granting program allows him to demarcate where composition studies properly begins and ends much more clearly (though perhaps arbitrarily so) than people who work at other sorts of institutions. Second, I am disappointed that I did not clarify the issue more. Perhaps I should have made clearer from the start that I believe Olson's argument is as much about who—and under what institutional banner—is authorized to "do" theory as it is about which particular theories are espoused and "used" in English studies. At the same time, Olson's response to me, in which he points out that we may "actually agree on many substantive issues" ("Struggling" 454), leaves me hopeful that more people might, in the near future, be willing to confront and challenge institutionally sustained stereotypes—reductive and counterproductive—about different stands of English studies and those who work within (or between) them.

If some compositionists go too far in guarding the perceived boundaries of composition studies, perhaps others go too far (or at least in the wrong direction) in arguing for a blurring of such boundaries, especially those with literary studies. Johanna Schmertz's 2002 essay "Identity Wars: 'Passing' Through the Lit/Comp Gap" is perhaps the most interesting recent example of this trend. Schmertz's argument is framed within her experience as a "newbie" and a "retread" at the 1997 CCCC convention. Her most compelling memory of this conference is that compositionists, both established and emerging scholars, routinely made "anti-MLA jokes" and poked fun at literature faculty (61–62, 68). Schmertz reads these jokes as evidence that compositionists attempt to create a stable identity for their methodologically and intellectually disunified field by claiming a collective identity against literary studies. Ultimately, as an aspiring compositionist who was once a literature person herself, Schmertz finds this gesture unproductive and potentially harmful, as it causes her to want to embrace and defend her older identity as a literature specialist. She instead urges compositionists to practice the art of "passing" in order to bring their concerns to forums like the Modern Language Association (MLA). In so doing, she allies herself with W. Ross Winterowd's argument that compositionists should learn to use the MLA to advance their own agendas, a position Winterowd later abandoned (unfortunately, in Schmertz's view) in favor of a more aggressive press by compositionists to assert their power and demand prestige within English departments (Schmertz 76). I have several difficulties with Schmertz's argument, difficulties that lead me to embrace (unlike Schmertz) the "post-1997" Winterowd position as opposed to the "pre-1997" one. First, I believe Schmertz misunderstands the significance of anti-MLA sentiment among compositionists. While she is correct that telling jokes about literature people probably doesn't accomplish much, I think she vastly overestimates the extent to which these jokes are an identity-forming mechanism and vastly underestimates the extent to which they are a genuine expression of the subjugation felt by compositionists within English departments.[4] Second, I believe Schmertz overestimates the potential for "passing" activities to bring about productive change as long as the "privilege of unknowing" that accrues to literature faculty goes unchallenged. Finally, Schmertz, like so many other reform-minded scholars and teachers, implicitly accepts a binary and simplistic model of the division within English studies. She completely ignores the potential role creative writing might play in efforts to reform English. This is puzzling, as many graduate students and new professors have moved from literary studies to creative writing and in some cases from creative writing to composition studies—not only from literary to composition studies, as Schmertz has. Ultimately, I believe, compositionists and creative writers currently interested in reforming English studies ought to be very wary of the temptation to reconcile their fields with literary studies, given the probability that such reconciliation is only likely to reinforce the dominance of interpretation as the central methodological focus of the discipline.

What Is (or Can Be) "Writing Studies"?

If composition and creative writing are indeed poised for some kind of alliance, where might this alliance lead, and how might it transform the two fields as we now know them? Is it possible that a "new" field of inquiry may emerge if composition and creative writing are joined together? I can certainly imagine such a possibility, and I hope that many readers of this book can too. Composition and creative writing together may become "writing studies," a hybridized field of inquiry that bears traces of its origins but also exhibits significant differences from its predecessors. (Of course, the name "writing studies" is not new to this book. It is already in use at several visionary programs around the country.)

If the primary potential bridges between creative writers and compositionists are theoretical (in their shared concerns), the primary barriers are institutional, in the departmental structures that so often keep the two areas separate. Because first-year composition courses are usually required of all students, whereas creative writing courses are not, the institutional difference between the two enterprises is perhaps most obvious in introductory-level courses. Because students in creative writing courses, for one reason or another, *want* to be in those courses, they differ from many composition students, who are in those courses because they have to be or because they think those courses will be good for them. Creative writing students, then, are far more likely to think of themselves as writers and to enjoy writing. And while this may be true of a few composition students as well, they tend not to be surrounded by like-minded peers. Classroom dynamics in creative writing and composition courses thus tend to be very different.[5] Classroom differences, though, are symptoms or evidence of deeper differences—differences woven into the fabrics of each enterprise; differences arising from their separate institutional histories; differences that might not be overcome simply by adjusting particular institutional conditions, like, for instance, requiring all students to take a creative writing as well as a composition course. Historical investments, both theoretical and pedagogical, need to be examined, articulated, and questioned—though this does not, of course, mean that these investments must always be rejected.

Consider, for example, creative writing's persistent investment in romanticism. By "romanticism" here, I mean the belief that writing ability is fundamentally a matter of individual psychology or selfhood, something certain individuals are born with while others are not. Many creative writing teachers openly acknowledge this investment, claiming to help students find, through writing, their true, individual, and unique selves beneath the layers of corruption heaped upon them by society. Such teachers are likely to regard theory and criticism with disdain, as contaminants to the true and pure art of writing. Yet even when creative writers question this wisdom and reject the romantic, individualist notion of selfhood, they sometimes slip back into rhetoric that might reinforce such a notion. In the previous chapter, I quote with approval Heather McHugh's description of her writing habits: "I suppose I have a gift for listening to language before I make it listen to me: it's a habit of resisting habit, and it keeps me (as I grow older and more patient) from some of the more presumptuous familiarities. As a daily aesthetic, it goes beyond rhetorical exercise: the main discipline is to keep finding life strange" ("Preface" xiv–xv). Though McHugh elsewhere explicitly rejects the notion of a coherent and unified poetic self (*Broken English* 56), this particular passage might be read as saturated with romantic ideology—as in the poet having a "gift" that others do not have, "going beyond" everyday habits and rhetoric, in effect standing outside of the conditions that entrap so many others. I sincerely doubt that McHugh wants to paint such a picture of herself or of any poet. But perhaps the discourse about creative writing has been so thoroughly shot through with romanticism that romanticism emerges even sometimes when writers are trying to avoid it.

There is also another possibility. Perhaps McHugh is struggling to articulate her writing practice—to theorize—in a way that posits neither a self-contained, totally autonomous, prediscursive writing subject nor an entirely contained (and thus entirely constrained), socially constituted writing subject. In other words, McHugh's craft criticism—her writing about writing—may contain the basis of a theory that would allow us to move beyond the dichotomy between complete autonomy and complete constraint. Anis S. Bawarshi has called for the development and articulation of such a "theory of divergence" in composition studies, a theory in which "writers not only derive from generic, ideological, and discursive conventions, but also . . . diverge from these conventions" (80). According to Bawarshi, the seemingly irreconcilable divide between expressivism and social constructionism in composition studies is a symptom of the lack of such a "divergence theory," a theory that might allow elements of both expressivism and social constructionism to coexist. The new theory might draw upon, among other things, genre theory and creativity theory (Bawarshi 79–81). In light of the concerns I raise here, however, we might reasonably ask why the pursuit of such a theory should be limited to composition studies, since the craft critics I have considered would be well positioned to work toward such a theory as well and since such a theory would be helpful to the academic enterprise of creative writing. A theory (or theories) of text production that could "reconcile the autonomous self and the constituted self" (Bawarshi 80) might be a capstone achievement for a joint enterprise between composition and creative writing. With such a theory, it might become easier to recognize that while certain absolutist interpretations (and pedagogical applications) of autonomy and constitution are problematic, so too are reflex rejections of any form of such theories. In the insterstices between expressivism and social constructionism, between the supposed autonomy of "the writer" and the supposed dehumanizing nature of "theory," might lie an epistemology of writing that would be useful for both creative writing and composition—for writing studies in general.

The articulation of such an epistemology might certainly shed new light on some persistent problems in the discourses of creative writing. Creative writers—poets in particular—are often acutely aware of, and interested in, the association of writing with "mystery." I can think of no more adequate term here, though for my argument's sake I wish I could find one. But I would like to draw a very subtle distinction—between mystery and mystification. *Mystery* is any thing (or quality) hitherto unknown or unexpected, which the act of writing may touch upon, or suggest, or lead to, at any time. *Mystification* is the act of shrouding a writing process in calculated uncertainty. It is an assertion, in effect, that the generation of discourse cannot be explained, and it often contains the implicit or explicit admonition that any attempt at such explanation is counterproductive and dangerous to the generative process itself and should therefore not even be attempted or should be left to those who are incapable of accessing the generative process in the first place. Mystification is, in other words, the belated revenge of "poets" upon "critics." I use quotation marks here to indicate the way in which such identities become—so easily—essentialized. I have been clear throughout, I think, that I take such identities to be constructed (socially, politically, economically, institutionally) rather than essential or immanent to individuals, even though individuals may to some extent "choose" from among the identities made available to them. It follows, then, that any piece of writing is a constructed artifact—bound up inextricably with the constructed identities of its writer and the myriad forces (social, political, economical, institutional) that serve to construct those identities. But does it necessarily follow that everything within a given piece of writing can be explained (or explained away, as the case may be) in terms of these constructions? This is a question that concerns Paul H. Fry in *A Defense of Poetry: Reflections on the Occasion of Writing.* Fry's purpose is to define "literature" or, to put the matter more clearly, to define that particular element of texts that might be called "literary." In a complex (and at times perhaps even convoluted) argument, Fry repeatedly maintains that although virtually all linguistic activity bears the marks of its own social, ideological, historical, and political constructedness, and can therefore be *interpreted* in terms of these things, there still exists a phenomenon called "ostension" in which the act of writing occasionally hurls the writer (and by extension the reader) into an ontologically prehermeneutic realm—a "place" where there is no meaning, only existence. It is not appropriate here to debate the merits of Fry's argument.

But it is worth noting that Fry may be attempting to articulate something about writing for which there is no room, and no language, within interpretive literary study.

It is possible, I believe, to demystify the writing of poetry (or any kind of writing, for that matter) without closing off the pathways between writing and mystery. This will not be easy, but it might very well be one of the ongoing projects of the hybridized field of inquiry called writing studies. An early attempt to do just what I am suggesting here might be found in Patrick Bizzaro's *Responding to Student Poems: Applications of Critical Theory.* Bizzaro rightfully criticizes those who would purposely mystify the process(es) of poetic composition. But he shies away from the temptation to deny or erase the possibility that the writing of poetry may involve mystery:

> Naturally, many poets who teach students to write do not want to demystify the process of making a poem, which is not to say that they do not want their students to write well. Rather, they do not trust the language of pedagogy; the use of "methods" or "procedures" in helping students to write poems might seem to many practicing poets as contradictory at best and dishonest at worst. Who would deny that poetry arises from some mysterious source? No doubt most teachers of writing would agree that the most difficult gift from nature to duplicate through artificial means is talent.... Acknowledging the unique and special nature of poetry writing should not prevent us from making the necessary inquiries into what results in the most effective teaching of it. (xvi)

It appears that Bizzaro wants to cast aside an *effect* (the notion that poetic creation is unteachable) without casting aside the underlying *cause* (the assumption that "talent" is something natural or innate, something some people are born with while others are born without it). Having read Bizzaro's book, though, I wonder if he really believes in the adage that writers are born and not made. I wonder if he really believes in talent and mystery and all of their affiliated concepts and practices, handed down to us from Romanticism, still firmly anchored within the discourse of creative writing. Or does Bizzaro— as rhetorician—simply believe he is writing for an audience where questioning such things would be futile? Or does he, like the philosopher-poet John Koethe, regard the myths of romanticism as a necessary fiction to which the writer must temporarily and self-consciously submit in order to compose certain kinds of texts? Certainly these are all questions that could be explored in much more detail in the kind of writing studies I am envisioning here.

Bizzaro's hands-off approach to the question of the relationship of writing to mystery (which might also be called the question of talent or inspiration) is perhaps typical of those who would dare to venture into examinations of creative writing pedagogy. Joseph Moxley, as editor, begins the preface to *Creative Writing in America: Theory and Pedagogy* by writing, "This book is for high school and college teachers who are interested in how creative writing can be taught effectively" (xi). Yet he ends this preface by noting that his book "is not meant to be a cookbook for producing literary luminaries. . . . Inspiration, talent, originality—these are elusive qualities that teachers cannot dispense. Yet, to prepare our students to plumb the depths and mysteries of their own creative processes and talents, we must establish a supportive environment for experimentation and discovery; we must assure that we have provided students with knowledge of the composing process, the fundamental techniques of creative writing, literature and critical reading" (xxi). This is, of course, another version of the refrain that should be familiar to anyone conversant with this discourse of creative writing: We can't teach students to be creative writers, but we can teach them *something*. In Moxley's formulation, this something takes two forms—a supportive environment and a body of specialized knowledge. The environmental part seems self-explanatory enough: students must be offered the freedom to explore and discover their own talents and inspirations, presumably in a supportive and nonprescriptive manner. The knowledge part is worthy of some unpacking, for it includes two elements related to composing that might be considered both prescriptive and reductively technical. "Knowledge of *the* composing process" seems an ironic phrase coming from an author who appears to be arguing against prescriptive pedagogies. Presumably, if students are to be allowed to discover their own ways toward writing, wouldn't it make more sense to refer to composing process*es*? "Fundamental techniques of creative writing" also seems to imply prescriptiveness. At the same time, it tends to reduce creative writing to a purely technical level—much the same way that an exclusive focus on grammar and mechanics reduces composition to a purely technical level. "Literature and critical reading," the other two things about which creative writing students must be provided with knowledge, are of course those things that have been most consistently valorized in English studies. It is perhaps fitting, then, that an attempt at truly transformative inquiry gets wrapped right back into the orbit of English studies as it has so long existed—with composition and creative writing reduced to marginal and technical status while "literature" and the critical reading practices appropriate to it are placed in a superior position, toward which composition and creative writing should aspire but that they will never, ultimately, attain.

A crucial task for writing studies would be to go beyond Bizzaro's and Moxley's formulations, to throw the notion of talent, of a naturally occurring "voice" possessed by talented writers, and other related notions into question —to transform, rather than merely redescribe, English studies. But let me stop here for an important clarification. I do not mean that things like "talent" and "inspiration" and "voice" don't exist. I mean that perhaps they can be explained in less troublesome and problematic ways than they have been before. Talent, for instance, might be viewed not as something a few lucky people are born with, but rather as something that develops or is ingrained, perhaps at a very early age, in very idiosyncratic and at times apparently untraceable ways. "Voice," likewise, might be viewed not as the enactment in language of unique self-qualities or an individual's artistic vision, but rather as a rhetorical device developed through conscious or unconscious absorption of, or resistance to, other such rhetorical devices. "Finding one's voice," then—the dream of many dedicated students of creative writing—may be a rhetorical rather than a spiritual exercise. Perhaps it is far more akin to finding a couple of lost puzzle pieces than it is to discovering the Holy Grail.

Another of creative writing's problematic investments—the investment in formalism—is also worthy of exploration along these lines. In the previous chapter's discussion, this investment is probably most obvious in the writings of Wayne Dodd. Oddly enough, Dodd's formalism emerges while he is critiquing a formalism of another kind. Dodd runs into problems, I think, by suggesting throughout *Toward the End of the Century* that the poetic ideology he prefers—the acceptance of uncertainty rather than the striving toward formally predetermined certainty—inheres in the *form* of the free-verse line. In this, I believe Dodd falls victim to what Vernon Shetley—in critiquing both the Language Poets and the New Formalists—calls "that curiously persistent American poetic myth . . . that one might term 'technological determinism,' which takes the decision to write in 'open' or 'closed' forms as the crucial, defining poetic choice" (136). Dodd is clearly disturbed by the insistence of

New Formalists and other conservative critics that poets must return to received poetic forms in order to revitalize poetry. Perhaps he is also disturbed by the Language Poets' (and their academic admirers') apparent reduction of poetry to a mere instrument in a struggle for political transformation. So for these reasons, Dodd embarks on a defense of the mischaracterized poetic "mainstream." While he rightly bristles at the reductiveness of the critiques leveled at free verse, he makes a serious mistake, I think, by suggesting that certain ideologies always inhere in specific poetic forms.

But just as there are challenges, within craft criticism and within the professional discourses of creative writing, to the most extreme and absolutist forms of romanticism, so too are there challenges to absolute brands of formalism. Consider, for example, the following statements by Michael Heller:

> Our attempts to retreat into sincerity or advance into formalism (where art becomes the only category) are suddenly impoverished by our memory, our irony, and our sense of the artificiality of the categories. . . . Uncertainty has become the only promise which the activity of writing can guarantee. In this regard, it might well be the first duty of a writer to resist violently the culture's language games, including a duty to resist the fashionable romance of resistances which is often part of the ongoing mythologizing of one's times. Suddenly, vigilantly, the writer is required to employ a kind of knowing yet willed refusal, one which is still full with the knowledge of art and language. In such a knowing refusal, all language . . . again becomes completely available. (14)

Heller is suggesting that all forms must remain available to the poet because no ideology always inheres in any particular form. Rather, the function of forms changes along with changes in historical and material conditions. Heller's view of poetry, then, is far more rhetorical and far less formal than Dodd's. Heller continues: "The poet needs, it would seem, to cultivate, at minimum, a hypersensitivity to the 'mythologies' of poetic craft, including those narcotics we call beauty, harmony, symmetry. In this sense, the poet cannot afford to be merely a literary figure. [The poet's] field of activity is the entire language production of the available culture. . . . Indeed, a more complete understanding of rhetoric seems now to be essential to poesis" (15). So while Heller is clearly allied with others like Santos, McHugh, and Dodd in attempting to enrich and refigure the concept of poetic craft, he pursues an avenue none of these other critics does: the relation of poetic craft to rhetoric. To my mind, this is a potentially productive direction. Closer attention to rhetoric—to poetry's potential for persuasion or to the myriad variations in audiences for poetry, for example—would not force poets, in their institutional roles as teachers of creative writing, to abandon any concern with formalism. But it would certainly move formalism into a different context. Assuming a rhetorical perspective on poetic production would compel those in creative writing to consider poetry as a social practice, to consider the material conditions that regulate the publication of poetry, and to work through the consequences of these conditions for those who write poetry and those who read it. In short, the rhetorical perspective Heller argues for would align creative writers much more clearly with their colleagues in composition. Indeed, rhetoric (as Heller uses the term) would lie at the center of a writing studies created through the merging of the fields of composition and creative writing.

Individual Texts, Collective Consequences

That there is the potential for a theoretical convergence between composition and creative writing should now be virtually beyond dispute. The possibility exists that these two strands of English studies, if willing to cast aside institutional stereotypes, might engage in collaborative work—work that will be very significant to any attempt to refigure English studies and reform the English curriculum. If established institutional boundaries and practices in English are problematic, then they need to be questioned, resisted, challenged, and in some cases employed strategically. But how, precisely, can this be done in such a way as to achieve maximum effect? Anyone interested in change at institutional and curricular levels must pay particular attention to the mechanisms by which such change might take place and to the general assumptions underlying any particular program for change. Those working for change must pay attention, in other words, to both theoretical and structural matters. They also must attempt to find projects that harbor the promise of effecting significant change.

Many craft critics and composition theorists have, of course, begun to challenge some of English studies' commonplace assumptions and institutional boundaries. How might these challenges be channeled together to provide impetus for change? I will turn next to a composition theorist and a craft critic who endeavor not only to challenge institutional arrangements in English studies but also to consider how such challenges might be fashioned into workable programs for change. The similarities in their work suggest that reform-minded professionals in English studies should pay close attention to the way individual acts of resistance on the part of students and teachers can be wound together into reform programs that have a real chance of working.

In an essay entitled "Marxist Ideas in Composition Studies," Patricia Bizzell explores some of the possible consequences of challenges to institutional regulations. In so doing, she draws upon Henry Giroux's distinction between "opposition" and "resistance." Both are "deliberate subversions of routine," but opposition occurs "in isolation and without much reflection," while "acts of resistance encompass self-reflective and collective dimensions" (Bizzell, "Marxist" 61). Here is an example Bizzell uses to illustrate her point: "A break in the educational process happens when a student or teacher refuses to play by the rules and chooses instead to violate academic norms. For example, a student in a writing classroom submits a rambling personal narrative in place of the cogently argued essay the teacher asked for; or a teacher gives such a paper a high grade even though writing it may not have prepared the author for the impending multiple-choice grammar exit exam" (61). Such acts performed in isolation and without reflection would be oppositional, while if they were performed with a view toward how they might "become the basis for further action," they would be resistant (61). In other words, to press on a little further with this example, resistance in this case would require that either the teacher or the student (and probably both) consider the larger institutional context of the act(s) and how the act(s) might lead to change in the educational process.

What I find particularly interesting about Bizzell's scenario is that it leaves certain institutional boundaries intact even as it challenges others. Would the scenario be significantly different, I wonder, if in place of "rambling personal narrative," Bizzell had written, "poem," "short story," or "screenplay"? Personal narratives (though perhaps not rambling ones) are acceptable—and even required—in many composition courses, whereas the traditionally understood creative genres usually are not. Handing in a poem instead of a research paper might be an even sharper example of opposition (or resistance). Nonetheless, her larger point remains significant: Such acts cannot bring about institutional change if they are performed in isolation. Their significance would have to be addressed in many forums—in the classroom itself, in committee meetings regarding the curriculum, and at professional conferences and in journals. Those interested in opposition as a catalyst for change would need to pay close attention to how such individual acts might move English studies in particular directions over long periods of time.

Bob Perelman, a craft critic associated with the Language Poetry movement, is also interested in individual acts of resistance and their potential institutional consequences. Specifically, Perelman wishes to challenge traditional boundaries between poetry and prose, as well as to interrogate conceptual categories like literary history. He begins his book *The Marginalization of Poetry: Language Writing and Literary History* with a hybrid poem/essay called "The Marginalization of Poetry." This piece is—among other things—a sharply self-reflexive meditation on the relationship between poetry and academic discourse (specifically, literary criticism). Here is a selection:

> "The Marginalization of Poetry": the words
> themselves display the dominant *lingua franca*
>
> of the academic disciplines and, conversely,
> the abject object status of poetry:
>
> it's hard to think of any
> poem where the word "marginalization" occurs.
>
> It is being used here, but
> this may or may not be
>
> a poem: the couplets of six-
> word lines don't establish an audible
>
> rhythm; perhaps they aren't, to use
> the Calvinist mercantile metaphor, "earning" their

right to exist in their present
form—is this a line break

or am I simply chopping up
ineradicable prose? But to defend this

(poem) from its own attack, I'll
say that both the flush left

and irregular right margins constantly loom
as significant events, often interrupting what

I thought I was about to
write and making me write something

else entirely. Even though I'm going
back and rewriting, the problem still

reappears every six words. So this,
and every poem, is a marginal

work in a quite literal sense. (4)[6]

Perelman, by employing devices common to poetry and academic criticism, disrupts both categories even as he attempts to unite them. For example, he uses the word *marginal* in a far more literal and traditional sense than the one in which it is most often encountered within academic discourse today, and he also questions whether the simple act of using line breaks in a syllabic metrical scheme can make a piece of writing into a poem. While Perelman subjects the category of poetry to scrutiny, he also questions the apparently unitary conception of prose:

Do I really want to lump
The Closing of the American Mind,

Walter Jackson Bate's biography of Keats,

and *Anti-Oedipus* together and oppose them

to any poem which happens to

be written in lines? Doesn't this

essentialize poetry in a big way? (6)

Clearly, Perelman is challenging established categories, exploring the boundaries between poetry and prose and wondering if those very categories are accurate or useful in any sense. Without any kind of reflection or consideration of consequences, Bizzell might suggest, such an act is merely oppositional —an act of defiance without any institutional consequences. But Perelman is well aware of the limits of his own defiance. This is evident in his willingness to question his own practice in "The Marginalization of Poetry" and also in the more traditional (in appearance, at least) piece of commentary that follows it: an essay entitled "Language Writing and Literary History." Perelman begins this essay by acknowledging some of the problems facing a project such as his own. In a piece such as "The Marginalization of Poetry," Perelman admits, what the writer wants to do may not have much correlation with what is actually accomplished: "Literary history is normally a retrospective category of bureaucratic struggle and consensus, and not a site for active writing. Writers write and get sorted out later: good, bad, modernist, postmodernist, novelist, poet. But 'The Marginalization of Poetry' wants to reconfigure the categories of literary history. As a performative gesture such a task is, of course, chancy" (11).

Perelman also questions the potential effectiveness of his own practice by pointing out some of the barriers that might block the kinds of changes he envisions. "The Marginalization of Poetry," he points out,

creates an opposition, however ironically poised, between poetry that is timeless and criticism that is set firmly, even fashionably, in history. Yet the poem wants to unite the two spheres, and it ends with the hope that "a self-critical poetry . . . might dissolve the antinomies of marginality"— that it might redraw or undo generic boundaries between poetry and criticism. By displaying its arbitrary form, the piece is willful in challenging distinctions, claiming that, as far as genre is concerned, the act of writing confers an automatic power of definition. But the conditional "might dissolve" registers the difficulties. The rifts between poetry and criticism, writing and theory, are not easily spanned. Literature and creative-writing departments are well-established regimes that generate a continuing proliferation of marginalities, antinomies, and linguistic specializations. The spread of the self-fashioning of genre envisioned by the poem depends on more than any single act of modeling: it needs to be supplemented by many acts in many contexts. (11)

In one sense, Perelman here is challenging the myth of individualism, the notion that one person, if s/he really wants to and tries hard enough, can make a difference. Change, if it is to happen, must be sought collectively. But this does not mean that those interested in change must fall into lockstep with a group of identically minded others. In this specific case, that of Language Poetry and its relation to institutionalized literary history and creative writing programs, the Language Poets are not a cohesive enough group to formulate "a uniform literary program," but they do share enough in common, especially "aggressive dismissals of self-expressive mainstream poetics," to have brought about some degree of change (Perelman 12–13). The publication of Perelman's book by an Ivy League university press might serve as an indication of such change. Still, though, the persistence of the generic and institutional boundaries Perelman critiques indicates that the process of change is still, at best, underway.

Neither Bizzell nor Perelman raises the possibility of any alliance between creative writers and compositionists. Bizzell focuses on resistance and opposition only in the setting of the composition classroom (though she does ponder the significance of such acts beyond the walls of the academy) while Perelman concentrates exclusively on resistance to boundaries between creative writing and literature programs. Yet Bizzell and Perelman (intentionally or not) do open up a space in which alliances between creative writers and compositionists might be considered. Both would agree that changes in institutional habits and structures are unlikely to be brought about by heroic individuals standing up defiantly against an unacceptable system. Rather, change will be brought about—if at all—through reflective and collective action, through individuals who are able to recognize similarities between their own projects and those of others. If established institutional boundaries (like those between literature, composition, and creative writing) or regulatory concepts (like literary history) are to be effectively challenged, they must be challenged by interested groups of people with clear knowledge of the goals they strive toward. And since compositionists and creative writers share many of the same goals, such as challenging the dominance of interpretive literary study in many particular English departments, they seem compatible partners in any attempt to reform the curriculum. It seems possible that creative writers and compositionists, perhaps working together under the banner of writing studies, could examine local acts of opposition and attempts at curricular reform in order to determine their effectiveness. This, of course, would require communication across traditional disciplinary boundaries, which in itself might help to blur, and perhaps even eradicate, those boundaries.

Starting Somewhere

What may feel at any given moment like a small, localized effort to "move a mountain" can, over time, accu-
mulate into significant changes in the institutional
ecologies in which we work.

Jennifer Beech and Julie Lindquist, "The Work before Us:
Attending to English Departments' Poor Relations"

THROUGHOUT THIS BOOK, ONE OF my central claims—both implicit and
explicit—is that theoretical change in English studies, however radical and
interesting it may seem at any given moment, will never realize its potential
without accompanying structural change. The greatest danger in theoretical
reform proposals, in other words, is not that they will radically transform
English studies, but that by themselves they *cannot* transform English studies,
except in fleeting and illusory ways. Structural change, however, cannot take
place by itself. It must always have a theoretical, self-reflective component.
Thus, theoretical explorations—in this book the mapping out of potential
connections between composition theory and creative writing (particularly
craft criticism)—must continually lay the groundwork for structural change
in English studies. And in a very real sense, moving any reform proposal into
the structural realm is more "difficult" than any theoretical exploration could
ever be. In fact, the alleged "difficulty" of theory, which has been both derided

and celebrated within the various strands of English studies, has, at least in one sense, prevented whatever transformative potential theory may harbor from having been realized. In other words, the "theory wars" in English studies have been largely about how theory might (or might not) be "understood" or interpreted or how it might be used as an instrument for interpretation. The theory wars have never really touched upon the question of whether or not English studies ought to be primarily an interpretive field of inquiry in the first place. Here, I hope to overcome that limitation by outlining several ways in which theoretical and structural change within English studies might, in the short term and the long term, happen together and sustain each other. The "blueprints for change" that follow, then, should not be taken as an infallible map of where English studies should be headed, but rather as a constant reminder that any real or meaningful change within the discipline will have to take place at many sites; must involve the efforts of many committed individuals; and will touch upon every aspect of what English studies "is," both inside and outside the classroom. Certainly "theory," as enacted in the professional discourses of composition studies and creative writing, can lead to almost immediate changes in classroom practice, so my analysis here will include an overview of some changes that are possible now, that is, changes in the ways existing English courses are taught. But structural change cannot take place solely in classrooms; attendant changes are also necessary in curricula, hiring practices, and professional organizations.

The most productive and potentially valuable type of transformation, to my way of thinking, has already been enacted or is underway at a relative handful of institutions. I am referring here to those places where writing programs have become independent departments, severing their ties with English. Clearly, I believe, this is the best way for writing programs to flourish and develop and to prevent themselves from being territorialized either by literary studies or, more broadly, by the methodological dynamic of literary studies, where textual production becomes a service activity in support of textual interpretation. The departments and programs described in *A Field of Dreams: Independent Writing Programs and the Future of Composition Studies* (O'Neill, Crow, and Burton) are all excellent examples of independent writing units, but that volume also offers at least two cautionary notes. First, there is not yet (and may never be) a single structural or theoretical model for writing departments existing outside of English departments. Local conditions and the vagaries of institutional history often guide much of the decision making that goes into crafting a new department. Some independent writing departments bring together creative writing and composition and rhetoric; some do not. Some include areas such as journalism and linguistics; some do not. My argument, of course, suggests that creative writing and composition should be joined together wherever and whenever possible, but there are also many barriers to such a joining that cannot or will not be easily overcome, at least not immediately. The second caution offered by *A Field of Dreams* is that both the creation and the continued existence of independent writing departments often create stern opposition from literature faculty who consciously or unconsciously perceive such departments as a threat to their own interests and occasionally from administrators who do not understand the complicated historical dynamics that have led to the desire for independent writing departments in the first place. Chris Anson's compelling contribution to the volume narrates a case in which a highly regarded and successful independent writing program was taken back (or reterritorialized) by an English department while its director was away on sabbatical. Independent writing departments then, desirable as they may be, are not yet possible everywhere, and those nonetheless interested in change are left to decide what other options they may have.

One such option is a milder or less dramatic version of the independent writing department—that is, a minor or major "track" or "option" or "concentration" in writing existing *within* an English department. This option obviously appeals more to those who, for whatever reasons, believe writing courses and programs ought to remain part of English. And perhaps because it is less prone to drawing opposition, it may be an easier endeavor to undertake. Further, it certainly opens the door for a future independent writing department if it is successful in terms of student enrollment and interest. Here, however, I will be concerned with more immediate possibilities—the kinds of things interested readers may be able to pursue right now, whether or not they are also engaged in long-term curricular and departmental reform efforts. As Thomas P. Miller demonstrates so vividly in *The Formation of College English,* change often originates with individuals and groups laboring within localized conditions, attempting to meet the needs of varied student constituencies.

Change also takes place in a top-down fashion, administratively or departmentally. And ultimately, efforts are required at all levels to realize genuine change.

A Blueprint for Change, Part 1: In the Existing English Classroom

Creating new courses is one of the major ways of enacting change within academic departments, and indeed, my analysis suggests an extraordinary need for new courses to be created. Perhaps the richest existing guide to creating new courses in writing is *Coming of Age: The Advanced Writing Curriculum* (Shamoon et al.). Many of the courses described therein would make wonderful additions to most English or writing departments. But the creation of new courses often takes time, as anyone who has done so (or attempted to do so) can probably attest. It sometimes takes years for a well-designed course proposal to find its way onto a college's or university's list of available courses, and it often takes much longer for that course to find its way into the realm of a department's requirements for majors—if in fact it ever gets there. Also, there is always the danger that new courses added to a department's offerings will not have a significant impact on the way students come to understand the discipline's methodologies and subject matter; several of Gerald Graff's works warn that new course additions can become mere "cafeteria counter" items, or additional choices that exert no fundamental influence on the overarching disciplinary structure.

So while the development of new courses is essential to any program of disciplinary change, there must also be changes (sometimes more immediate ones) to existing courses. The following, then, considers how a convergence between composition studies and creative writing might transform classroom practices in three extremely common college-level English courses: (1) the required first-year composition course; (2) the introductory course in creative writing; and (3) the writing-about-literature course.[1] Thus, the changes suggested would be *theoretical* changes—changes that occur within established institutional boundaries and do not necessarily erase or blur those boundaries. But these changes would be intended to lay the groundwork for *structural* changes, in which institutional boundaries would be challenged and redrawn. In all of the following course descriptions, I will advocate the use of portfolios as a means of soliciting, responding to, and evaluating student writing, because portfolios are specifically geared toward revision and reflection as essential elements of students' writing processes; at the same time, I acknowledge that much of what I advocate here may be possible without the use of portfolios per se, as long as there is a significant element of self-reflexive writing built into any given course and as long as revision is emphasized as a key element of students' writing processes. All of these course descriptions are also guided by one basic principle—that the fundamental way to enact significant change within existing English courses is not to allow such courses to be arenas where the textual production of students is merely a means of showcasing textual interpretation. Traditionally, of course, this has been done in literature classes whenever the interpretation of literary texts is the only kind of writing solicited from students. But it has also often happened in composition classes—even in apparently progressive ones—whenever student writing focuses solely on the interpretation of "nonliterary" artifacts like television commercials, movies, clothing, and so on.

The Required First-Year Composition Course

For a number of reasons, the required first-year composition course may be the most difficult place to put into practice some of the basic notions discussed in this book. Many composition teachers have very little freedom to design their own syllabus and drive the agenda of the class; likewise, institutional structures also often make it difficult for teachers to adjust their pedagogies during the course of any given semester in order to respond more effectively to particular student needs. Composition scholars, however, have long recognized the required first-year course as a potentially transformative site, at least in those instances where teachers and/or students—individually or collectively—have the opportunity to drive the course's agenda. The required first-year composition course can be perhaps the most important site at which theory can be allowed to engage practice, since so many students must take the course and since the course can be a place where students' notions about English studies are formed, solidified, or altered. There are two basic ways in which questions at the intersection of creative writing and composition theory can become relevant to classroom practice in the required first-year writing course.

The first, ironically enough, concerns the point at which creative writing seems initially to have no relevance at all—the point at which a unit of the composition course (or frequently the entire course) focuses on "academic writing" in order to prepare students for writing tasks they will face later in their college careers. Since creative writing is a fundamentally different type of writing than academic writing, one line of thought might run, it can be of no relevance to a composition course that focuses on academic writing. Yet I would hope by now to have problematized such lines of thinking. As I have already demonstrated, several composition theorists' work (even when rooted within the framework of academic writing) is animated by the same questions and concerns as the work of several craft critics. One of the stickiest problems for all of these writers and scholars is the conflation of writing with form or technique—which Heidegger would take to be a revealing of "the essence of technology," which Worsham calls "the technical interpretation of writing," and which—in the context of creative writing theory and instruction —I call the reductive interpretation of craft. First-year composition courses, as Worsham suggests, are always in danger of falling into a strictly instrumentalist, technical interpretation of writing and thus of closing off the potential for students to glimpse the "poetic," revelatory, and heuristic possibilities in writing. Approaching the problem from a somewhat different perspective in *The Methodical Memory: Invention in Current-Traditional Rhetoric*, Sharon Crowley shows how centuries of theory about discourse and writing reduced invention—potentially the richest and most mysterious of the traditional rhetorical canons—to a dry, formulaic affair. The most tangible result of this progression (or perhaps *regression* is a more apt term) is the five-paragraph theme. In the five-paragraph theme, and its grown-up cousin the "research paper," the writer supposedly begins writing only after having thought the topic through completely. As Crowley argues, such a notion is bankrupt and untenable.

Still, many composition teachers are required, or feel themselves professionally obligated, to teach students how to write papers for professors who tend to view writing as an instrument for the transmission of already existing knowledge, not a vehicle for discovering new knowledge. I understand that writing is an act of discovery, such a teacher might say, but I don't want to do my students a disservice by proceeding from a notion of writing their future professors will not share. I would like to suggest here that writing teachers need not face an either/or choice between teaching writing-as-discovery and writing-as-instrument, since writing is never simply one or the other, as W. Ross Winterowd argues ("Emerson" 38). Even in the most rigidly structured and regulated genres, writers might find language resisting them, apparently pulling itself into unexpected shapes and forms, suggesting previously un-considered ideas. This might be termed the "poetic" tendency of all writing. Rather than covering over one possibility or another, writing teachers can urge students to be aware of the dialectical interplay between planning and discovery. Even in a composition course that focuses exclusively on the aca-demic, analytical, interpretive essay, students can be invited to discuss and write about this interplay. Questions directed toward student writing might include: How did you plan for these pieces to look before you wrote them? In what instances did this planning work out well? In what places did it not work out well? Did you discover anything new as you wrote? Did anything you dis-covered in such a way help you to rewrite, rethink, revise? What aspects of your writing might you identify as poetic? Ideally, these questions might allow students to find the poetic elements even in the most rigidly structured types of writing; to learn not always to resist or shy away from these elements; and to understand writing processes for the unwieldy, context-specific, vari-able, and mutable things they are.

The second basic way in which the connections between creative writing and composition theory might become relevant to the first-year writing course would be in those courses that include poetry writing or some other form of creative writing. In many cases, poetry writing (or, for that matter, most of what is commonly called "creative" writing) is considered out-of-bounds in the required first-year college writing course.[2] The reasons for this are numerous, and many of them have been touched upon at various points in this book. However, some teachers and scholars have recognized the po-tentially transformative power of creative genres in the composition classroom. Especially worthy of mention in this regard is James Seitz's account, in *Motives for Metaphor*, of his attempt to raise provocative and challenging questions about the interplay between figurative and literal uses of language by having his students write short novels in a composition course. While such an effort may seem impractical or even impossible to many composition teachers, Seitz's account certainly illustrates some of the possibilities for incorporating creative writing into the composition classroom.

In practice, of course, individual composition classes, despite their overwhelming similarities, also differ in many important ways. Some focus exclusively on one particular type of writing, such as the argumentative essay. Others, though, include several different types of writing, such as the personal essay. The self-reflexiveness encouraged by a portfolio pedagogy is particularly helpful in a composition course that includes multiple genres. In a composition course that employs portfolios, different genres operate not only as separate tasks that require particular blends of skills, and that students are expected to master (at least in a preliminary way) after one or two tries, but also as varieties of composing that might, despite their differences, be related to one another. Students revise throughout the semester and are invited to consider in their cover letters or reflective essays how and why particular revision choices may have been made and how their overall development as writers might be encapsulated in their attempts to write in various genres.

I would like to argue that if the teacher of a first-year composition course allows or requires students to write poetry or fiction, then these genres must be integrated into the course in a meaningful way. They must not be presented as a cordoned-off area reserved for the expression of emotion, or as a break from the more "serious" work of academic writing, or as a type of writing in which the aesthetic autonomy of the completely coherent creative self is put on display. Of course, I do not mean to suggest that these possibilities (or something like them) never operate within the sphere of activity commonly designated as "creative writing." But I do mean to suggest that received ideas about poetry and fiction (and, by extension, about all other genres students are invited to work in) should be called into question and that the potential relationships among genres—their similarities as well as their differences—should be continually questioned as part of an ongoing pedagogical project. In this regard, craft criticism is a vital resource for students and teachers, since craft critics challenge received notions about genre—as, of course, do many composition theorists.

I have attempted, in first-year composition courses, to afford students the opportunity to write in genres other than the interpretive-analytical essay. I have never required students to write poems or stories in these courses; initially poems were one choice among many in an assignment that basically asked students to hand in a piece of writing in any form they might choose and concerning any subject matter they might choose. When I first tried this a number of years ago, I noticed that only about a quarter of the students in my classes chose to turn in a poem in response to this "free" assignment. Those poems that did appear on my desk initially struck me as being of particularly low quality in relationship to the interpretive essays previously written by the same students. My immediate visceral reaction was that these students must simply not have worked as hard on their poems as they had on other types of writing. But now I certainly do not think that explanation ultimately goes very far toward understanding what might have gone "wrong," if anything.

The problems I initially encountered seem to me, after some reflection, to have arisen from at least three basic factors. First, some students may have had little contact with poetry, either in or out of school. Second, many students who have been exposed to poetry are accustomed to approaching it as something that must be interpretively dissected and/or appreciated as exhibiting the genius of its writer; this is not, in my experience, a particularly apt mind-set for approaching poetry's composition. Third (and this is perhaps more important), the assignment as I originally devised it—simply instructing students to write about whatever they wanted, in whatever form they wanted—differed dramatically from the other assignments the students had written insofar as there were no specific, detailed guidelines. Some students relished this, of course. Others, though, may have felt lost—unsure about what was to be done in the absence of rigid constraints. This confusion, perhaps in combination with a more general confusion about what might actually constitute a poem, probably led to the student poems with which I, as a teacher, was so dissatisfied. The blame for this situation (if indeed blame should be assigned) fell at least as heavily on my shoulders, if not more so, than on those of the students. Unintentionally, I had segregated poetry and fiction (and, in fact, *any* genres other than the analytical-interpretive essay) into an "extra" area, seemingly tacked on to the end of the semester. It is easy to think, in retrospect, that I should have known better.

But what could I have done? An easy response to this question would be that I should have spent more in-class time considering poetry, and other genres, than I did. To go too far in that direction, however, might be irresponsible. The first-year composition course at most institutions exists primarily to allow students to practice writing skills that (presumably) they will need later in their academic and professional careers. But teachers who are interested in including poetry and fiction in their composition classes, I would suggest, need to consider how the particular problems surrounding poetic and fictional composition might be addressed. Specifically, I mean that teachers might solicit student poems or stories by asking students—before they write and/or as they write—to think about two broad questions: How are poems and stories written? and, Why are poems and stories written? Requiring or recommending that students read some craft criticism would be one way (though certainly not the only way) to get students thinking about these questions. Reading the work of craft critics, at the very least, would allow students to see that for some people, the issues of how and why poems and stories are (and should be) written are vital. And the work of particular craft critics, especially those who challenge dominant neoromantic ideas about writerly identities, would alert students that writing poetry and fiction is a more complicated affair than it might initially appear.

In my current position, I rarely teach the university's required first-year composition course. But unlike many institutions, mine also has a required third-year composition course, and I teach several sections of this course every academic year. In this course, I have continued to experiment with integrating poetic composition with other kinds of composition. (Unfortunately, I have yet to find a way to integrate fiction writing meaningfully into the course structure.) My advanced composition courses currently function not only as "skills" courses but also as sustained inquiries into how writing functions (and has functioned) politically, socially, and economically in the world. Through writing, reading, and discussion, my students and I focus on three "sites of contention"—education, technology, and the self—at which writing assumes particular importance. Poetic composition enters the course (as an option, not a requirement) when we examine writing and its relationship to "the self." And since poetry is often thought of (often reductively) as "self-expression," I try to complicate this notion—or at least encourage students to articulate what "self-expression" means, either in the composition of poetry or in the composition of other sorts of writing, like resumes and job-application cover letters, which purport to express or present a "self." Although relatively few students choose to write poetry in my current advanced composition courses, it seems to me that students' attempts at poetic composition are considerably enriched by their integration into a sustained inquiry about how all sorts of writing actually function in the world.

The Introductory Creative Writing Course

The introductory creative writing course would seem to be an ideal place for an exploration of the concerns outlined in this book—concerns that appear at the intersection of craft criticism and composition theory. In my experience, though, the introductory creative writing course has not served such a purpose; rather, nearly all the creative writing courses I have taken have focused so sharply on the student text as to obscure any questions about whether, and how, the individual student text might fit into a larger textual network. In other words, my experience in creative writing classes has been governed by the implicit understanding that the student text, though worthy of intense scrutiny and criticism, should be conceived as occupying a sphere all its own, largely outside the bounds of economic, social, and material realities, largely outside of any rhetorical relationship to the world in which it presumably must operate. It might even be said that the New Critics' insistence on the autonomy of the poem persists more tenaciously in creative writing classrooms than anywhere else. This does not mean that all creative writing teachers bring New Critical sensibilities to their classrooms, nor does it mean that social and political aspects of creative text production and reception are never addressed. What I do mean to suggest is that creative writing pedagogy, in my experience and in the experience of many I have spoken to, primarily focuses on the text's formal and aesthetic qualities, letting social and political considerations into classroom discourse infrequently, intermittently, and usually only with the implication that such considerations are of a lower order than formal and aesthetic ones.

To illustrate my point, I would like to share an anecdote about how one of my own poems was received in a creative writing course I took as an undergraduate and how it was revised according to the suggestions I received. I will tell the story of this particular creative writing workshop session, what *did happen*, in order to speculate about what *might have happened* had the workshop session been more explicitly animated by some of the questions discussed here, questions that mark some of the terrain where craft criticism and composition theory come together. The version of the poem I handed in for consideration on the classroom worksheet, and that the professor reproduced on that worksheet, was entitled "Close to Home" and read as follows:

Damp newspapers rustle in the warm breeze;
I lean back against these damp bricks & sigh
as a solitary set of headlights
comes, passes, fades into silence
around the corner, & is gone.

City lights glitter
on the surface of the brackish channel
behind darkened houses across the street,
shining like high-beams
& obscuring whatever lies behind.

Two girls sing a song of loneliness
somewhere off in the darkness.
Their voices reach me, disembodied
& calm like the eyes of hurricanes.

I gaze toward a backlit
second-floor bedroom window. It
blinks out, & I turn to walk away as
a ship's horn wails
over miles of moon-sparkled water.

On the day of the workshop, I read the poem aloud, per established classroom procedure, and then my fellow students and the professor began commenting on it. Most thought it was a good poem but also had suggestions for changes. One student thought light imagery was "overused" in the poem, with mention of headlights in the first stanza, city lights in the second, and the bedroom window and the moon in the final stanza. He suggested getting rid of one or more of these images. Another student agreed in part but thought the problem was not with too many light images, but rather with some of the words used to describe light, particularly "glitter." She suggested finding words to replace "glitter" and "sparkled." The professor agreed. He suggested replacing the two words in question with "glimmer" and "sprinkled," which, he said, were more fresh and surprising than the words I had chosen. Other students thought the first stanza was somewhat excessive and repetitive. They suggested removing "& sigh" and "& is gone," which, they claimed, were unnecessary and added nothing to the poem.

The discussion went on like this for about fifteen minutes, with my classmates offering numerous suggestions for word changes and excisions. Finally, the professor said, "I think you've gotten a number of good suggestions here. If you make some of those changes, you probably have a finished poem." By "finished poem," he meant one that could be sent out in the mail for possible publication, one that could hold its own with most of what appeared in the mailboxes of literary journals. Then the professor paused a moment, looking back over the poem. "You know, when I first read this," he said, "I half expected to hear a jazz saxophone in the background. I suppose some people might think of this kind of poem as high art. Others might think it's just a better way to sell wine coolers." At that, a few people in the class chuckled, including me, and we moved on to the next student poem.

Perhaps the most interesting avenues of discussion about the poem were implied in the professor's seemingly off-the-cuff remarks before we moved on to the next poem, but these avenues were never pursued in class that day. Before exploring this in more detail, though, I will include the revised version of the poem, the one that appeared as part of a collection of poems that I turned in as a senior honors project. This version also bears the title "Close to Home" and reads as follows:

> Today's newspapers rustle in the warm breeze.
> I lean against damp bricks
> as a solitary set of headlights
> approaches, passes, fades into silence
> around the corner.
>
> City lights glimmer
> on the surface of the brackish channel
> behind blackened houses across the street,
> shining like high-beams
> & obscuring whatever lies behind.

Two girls sing a song of loneliness
somewhere off in the darkness.
Their voices reach me, disembodied,
calm like the eyes of hurricanes.

I gaze toward a backlit
second-floor bedroom window. It
blinks out, & I turn to walk away as
a ship's horn wails
over miles of moon-sprinkled water.

I think the suggestions for word changes and excisions helped me make the poem "better" in a rather limited sense. That is, they allowed me to compose a poem that was more technically adept than the earlier version. The vast majority of workshop commentary that day led me in this direction. In one sense, then, this workshop was more an editing workshop than a revision workshop. But the professor's closing comments, as I have already suggested, hinted at concerns that venture beyond the sphere of mere technique and into the wider sphere of rhetoric. These wider concerns were not pursued in class that day, but I would like to speculate about what might have happened if they were.

When the professor suggested, however subtly, that the poem "Close to Home" might bear some similarities to wine-cooler commercials, he touched upon a vital issue—or even a vital cluster of issues. His comments seemed to cut down to some part of the poem that could never be accessed through a simple attention to technique or image presentation. At the same time, though, the comment was frustrating, because it seemed that the possibility of a connection between the poem and wine-cooler commercials was merely suggested, but never explored in any kind of detail. Clearly, we needed to move on and consider other poems. But had the connection between poetry and other media been raised as a more general issue, it could have animated our discussions of many student poems, along with the aesthetic and formal issues that animated all our other workshop discussions.

The practical outcome of the workshop session, as I have already mentioned, was that I took into account many of the technique-oriented suggestions offered by my classmates and the professor, revised the poem, and included it as part of my senior honors project and a small collection of poems that I submitted as part of my application to the MA program in creative writing at SUNY Binghamton, to which I was admitted. In a very important way, then, the poem was a success. The wine-cooler connection, though, if I may call it that, continued to nag at me. When I began regularly mailing groups of poems to journal and magazine editors for consideration, "Close to Home" was often included among them. But the poem was always rejected, even though it occasionally accompanied others that were accepted for publication, and eventually I decided it was probably not publishable, and I stuck it in a folder, moving on to write and revise other poems.

Closer attention to the wine-cooler connection, though, might have allowed me to think about (and perhaps revise) the poem in other ways. What did it mean that the professor sensed a similarity between my poem and wine-cooler commercials? What imagery and topoi might the poem have shared with certain kinds of advertisements? Looking back at it now, I think I have some clearer answers to those questions. It now seems, for example, that one aspect of the poem that might have contributed to this sensed similarity is the poem's "I." This "I" might be recognized under a number of names: voice, narrator, speaker (in New Critical parlance), speaking subject, or subjectivity. Under any of these names, this "I" is worth examination. What kind of self or person is it? Is it similar to any other recognizable selves, persons, subjectivities? What might be at stake in the activation (or "use") of such a self or subjectivity in this particular poem? What kinds of readers might respond favorably to such a speaker? What kinds of readers might respond unfavorably? Why would they respond in these ways? Any of these questions might provide a way to begin examining the poem's "I."

This "I," which I believe remains completely intact from the first version of the poem to the second, seems alone, isolated, alienated, and self-aware. This "I" apparently seeks contact with another but is for some reason denied this contact. And this seeking after and denial of contact are, at least in one sense, what the poem is about. What the professor seemed to suggest was that a character very much like this might turn up in a wine-cooler commercial, although such an advertisement would not be the only place a character like this might appear. Such an "I" might also be found in other poems, in novels, in films, in songs, in advertisements for products other than wine coolers. Perhaps a quite useful avenue of discussion about this poem might have begun with the following questions: Why does this kind of "I" appear in the poem?

What purposes does it serve? Could you imagine the poem without this "I"? Might this "I" be altered or changed in any way, and if so, to what effect? What kinds of readers might respond favorably (or unfavorably) to this "I," and why? I do not know how the class discussion might have progressed that day if these questions were brought up, but I do think it would have been dramatically different. Had I been asked these questions, and had I been required to write a cover letter or reflective essay articulating the processes of revision employed in my poetry throughout the semester, I might have rewritten the poem far differently than I actually did.

The implications of this narrative are worth clarifying. Most, though not all, of the workshop commentary on my poem reinforced the notion of craft as technique. The revisions I made also reinforced this notion. Those comments that could have moved the discussion beyond the realm of technique into the much broader realm of rhetoric were never pursued extensively. These same comments, had they been pursued more extensively, might have led to much more radical revisions than the technique-oriented comments did. While it is important to recognize this narrative for what it is—an account of the responses to a single poem in a single creative writing course—I think the incident is representative of American creative writing pedagogy in a number of ways. The professor, a graduate of the prestigious University of Iowa MFA program, probably modeled his poetry workshops—at least partly—after those he took as a graduate student. The technique-oriented Iowa workshop model worked very well for many of its students, helping them toward revisions that enabled them to publish their creative work and, in some cases, helping them earn credentials that landed them jobs as professors of creative writing. And for some students, the Iowa workshop model continues to work this way. But I think we have arrived at a time where creative writing pedagogy needs to be reexamined and refigured, not in order to eliminate the emphasis on technique but in order to imagine technique as only one among many concerns vital to practicing writers. In an age when most creative writing MFA and Ph.D. graduates will not find employment solely as teachers of creative writing (those who remain in the university will most likely teach composition courses and perhaps other types of writing and literature courses), it is imperative that creative writing programs encourage their students to study scholarship in other areas of English studies, particularly composition. Writing teachers of all types must continually question what it means to write, and to teach writing. In this regard, creative writers and compositionists, despite their inevitable disagreements, can and should work as allies.

It is also worth noting here that in the course of revisiting this particular episode, and thinking through the composition of this particular poem, I found myself led to attempt another revision, one that might more explicitly acknowledge the poem's use of familiar types of character and scene. I wanted to introduce a subtle element of self-parody into the poem and to tone down what now strikes me as a strained attempt toward mythologizing a rather mundane experience in the earlier versions. The poem, now entitled "Love Lyric of a South Amboy Teenager, set to the accompaniment of an imaginary jazz saxophone," reads as follows. I leave it to readers to decide whether or not this revision makes the poem any "better":

> Newspapers rustle in the breeze.
> My back against damp bricks, I watch
> a set of headlights
> approach, pass, fade into silence
> around the corner.
>
> City lights glimmer
> on the surface of the brackish channel
> behind dark houses,
> the shapes of buildings warped
> by the water's indistinction.
>
> Two girls sing
> somewhere nearby—on a
> porch, in a driveway, perhaps—
> their voices smooth, their
> rhythm solemn, heavy.
>
> Across the street, an
> upstairs bedroom windowframe
> winks out. I turn away.
> A ship's horn wails
> over miles of moon-sprinkled water.

This current version may still be only superficially different from the earlier ones. But the issues that arose during this discussion may well shape some of the choices I make in composing and revising future poems.

Another example of a creative writing workshop that misses an opportunity to consider compelling rhetorical issues can be found in an account by Lucia Perillo of a particular kind of problem she has noticed in her poetry workshops. Perillo is very clear about what she feels her role as a creative writing teacher is: "Although the assignments that I give are meant to elicit various principles of craft, they are not prescriptive when it comes to subject. Often, students choose to write about intimate matters, and my assumption (which I confirm to them later, privately) is that we are gathered to work on the poems only; working on the psychic turmoil must be handled elsewhere, since my expertise pertains only to my students' writing, not to their lives" (A56). In one sense, this comment is fair and sensible; writing teachers are not therapists, nor should they be asked to fill such a role. In another sense, though, this comment opens up a number of troubling but important questions. What exactly is the difference between "craft" and "subject"? What is the nature of the relationship between them? Where, precisely, does one draw the line between students' poems and their lives? Is it possible to do so in harmful or detrimental ways?

The specific classroom problem Perillo describes involves the kinds of tensions evident in her comments above: "One of the first batches of their work read out loud in class included a poem by an older female student, detailing her sexual molestation by an uncle many years ago" (A56). The class, unsure of what to do, waited in uncomfortable silence for Perillo, in her teacherly role, to begin speaking. After praising the poem for its display of technical skill, Perillo began talking about some possible structural problems. Very quickly, she was cut off by "a young female student" who "stood up to deliver an impassioned speech about the courage the writer had demonstrated and how she ought to be applauded for sharing her experience" (A56). The class had arrived at an impasse: "After she sat down, the class looked my way accusatorially, no doubt wondering why I wasn't the one who'd said these things. I tried blustering a bit about the difference between poetry's therapeutic and aesthetic uses, but, before I could even make the terms of that distinction clear, I realized that no one was listening. *Not* to applaud the confession flew in the face of everything my students had learned from popular culture.

Trailing off into inaudibility, I had the feeling that we had all somehow astral-traveled to Oprah Winfrey's studio. And I was the bad guest, the expert who'd been brought in for the audience members to attack" (A56).

The problem Perillo describes here is very serious indeed, not only for creative writing teachers but also for composition teachers whose students write personal essays. Perillo is well aware that her classroom is not a sheltered space, that her students bring predispositions toward confession with them, predispositions that are formed and fed by a public fascination with confession. But the impasse reached by her class might have arisen, at least in part, from the way Perillo frames the entire issue. In her account, Perillo is faced with two imperfect options. She can either respond on a personal level to the events described in the poem, and thereby overstep her professional boundaries, or she can restrict her comments to structural and aesthetic elements of the poem, and thereby appear to be cold and unfeeling. I don't think these are the only options.

Instead, I would suggest that this situation Perillo describes provides an excellent opportunity to raise questions about the function of poetry within the larger culture. Such a poem—a narrative of abuse—can provide an entry point for class discussion about confessional rhetoric in poetry, discussion geared toward clarifying the uses and purposes toward which such rhetoric might be employed. Students might be asked to consider, for instance, whether there is a significant difference between narrating childhood abuse in a poem —then submitting the poem for consideration in the rhetorical context of the classroom—and talking about such abuse on a daytime talk show or in a support group. Students might be asked to consider the rhetorical effects of submitting such a poem for classroom discussion. The issue must be raised that—*whether the student writer intended it or not*—her poem effectively silenced the rest of the class or at least restricted the kinds of responses they might offer. She had managed, within the restricted space of the classroom, to harness media-fueled public attitudes about child abuse in order to restrict her classmates' comments about the poem—to leave her classmates with no other options than to praise her courage, remain silent, or focus instead on simple matters of technique. But as a teacher, Perillo might have asked the class members to think critically about their own initial reactions to the poem. Why were they inclined toward silence or praise? Ultimately, the class could consider the following questions: Is poetry a particularly effective medium for confession or for narratives of abuse? How does poetry differ from other media in this regard? When someone writes a narrative of abuse in the form of a poem, what social and rhetorical consequences are being sought? In the case of this particular poem, what—if anything—must be done in order for such consequences to be realized? These are not easy questions to ask or to answer. But if creative writing teachers and students want poetry to matter, in the words of Dana Gioia, to have some impact in the public sphere, then these are essential questions to ask and to answer.

Perhaps the workshop format itself, with its near-constant direct focus on the student text, works against the consideration of such essential questions. Perhaps creative writing teachers who rely exclusively on workshops need to begin devising alternative activities for their classes—activities that, as a supplement to workshops, would allow for sustained reflection on the very enterprise of creative writing as it relates to larger social, political, and rhetorical trends. At the very least, creative writing courses should, if they do not already, begin to locate poetry and fiction writing within the extensive and complex nexus of forces in which composition studies, over the last thirty years or so, has begun to locate other forms and genres of writing. Thus, in my most recent creative writing courses I have invited students to attempt to articulate what "creative writing" means and to situate their own poetry and fiction writing within larger contexts. One of the most successful activities in this regard—one that students seem to enjoy a great deal—is an assignment in which small groups of students research, and later present to the class, journals and magazines that publish short stories and poems. The assignment is most successful when the publications in question represent divergent editorial philosophies and aesthetic and political sensibilities. This allows students to see that the production of fiction and poetry is contested terrain today, as it has always been. It also allows students to see themselves as potential agents in this sphere of activity.

Some creative writing teachers might object that time not spent on workshops in creative writing classes actually robs students of what they came to the class for in the first place—sustained and detailed attention to their own writing. Or, as one impassioned creative writing teacher once said to me: "There's no other class where my students can *get* that kind of time spent on their own writing. How can I take it away from them?" While there is merit to this sentiment, I believe it obscures a much more important question: why aren't there more opportunities for sustained attention to student writing (at least in some institutions) across the English curriculum—especially in literature classes? It may be that the attempted "preservation" of the creative writing course as one of the only (or few) sites for sustained attention to student writing actually makes the status quo much easier to maintain. Just as "critical" practices are sorely needed in many creative writing classrooms, "creative" practices are sorely needed in other classrooms across the spectrum of English studies. Larger changes cannot be made if too many teachers are intent on preserving their own comfort zones within the status quo.

The Writing-about-Literature Course

As Robert Scholes and Wendy Bishop both note, the introductory course in literary analysis is a course where separate strands of English studies—literature, composition, and creative writing—both converge and diverge.[3] It is a course where (at least presumably) students are expected to gain a brief introduction to the discipline of English studies and some of its many institutional practices. It is also a course where teachers tend to present the concerns and methodologies of English studies through the lens of whichever particular strand they might be associated with. For these reasons, Bishop and Scholes recognize (and I certainly agree with them) that any scholar or teacher attempting to refigure English studies should regard the writing-about-literature course as a vital site of action. It is a site at which the different kinds of assumptions and questions that undergird the separate strands of English studies can be put into play. The fact that a "creative writer" might choose to approach texts differently than a "critical theorist" can be not only observed but questioned. These differences, and the kinds of implicit and explicit debates they characterize, can become part of the focus of the course. Students can be invited not only to act as spectators but to consider whether and why they themselves might like to take part in the debates.

The writing-about-literature course may be an institutional remnant at many colleges and universities, a throwback to the time when literary analysis seemed the "natural" content of a college writing course, either because all professors' training was exclusively in literary analysis or because literary texts were thought to be the best available examples of "great" writing. In many cases, the course itself may have survived even though its initial enabling conditions no longer exist. I would now like to outline in general terms a plan for organizing a writing-about-literature course so that some of the tensions and shared concerns between creative writers and composition theorists might be brought into play. Such a course would have several general features. First, all required readings would be contemporary—published within approximately the last ten years; these readings would be chosen both by the students and by the teacher. Second, students would be required to read and write in numerous genres. Third, a portfolio pedagogy would be employed so that students might have the opportunity to explore connections between the different types of reading and writing required of them, and students would be encouraged to continually question, and work to define and redefine, some of the key words of English studies, like *poetry, literature, writing,* and *criticism.*

Focusing solely on contemporary writing, as I advise, obviously has its advantages and disadvantages. But I think the advantages, especially in the context of a course like this, outweigh the disadvantages. The primary advantage is that "literature" is treated as a vital and ongoing sphere of activity, a sphere in which students might, if they wish, become involved. Literature is not figured as a collection of perfected works by (mostly) dead authors; literature is not figured as a storehouse of cultural capital about which students need to attain a certain degree of knowledge if they are to be considered educated. While this approach does veer away from inculcating students with factual knowledge about canonical literary works, it does not by any means preclude all the concerns of traditional literary study. In fact, many of these concerns can be addressed just as easily through contemporary texts as they can through canonical ones. To cite just one example, I might note that the structure of the sonnet, its formal techniques, and potential variations can be illustrated just as easily through a sonnet culled from the most recent issue of the *American Poetry Review* as they can through a sonnet by Shakespeare or Browning. Also, the contemporary piece allows a sharper focus on rhetorical, in addition to structural, concerns. Specifically, students and teachers can consider how formalistic verse fits into the contemporary poetic landscape— which kinds of poets write it and which kinds of journals publish it. Taking canonical authors like Shakespeare and Browning out of the writing-about-literature course does not mean banishing them from the English curriculum entirely, nor does it eliminate the possibility that a student particularly interested in the sonnet form might seek out sonnets by Shakespeare and Browning on her/his own or at the direction of the teacher.

Focusing squarely on contemporary writing might seem to pose a logistical problem, insofar as no writing-about-literature textbook (so far as I know) is available to accommodate such a task. In my experience, though, this too is an advantage. In the last two writing-about-literature courses I taught, the university library's current periodicals room became the primary resource for me and my students. Early in the semester, I took my class to the current periodicals room and pointed out most of the available journals that publish contemporary poetry, fiction, and drama. These, I explained to the class, were where nearly all of our required "literary" readings would come from. I encouraged students to visit the room frequently, not only to locate the pieces I might assign but also to find pieces they might like to suggest for class discussion or about which they might like to write. Instead of having a textbook with a rather static set of readings we might choose from, the class had a dynamic, continually changing, and ultimately uncontainable storehouse of texts, a storehouse through which students were encouraged, primarily, to seek their own paths.

The contemporary focus can encompass numerous genres, since most literary journals contain not only poems, stories, and plays but also book reviews, interviews, and critical essays. Students can be encouraged or required to write in these genres, and the current periodicals provide them with numerous —and even conflicting—models for such writing. Because contemporary literature is such a contested terrain, students get a sense of literature not as something that is (and has been) defined and identified once and for all, but as a ground of contention, an area under dispute. They come to see how *literature* is a term that, despite its instabilities, bears a degree of cultural power— power that is worth continued arguments and definitions about what literature might be. To help students gain a grasp of the histories and implications of some of these arguments, I supplemented the readings from literary journals with selections from Frank Lentricchia and Thomas McLaughlin's *Critical Terms for Literary Study.* These selections, at times very difficult for students to read, at least allowed them to see, grapple with, and even complain about what it might mean to "theorize" in English studies. I also included several pieces of craft criticism in order to provide opportunities for students to discuss the possible differences between the perspectives of those identified as "writers" and those identified as "theorists" or "critics." I tried, with varying degrees of success, to allow some of these theoretical speculations to inflect our class discussions of contemporary poems and stories.

Students in this type of class are informed during the first days of the semester that they will be required to attempt, and then reattempt, a number of kinds of writing. In my own most recent class, for example, students were required to write in four genres: a definition of the term *literature;* an analytical-interpretive essay about a particular poem or short story; a piece of "creative writing" (either a poem or a short story); and a book review (of a recently published book of poems, collection of stories, novel, or book of literary criticism). For their portfolios, students were required to revise any three of these pieces and to compose a cover letter articulating why they chose to include the particular pieces they chose; why they chose to omit the fourth piece; how their revision decisions were made; the relationships they saw developing among their various kinds of writing; and what kinds of "writerly" identity they felt most drawn toward or comfortable with, and why.

Classes of this sort need not focus only on the genres mentioned above. I offer them merely as an example of what *might* be required of students in a writing-about-literature course. Certainly, other genres might fit well in such a class. Should I teach such a course again, I may ask students to read brief histories of writing instruction, and of English studies, in order to contextualize the course itself within historical and institutional parameters. I may also ask students to compose "English studies autobiographies" in which they narrate their experiences in past English classes; compare and contrast them to their experiences in my class; and attempt to make sense of what "English," as a school subject, has meant to their lives. Teachers of courses along the lines of the one I am describing might also wish to include reading and writing assignments that emphasize the connections and discrepancies between traditionally understood "literature" and artifacts of contemporary popular culture, like songs, films, advertisements, and television programs. This would be one way to allow students to understand and take part in a movement that some scholars describe as a transition from literary study to cultural studies. But, more important, it would do so without remaining rooted within an exclusively interpretive framework. In a course such as the one I am describing, the possibilities are—to borrow from an old cliché—endless. But the most basic questions remain the same. What is "literature"? What is "writing"? What is a "text"? How should we read? How should we write? What is at stake in various acts of reading and writing?

If many of the ideas in this book are eventually put into classroom practice, the writing-about-literature course will probably disappear at some point, with its function migrating into other courses and other parts of the curriculum. If compositionists and creative writers can successfully challenge the centrality of the literary text (as an artifact to be interpreted) to English studies, such a course as writing-about-literature will no longer seem necessary. At the present moment, however, this course may be one of the more fruitful sites for enacting transformative practice in English studies.

A Blueprint for Change, Part 2: Across the English Curriculum

Ultimately, of course, the task of refiguring English studies—whether or not this involves the migration of writing studies into separate academic departments or units—will involve much more than redesigning the syllabi of existing courses. "Structural" change involves redrawing the boundaries between various areas of the discipline. Up to this point, I have been suggesting ways in which the boundaries between composition and creative writing might be redrawn, opening the space for an area called writing studies, in which acts of textual production and interpretation could be studied—and, of course, performed—with regard to both their generality and their specificity. In other words, writing studies would attempt to ascertain the ways in which any particular piece of writing differs from others, as well as the ways in which it is similar to others. A rhetorical perspective—a keen awareness of social, political, economic, and institutional contexts—would be a key element of writing studies. Relationships among genres would be brought into play in new ways, and this would have a significant impact on the English curriculum. The writing of poetry and fiction, for example, rather than being cordoned off within creative writing courses, might be integrated into all or most of the courses offered in English. I have already suggested ways in which creative genres might be integrated into first-year composition and introductory literature courses. But how might they be integrated into other kinds of courses?

Such integration of creative genres into other parts of the curriculum would not be governed by strict or uniform rules. Rather, it would depend upon the particular course, the knowledge of the instructor, and the needs and preferences of the students. James A. Berlin offers one possible plan for such integration in *Rhetorics, Poetics, and Cultures* when he outlines a course called "The Discourse of Revolution." This course is both an outgrowth of and a challenge to the traditional advanced undergraduate or graduate course in British literature of the eighteenth century. Having already asserted the importance of regarding the aesthetic, generic, and rhetorical dimensions of texts as interconnected (93), Berlin describes how these interconnections might be put into play in a course with a specific historical focus: "The heuristic to be employed in examining both rhetorical and poetical discourse requires looking at each text in its interacting generic, ideological, and socioeconomic environments. At each level, the reader attempts to locate the conflicts and contradictions addressed, resolved, ignored, or concealed with a view to considering their significance to the formation of subjects and to the larger culture. In the case of literary texts, the unique historical role of the aesthetic is a special concern" (132). By itself, such a strategy would certainly challenge some aspects of traditional literary study, but not others. The notion of textual interpretation as the primary purpose of literary study, for instance, might remain intact. Berlin is well aware of this and advises the following:

> Class members should also, of course, be involved in text production. They should keep journals, prepare position papers for the class, and even imitate and parody the materials of the late eighteenth century in an attempt to understand the methods of signification called upon and their relationship to economic, social, and political constructions. They should self-consciously pursue particular rhetorical devices, devices chosen because of their effectiveness in making a case. In other words, the rhetorics and rhetorical texts of the late eighteenth century must be seen in terms of their differences from contemporary constructions as well as their similarities. Students will learn that producing different utterances about a single event commonly involves producing different meanings. (136)

These tactics—foregrounding the interconnectedness of the rhetorical and the aesthetic and requiring students to write in many genres, including literary ones—could very well serve as guidelines for transforming the literature classroom. Craft criticism and composition theory would be relevant to such a transformation, as students and teachers would begin to consider not just what literary texts mean but also how they are produced and what factors might affect their publication, distribution, and reception. An ideologically grounded critique of Alexander Pope's *An Essay on Criticism,* for example, might be considerably enriched if its writer understands the specific difficulties of composing in heroic couplets.

Shifting the primary focus of the course from an arbitrarily specific kind of text (literature) or a specific historical time period (the eighteenth century) to the production of multiple kinds of discourse allows Berlin to alter some of the traditional dynamics of English studies without creating an entirely "new" course. "Literature" is not banished from consideration, nor is "the eighteenth century," but the reasons why these things are important seem to change rather dramatically. The eighteenth century, for instance, no longer serves as a discrete period marked by timeless texts and great authors, but rather as a historically dynamic and interesting site for the production of written discourse. A general shift of focus away from "fixed" time periods and texts and toward sites of written discourse production might have two very interesting effects. First, it might help to rescue certain aspects of the curriculum, like business writing and technical writing, from the excessive functionality to which they are usually consigned by the English curriculum. Second, in the long run, a focus on dynamic sites of written discourse production may very well change the ways in which literary texts "fit" into the English curriculum. Shakespeare's plays, for instance, might no longer appear in courses devoted entirely to Shakespeare or as a unit in a Renaissance literature course. Instead, they might crop up at various points in the curriculum, such as courses on the discourses of politics and power, or on the history of dramatic writing, or on the historical roots of film and television writing.

Of course, changes of that sort will probably occur in the long term rather than the short term. In the meantime, an emphasis on multiple genres, as well as a shifting of the balance between textual interpretation and production, might be possible within the frameworks of existing courses that are usually only functional, such as business, scientific, technical, and professional writing. The course in business writing, for example, might be supplemented or replaced by a course called "The Discourses of Business" or perhaps "The Rhetorics of Business." This kind of course would still involve the study and production of genres specific to business, like the memo and the résumé, but would also involve the consideration of larger issues related to business. As such, the course might well involve the study and production of genres not usually associated with business, like newspaper opinion columns, novels, poems, and films. The criterion for inclusion of particular texts would simply be whether they deal in some way with issues under consideration. To provide an example of how this might work, a specific unit of the course could address an issue relevant to those wishing to pursue careers in business or those interested in the social and political consequences of business practices, an issue like outsourcing. Consideration of outsourcing could easily require looking at many kinds of texts—corporate restructuring plans, memos to employees written by managers, and résumés prepared by employees who lose their jobs. But many other kinds of writing might also be relevant, including public defenses of outsourcing by corporate executives and boards or government officials; letters to the editor written by displaced workers; or stories, poems, songs, and films dealing with the issue. Students might be invited to choose to write in whatever genres seem most appropriate to them in dealing with the issue, or they might be required to write in many. They could also, in groups, conduct interviews with managers and employees of local businesses undergoing restructuring plans and attempt to prepare a comprehensive report on the problem, taking into account as many perspectives as possible. Students bound for careers in business would benefit from such projects not only by gaining functional knowledge of business-related writing but also by developing a keen social and political awareness of issues they will need to deal with in their careers. Ideally, they might begin to learn how they can shape and transform business practices, as well as how they personally will be shaped and transformed by such practices.

Eventually, shifting the focus of existing courses might lead to larger-scale changes across the curriculum, many of which I have hinted at here. Probably the most notable of these changes would be the movement of traditional literary texts into radically new contexts and frameworks. And while some people, particularly among the more institutionally conservative practitioners of literary studies, might regard these developments as a disaster, I would prefer to regard them otherwise. I would argue that my proposal does not represent the abandonment or destruction of the intellectual "traditions" of literary studies. Rather, I would maintain that this proposal—in full recognition of the historical and institutional constructedness of these traditions—represents a reinvention and reinvigoration of these traditions.

A Blueprint for Change, Part 3: Hiring and Personnel

The program of change for English studies I am outlining here would, without a doubt, require both long-term and short-term changes in faculty hiring. Most current faculty members, and most recipients of Ph.D.'s in English, would not be well prepared to implement and oversee the kind of curricula I have advocated here. Still, the fact remains that composition studies and, to a lesser extent, creative writing are fields pioneered for the most part by people with very traditional-looking backgrounds in literary studies. If English studies is to overcome its narrow and obsessive focus on textual interpretation—whether or not this involves changing its name to writing studies—the initial efforts in this direction (many of which have already begun) must be undertaken by those who are products of English studies as it currently exists. Perhaps one of the surest paths toward meaningful change in the discipline will be the creative reimagining of criteria for new hires. Rather than striving always to reproduce the past—replacing, for example, the retiring Miltonist with a much younger one—departments should strive more often to use new and renewed faculty lines to change the local focus of the discipline.

Of course, any attempt to change the direction of a particular department through hiring or staffing patterns may meet with stiff resistance. At the department where I teach, for instance, a pointed battle has waxed and waned for well over half a decade now. Unlike many departments, we have been fortunate to receive administrative approval for the hiring of new tenure-track faculty members during most of the years I have been here. This is due in part to a series of retirements and in part to a strong faculty union contract that places limits on the number of adjunct instructors any department may use, but it is also due to the desire of some administrators and faculty members to bring more writing specialists into a department traditionally populated almost exclusively by literature specialists. Because the English department houses both 100- and 300-level required writing courses, the majority of the sections it offers in any given semester (at least 65 percent, often more) are composition courses. It has been fairly easy, then, for the department to justify its need for tenure-track faculty members whose primary or exclusive teaching assignments consist of required composition courses. Agreeing as a department, however, about what kind of people should fill these positions has been anything but easy. When I was hired in 1998 as a compositionist with a secondary specialty in creative writing, I became, in effect, the department's fullest-fledged composition studies specialist. Only three others in the department of roughly twenty-five could claim any professional expertise (i.e., graduate coursework, publications, or conference presentations) in composition studies. Of these, one was a senior faculty member whose degree had been conferred in the late 1970s, a full decade before Stephen North's influential study called composition an "emerging field." The other two were junior faculty members who had been trained fairly extensively in composition studies but whose primary areas of responsibility lay in the area of English education. Along with these two other junior faculty members, then, I essentially "split time" (and still do) as a compositionist with responsibilities toward another field. And the senior "composition specialist" had chosen long ago to pursue departmental administrative work rather than to remain active as a participant in the professional discourse of composition studies—a common and quite understandable decision made by many faculty members at teaching-intensive institutions.

During each of my first two years on the job, I served on a search committee charged with identifying two candidates suitable for hire as tenure-track composition specialists. In each year, we were able to hire only one. During subsequent years, two other searches were canceled by the administration because search committees could not reach consensus about what would constitute appropriate qualifications for the positions. Finally, six years after the process began, the last available position was filled. All of these new hires have added valuable expertise to our department, but at the same time a disturbing trend has emerged. During this long process, some members of the search committees and other members of the department, with increasing volume and anger, repeatedly argued that we already have enough (or even too many) faculty members who have graduate training and scholarly credentials in composition studies and that what we need to do is start hiring people—to teach composition courses exclusively—who have degrees in literary studies. The alleged reason for this, at least according to one colleague with whom I spoke in the hallway, is that in a department that is already dominated (numerically speaking) by people who are literature specialists, the interests of "collegiality" are better served by hiring more of them. Thus, it is "appropriate" to hire a person with no formal training in writing to be a writing specialist, since just about everyone who holds an advanced degree in English has probably taught composition at one time or another anyway. For many compositionists, this story probably has an all too familiar ring. Composition, despite its dramatic growth as a field of research and inquiry, is still regarded by many professionals in English studies as entirely a teaching enterprise that (apparently unlike literature) requires no particular course of training or study. A couple of people in my department have even asserted—though they have not offered any evidence for this position—that "literature people" teach writing better than "composition people" do and should therefore be favored for positions teaching composition.

Bruce Horner describes, from his own department, developments that would seem on the surface to be diametrically opposed to those I have just narrated.[4] As I will argue shortly, though, the events Horner describes bear an uncanny similarity to those I have described. Horner writes: "In my own department, at least some faculty without claims to expertise in Composition have bitterly resisted efforts in the past to require them to teach one section per year of the composition course required of all first-year students. Pointing to the reputed expertise of 'the composition folk' among the faculty, they confessed their own ignorance about the subject and thus their unsuitability for teaching it" (17).

In one department, then, there is a bloc of faculty arguing that since composition expertise accrues to anyone who ever teaches composition courses, there is no need to hire people with specialized scholarly training or expertise. In another department, a bloc of faculty argues that their own expertise (presumably in literature) makes them unfit for teaching composition. My contention is that both blocs, despite the apparently radical differences in their arguments, are really after the same thing: the preservation of the integrity of literary studies as the conceptual center of English studies. The difference in their arguments lies more in the particular institutional locations in which they are made than it does in any deep conceptual or theoretical divide. In my department, those who wish to maintain the dominance of literary studies need to argue that composition is a field bereft of substance and that anyone who has ever taught composition has picked up enough "expertise" to be labeled a specialist. Because the department is economically dependent on composition courses (without which it would likely be less than half the size it is now), the dominance of literary studies can only be maintained by figuring composition as a pure "service" enterprise. In Horner's department, apparently, the dominance of literary studies can be maintained by "respecting," at least on the surface, the intellectual integrity of composition studies, if only so that literature professors can be rescued from the alleged drudgery of composition teaching. I have little doubt that some in my own department (and in many literature-dominated English departments at teaching-intensive institutions) would do the same thing if they believed it would not put their own jobs in danger.

Some readers might argue that tenure poses a major threat to my proposed reform plan for English studies, as it does for any academic reform plan. This is not an easily dismissed concern. Tenure does offer a degree of institutional power and leverage to those who might wish to obstruct, complicate, or subvert efforts at curricular reform and redesign. At the same time, tenure offers institutional power and leverage to those who favor such efforts. Perhaps, then, the issue is not tenure per se but rather the numerical balance of power in any department that may be negotiating curricular reform. And those who engage in unprofessional or illegal behavior in the pursuit of *any* end are not (or should not be) shielded by tenure from the legitimate consequences of their actions; college and university administrators have a responsibility to take action against tenured faculty members who violate the terms of their employment contracts. Further, the abolition of tenure would probably be a greater roadblock to curricular reform than any particular group of reactionary faculty members. Without reasonable long-term commitments from their institutions, how can faculty members be expected to invest time and effort in long-term projects for the benefit of their institutions? In short, while tenure might have the unfortunate short-term effect of slowing down curricular reform, its abolition would probably make meaningful curricular reform an impossibility.

A hypothetical example here will help clarify the hiring and staffing challenges faced by English departments today and demonstrate some of the ways in which hiring choices can hinder or help the effort to refigure English studies in general. Let us assume that the English department in a small- or medium-sized public or private university with a teaching load of four courses per semester wants to search for a tenure-track assistant professor whose teaching load—at least initially—will involve several different kinds of courses: the survey of British literature of the eighteenth century, which is offered during each fall semester and required for all English majors; a sophomore-level introduction to literature course for non–English majors, offered every semester, which this new hire would be asked to teach one section of during the spring and perhaps occasionally in the fall as needed; and the first-year composition course, required of all the university's students, which this hire would be asked to teach at least two, and sometimes three, sections of per semester, unless s/he were interested in teaching technical writing instead. This person would also be expected, over time, to propose and develop new courses.

We can infer a great deal about an English department by examining the way it chooses to define the sort of person it wants for this position. One option (let's call it the "literary-studies option") would be to allow only one of the potential professor's eight yearly courses—the eighteenth-century British literature survey—to drive the job description. In other words, the department would search for a specialist in eighteenth-century British literature, assuming that all of the other aspects of the position are incidental. It would be assumed, therefore, that feasible candidates would have extensive graduate training, dissertations, and probably even publications in eighteenth-century British literary studies. The new courses such candidates might develop for the department would likewise be expected in eighteenth-century British literary studies. The qualifications necessary for teaching composition, it would be assumed, would have been "taken care of" (if at all) through candidates' experience as graduate teaching assistants or temporary instructors elsewhere. The composition-teaching aspect of the position would be regarded by the department (and perhaps by many of the candidates as well) as a purely pedagogical or service-oriented enterprise—a time-consuming and regrettably necessary endeavor that would enable the "real" work of literary studies to take place. Throughout much of the twentieth century, most English departments would have approached such a hiring situation in exactly this way. And there may very well be many departments (or vocal members of departments) still inclined to do so. It is more likely now than, say, thirty years ago that the "literary-studies option" to hiring for such a position would be slightly revamped to account for the emergence of composition studies as a field of scholarly endeavor in its own right. Thus, departments might still view the literary component of the position (particularly in its hyperspecialized focus on a certain kind of writing produced in a single nation during a specific period of time) as its guiding intellectual focus. But in recognizing that the position would involve other sorts of teaching, some departments might require (or simply "prefer") that candidates also have scholarly credentials in composition studies as well as in eighteenth-century British literary studies. But the remarkable fact—that the position is primarily defined through only one of the courses that might be taught each year—would remain.

Another option for hiring in this scenario would, so to speak, turn the tables on the first. The "composition-studies option" would be based upon the notion that since composition would be the primary teaching responsibility (at least in terms of the number of sections taught), then composition studies should be the primary area of scholarly interest for job candidates. Likewise, it might well be expected that any (or at least most) new courses candidates might develop for the department would be in composition studies. Of course, the literary aspect of the position would exert some influence on the job description; candidates would likely be expected to have a secondary specialization in literature, as demonstrated by graduate coursework, comprehensive exams, conference presentations, publications, or some combination of these elements. It is highly unlikely, however, that such a secondary specialization in literature might be demonstrated through teaching experience alone. And it is likely that the most vocal arguments against such a proposition would issue from those who also argue that a so-called secondary specialization in composition studies *can* be gained through teaching experience alone. Still, I would argue that the "composition-studies option" is preferable to the "literary-studies option" in this hypothetical case.

The two options described above, though they might seem the most likely ones for departments in this kind of situation, are certainly not the only ones available. What if, for example, the department in question sought to hire (or at least consider) a novelist or poet who also had training in composition studies and a keen, demonstrated interest in eighteenth-century Britain because of its historical relevance to the production of fiction and/or poetry in English? Such a candidate might be more capable than either the "straight" composition or literature specialist of integrating the various aspects of this faculty position, both pedagogically and intellectually, and such a candidate might also be able to develop a wider array of new courses for the department than either of the other two sorts of candidates. Current graduate programs in English may produce very few candidates matching this sort of description, with the possible exception of "fusion-based" programs such as those described by Stephen North, and very few such programs currently exist. But there may be little impetus for the creation of more innovative graduate programs if colleges and universities of all kinds exhibit no willingness to hire candidates with nontraditional backgrounds. The fact that some schools may now be willing to hire compositionists for positions that also involve teaching literature is, as I have mentioned, a positive step. But departments can do more, certainly, in individual hiring situations to move the discipline of English studies toward an emphasis on writing in general. The most effective ways to do so will often vary, sometimes dramatically, along with local institutional conditions.

A Blueprint for Change, Part 4: Professional Organizations

The current divisions in English studies are perhaps most starkly represented by the existence of three distinct professional organizations—the MLA, the CCCC, and the AWP—that represent the discipline's three largest camps. While these organizations may have very little explicit power over what happens in any particular English department, they certainly operate as nationwide networks that tend, for the most part, to reinforce intradisciplinary boundaries rather than to challenge them. Thus, they serve as a powerful, institutionally conservative force, more often thwarting than enabling any localized attempts to blur the boundaries between the discipline's constituent strands. Certainly the MLA, among these three organizations, is the most powerful instrument of institutional conservatism. Periodically, of course, the MLA gets "bad press" (often based on little more than the titles of one or two conference presentations or journal articles) that portrays it as a band of radical misfits intent on destroying the revered cultural traditions of the Western world. In actuality, though, this kind of publicity obscures the fact that battles over what to interpret and how to interpret it—no matter how apparently radical—never move into the realm of questioning why English studies ought to be a discipline in which textual interpretation (of a very narrow sort) is routinely privileged over textual production (of any kind). The MLA stands, in effect, at the center of English studies, drawing much of its power from its position as a clearinghouse for most of the job advertisements and a de facto conductor of many of the early job interviews in English studies each year. Thus, many professionals and aspiring professionals who might feel much more comfortable with the CCCC and/or the AWP are effectively forced, at least temporarily, to join the MLA and help finance its activities. It becomes easy, then, for the MLA to stave off any real challenge to its authority. And its power is only exacerbated because its potential opposition, that is, the CCCC and the AWP, is essentially split.

In order for English studies to move toward a conception of itself in which textual production is not considered subservient to textual interpretation, the CCCC and AWP—the organizations representing the production side of the equation—probably need to cooperate and communicate more than they have done in the past. In the long run, these two organizations might find that they can effect more meaningful and lasting change by merging. At the present moment, such a merge would be difficult because the two organizations conceive of themselves in rather dramatically different ways. But working toward a merger between the CCCC and AWP might be a reasonable goal for the relatively few people who already "cross" between these two organizations. One of the first steps, of course, would be to convince other members of these organizations that compositionists and creative writers—at least at this moment in institutional history—have far more in common than many people might imagine. Certainly, there are differences between the two groups, and many of these differences ought to be respected and even, sometimes, preserved. I am not suggesting that the diverse ideas and practices of different kinds of "writing specialists" always ought to be flattened out or covered over. I am suggesting, though, that compositionists and creative writers alike suffer from the dominance of the MLA over all of English studies—a dominance that is the tangible, lingering effect of English studies' institutional history in America.

A merger or coalition between the CCCC and AWP would be beneficial in many ways. On the conceptual or theoretical level, it might lead to much richer investigations of, and debates about, writing theory and pedagogy. For example, the tensions between "expressivist" and "social constructivist" theories and pedagogies might become more productive if craft critics were active participants in the debate. But even greater benefits for compositionists and creative writers, at least in the short run, might be realized at the institutional level if the CCCC and AWP could possibly merge or work together. In fact, an interesting goal for a CCCC/AWP coalition could be to wrest one of English studies' most cherished and dreaded rituals—the annual publication of job announcements and the subsequent massive job interviews at an annual convention—away from the MLA. Many might argue that this ritual ought to be discarded altogether or at least radically changed. But as long as it is in the hands of the MLA, I suspect, such changes are not likely. A new writing-centered professional organization might find it necessary first to co-opt the ritual and then change it later. But the surest way *not* to change or alter any of this would be to allow English studies' three major professional organizations to continue to exist as they do now: separately but not equally.

Uncertain Future(s)

Predicting and influencing the future are uncertain and risky activities, even at best. There is certainly no guarantee, especially for people working in English studies, of any desired outcome. Yet at the same time, it seems perverse to do nothing, to resign ourselves to a fatalistic view of the future. The discipline's numerous histories suggest that English studies has been successful, at certain times and to certain degrees, in identifying and preserving its own intellectual interests while justifying its existence—however tenuously and difficultly at times—to an interested public. The ascent and institutionalization of literary studies is a key example of this trend.

Of course, the available histories contain stories of failure as well. The saga of Norman Foerster might be read as such a tale of failure. But such a reading, I would like to suggest, might be misleading insofar as it covers over an aspect of Foerster's legacy that interested professionals in English studies today might want to recuperate. Certainly Foerster's plans for institutional and disciplinary reform, especially at the University of Iowa, were never realized the way he intended them to be. Further, the successes he did have, insofar as he made creative writing a viable academic field and contributed to efforts to do the same for literary criticism, resulted in developments he would have hated. In short, Foerster wanted some kind of integration in English studies; the discipline, however, moved toward fragmentation and separation. Perhaps one of the present crises facing English studies, in the form of disciplinary fragmentation that at some institutions threatens to spiral out of control, could have been avoided had Foerster's efforts toward disciplinary integration taken hold during the first half of the twentieth century. A version of English studies in which textual production and interpretation were more firmly integrated might have been better able to move beyond Foerster's problematic "new humanist" ideology and allow emergent forms of "theory" to invigorate pedagogy as much as they tended to invigorate scholarly interpretation.

Another aspect of Foerster's thinking worth recuperating is the notion that scholarship ought to have some sort of noticeable public presence. This is not to say that scholarship should be "watered down" in order to make it "sell" better, but rather that the specialized discourses of scholarship should at least occasionally, and perhaps often, be carefully crafted for nonspecialist, but nonetheless keenly interested, stakeholders and observers both inside and outside academia. Perhaps the most notable attempt at such a feat from English studies is Mike Rose's *Lives on the Boundary*, a book that becomes particularly interesting in light of the arguments I make here. Rose manages to weave many of the important findings of composition scholarship—particularly with regard to writing apprehension and the influence of social class on students' successes and failures as college writers—into an engaging autobiographical story about his own academic struggles and successes, as well as those of many of the students he has worked with. Rose combines incisive scholarly and historical analysis with the kind of narrative pace and detail that any aspiring novelist might do well to imitate. In an era when higher education is coming under intense political and public scrutiny, and in which it is subject to increasingly vocal demands for "accountability," more efforts such as Rose's could have a dramatic impact on the public perception of English studies (or, if it transforms itself, writing studies). As such, these efforts could also affect the levels of funding available for writing instruction and writing scholarship. Professionals trained in both composition studies and creative writing, or in some future combination of the two, would be particularly well positioned to produce more books like Rose's.

In practice, transforming English studies will probably be an uneven and chaotic practice at times. No single plan will result in the quick and seamless integration of the discipline's separate strands. No easy blueprint is available for the transformation of every course at every institution. Barriers to reform are numerous, and they will need to be overcome in many ways, both intra- and interinstitutionally. What I have tried to suggest, though, is that some of these barriers prevent truly interesting and productive collaborations from coming about. The common isolation of creative writing from the rest of the English department is one such barrier. Creative writers have much in common with their colleagues in composition, particularly a commitment to teaching students to produce texts and an interest in studying the conditions that shape and mediate the production of texts. The intersections of craft criticism and composition theory indicate, I hope, the space in which collaboration might occur—an area of common concern that might be called writing studies. Work undertaken in such an area—in the classroom, in the pages of professional journals, and in public discussions of the functions and purposes of writing instruction—would resonate throughout English studies, especially as many scholars and teachers attempt to refigure the discipline so that English studies might have a more clearly articulated mission, a more cleanly integrated curriculum, and above all better ways to prepare teachers and students for their own futures as workers and citizens. Certainly it will be difficult at times to forge a meaningful alliance between composition and creative writing; practitioners in both areas will no doubt feel that something valuable about their chosen fields may be lost in the process. But clearly neither field has benefited much—and indeed, both have suffered much—from existing within English departments dominated by literary study and interpretive methodology. If a composition–creative writing alliance holds the promise of ending this dominance, through either the creation of stand-alone writing departments or a dramatic restructuring of English departments, the gains will far outweigh the losses.

Notes

Chapter 1: Composition, Creative Writing, and
the Shifting Boundaries of English Studies

1. As a brief aside, I should make clear that I do not blame *College English*'s editors for this situation in any way; I do not mean to suggest that they should not have published Richardson's article. In fact, the juxtaposition of Richardson's and Bizzaro's articles might be read as a brilliant yet subtle strategy by the editors, who choose pieces they know will appeal to various groups within their large and diverse audience. Many *College English* readers intrigued by Richardson's article, I suspect, would not be particularly interested in Bizzaro's, and vice versa. This also is a manifestation of one of the central problems of English studies today: only a small percentage of practitioners would seek to understand what it might mean that two such articles could be published back-to-back in the same journal. I would hope, though, that such practitioners might compose an important part of the audience for this book.

2. Those readers who prefer to locate composition's origin within the ancient tradition of rhetoric may disagree here, but I believe the accounts of those who warn against seeing such an easy continuation—especially Susan Miller and Sharon Crowley—are persuasive.

3. Stephen Wilbers's 1980 book on the Iowa Writers' Workshop might also be considered a history of academic creative writing, but since it focuses on only one program, it cannot provide the depth of analysis to be found in Myers's account.

4. In fact, the official journal of the Association of Writers and Writing Programs (AWP), the *Writer's Chronicle,* is subtitled "The magazine for serious writers."

5. To be fair, there are probably a great many teachers of creative writing who believe—like the early expressivists in composition studies—that everyone possesses creativity of one kind or another and that the task of a teacher is simply to "tap into" each student's creativity. Despite their differences, though, both positions conceive of creativity as something an individual *already has.* And thus, in both positions, creativity itself is entirely outside the realm of pedagogy. It cannot be taught.

6. Since I am citing the nonpaginated version of this essay from AWP's Web site (accessed 13 June 2001), my in-text citations contain no page numbers.

7. For an excellent summary of this essay, "Tradition and the Institutionalized Talent," and some of the many responses it engendered, see Berlin, *Rhetorics* 162–68.

8. While this characterization certainly holds true for Graff's "teach the conflicts" approach, as outlined in *Beyond the Culture Wars,* his more recent work, especially *Clueless in Academe,* seems to be moving toward the structural category.

Chapter 2: "Craft Criticism" and the Possibility of Theoretical Scholarship in Creative Writing

1. Indeed, as a faculty member with a 4-4 teaching load that consists almost exclusively of composition and creative writing courses, how could I believe otherwise?

2. I am reminded here of Truman Capote's well-known dismissal of the work of Beat writers: "That's not writing, it's typing."

3. In other words, I am more interested in opening up new possibilities than I am in shutting off existing ones. At the same time, I do not pretend to operate from a position of ideological innocence or neutrality. I have an argument to make, and I intend to make it persuasive to as many readers as I can. But I would prefer to present my findings as those that other scholars may not yet have noticed rather than (to employ a scholarly phrase I particularly dislike) those that others have "failed to recognize."

4. For a thorough explanation and historical treatment of what I mean by "academic literary criticism," see Gerald Graff's *Professing Literature: An Institutional History.*

5. This is probably most evident when Gioia begins an essay entitled "The Dilemma of the Long Poem" by wondering what an "intelligent eighteenth-century reader," a "long-suffering gentleman . . . would conclude if he surveyed the several hundred books of poetry published in America in an average year" (24). Gioia gives little indication about why he believes such a reader could offer a "true" perspective on current American poetry. Presumably, though, this eighteenth-century reader serves as the model for the "general reader" Gioia claims to be writing for.

6. Interestingly, Vernon Shetley also recommends a renewal of the relationship between poet and audience like the one that characterized Modernism. He differs from Bernstein, of course, in terms of how he believes poets and audiences might get there.

7. Wenderoth's target of criticism seems to be the "mainstream" poetic sensibility, the same sensibility rejected (for differing reasons) by the New Formalist and Language Poets. Yet Wenderoth's essay appears in the *American Poetry Review,* one of the nation's premiere mainstream poetry journals. His essay is an indication, I think, that some mainstream poet-critics have come to terms with the critiques leveled by the New Formalists and Language Poets. But rather than "jumping camps," writers like Wenderoth have begun to stake out new positions within the mainstream.

8. Perceptive readers might now be thinking, "Wait a minute! Isn't this *interpretive* criticism?" And my answer would be, "Yes *and* no." Clearly, Wenderoth is interpreting in order to make a larger point about textual production. In his essay, interpretation operates *at the service of* questions about production. This dynamic is exactly the opposite of that which operates in academic literary criticism—and in most of English studies in general.

Chapter 3: Writing, Reading, Thinking, and the Question Concerning Craft

1. All citations to Heidegger's works refer to the English translations. I employ the following abbreviations to refer to these works: *BT: Being and Time; OWL: On the Way*

to Language; QCT: The Question Concerning Technology and Other Essays; PLT: Poetry, Language, Thought; WCT: What Is Called Thinking? There are two English translations of *Being and Time.* The first is by John Macquarrie and Edward Robinson (1962), and the second is by Joan Stambaugh (1996). In this book, all citations of *Being and Time* refer to the Stambaugh translation.

2. I am not the first to make this contention. The issue of whether or not Heidegger's thought underwent a "turn" has been debated by scholars for years. A fairly concise description of how Heidegger's thought may have "turned" or "reversed" upon itself can be found in J. L. Mehta's *Martin Heidegger: The Way and the Vision* (315–44). Joan Stambaugh is among those scholars who find continuity from Heidegger's early work to his later work. Stambaugh's new translation of *Being and Time* is partly motivated by an attempt to make this continuity clearer than it once was.

3. Much has been written recently about Heidegger's involvement with Nazism and its potential implications for his thinking. Interested readers might wish to consult Richard Wolin's edited collection *The Heidegger Controversy* (1991), which serves as an excellent sourcebook for the debate; William V. Spanos's *Heidegger and Criticism: Retrieving the Cultural Politics of Destruction* (1993); or Rüdiger Safranski's ambitious "intellectual biography" *Martin Heidegger: Between Good and Evil* (1998). Also, David Farrell Krell's introduction to the paperback edition of his translation of Heidegger's lectures on Nietzsche contains an excellent analysis of Heidegger's involvement with Nazism; Krell refuses both of the easy solutions to the problem—ignoring Heidegger's politics altogether or using those politics as an excuse to reject Heidegger's thinking outright. Krell sums up his analysis succinctly by describing Heidegger as "a thinker who is repelled by the biologism and racism of his party, yet one whose nationalism almost always gets the better of him. It is not yet a chauvinism, not yet a xenophobia, but a nationalism that conforms to the nation of thinkers and poets, a nationalism of the German academic aristocracy of which Heidegger yearned to be a part. . . . Heidegger's nationalism is not of the flag-waving variety. It is a nationalism of high cultural expectations and intellectual demands" (xii–xiii).

4. This essay is also reprinted in Santos's essay collection entitled *A Poetry of Two Minds.* The reprinted version of the essay has a slightly different subtitle, "How Does Poetry Think?"

5. My guess is that this comment is primarily aimed at John Updike.

6. Lauterbach teaches at the City College of New York.

7. I suspect Worsham might argue that clear, easy-to-grasp explanations (and the desire for them) are symptomatic of technological thinking. So attempting to outline clearly her alternative approach to writing would pull this notion back inside the realm of technological thinking.

Chapter 4: Terms of an Alliance

1. For an extensive treatment of the subtle yet crucial and always shifting meanings of these words early in the twentieth century, see Graff's *Professing Literature.*

2. I am aware that instructors may use texts in ways that do not exactly parallel, and

sometimes even subvert, the aims of the texts' editors and/or authors. At the same time, I am convinced that classroom texts reflect large trends and tendencies within the profession.

3. To be fair, O'Dair is elsewhere much kinder to composition students and composition studies than she seems to be here. In "Academostars Are the Symptom; What's the Disease?" she critiques the persistent overproduction of doctorates in literary studies and suggests that the most effective graduate programs right now may be the ones that specifically train their students in both composition studies and literary studies with a specific focus on how they relate to teaching.

4. At the 2004 CCCC convention, in my experience, the antiliterature sentiment was still palpable, but it seemed to coalesce around two related issues. First, many compositionists—especially new assistant professors—complained that their attempts at curricular development in their home departments were routinely blocked by literature faculty. Most disturbing about this trend was that literature faculty apparently felt no need to argue in intellectual terms against the development of new courses and programs in writing; they argued instead through baseless assertions and ad hominem attacks and ultimately used the power of their voting blocs to quash reform. Second, and more on the positive side, many speakers argued eloquently that the time has come for fully developed undergraduate major programs in rhetoric and composition.

5. For more on the differences in classroom dynamics between creative writing and composition, see McFarland.

6. By "earning," Perelman is referring to a notion that, in my experience, prevails in many creative writing workshops. The idea goes something like this: a poet cannot simply "get away" with something like a flat, declarative, or abstract statement. Such a statement must be "earned" by skillful use of particular techniques, like the vivid and colorful description of visual scenes, elsewhere in the poem.

Chapter 5: Starting Somewhere

1. These courses may often be found under different names at different institutions, but they certainly represent three very distinctive and commonly available types of courses in English departments.

2. The most likely exception here is the personal essay, common in many "expressivist" composition courses and considered by many to belong to a loosely defined genre called "creative nonfiction." For many years, "creative nonfiction" was not one of the genres covered in creative writing programs, at either the undergraduate or graduate level, but this has certainly begun to change in recent years, perhaps because so many writers have begun to enjoy commercial success in the genre. Creative nonfiction has also engendered some very recent scholarly debate as it has come to be recognized as a site where concerns from the three strands of English studies may intersect. I will not consider the implications of this particular intersection point in this book because I believe it requires a more extensive analysis than the current context allows.

3. The introductory course in literary analysis goes by a number of names, depending on the department where it is taught. These names include "Writing about Litera-

ture," "Writing with Literature," and "Introduction to Literature," among others. I will refer to it here consistently as the writing-about-literature course. At some institutions, like the one where I currently teach, there may be more than one course that fits into this category. Where I work, "Introduction to Literature" is offered to non–English majors, while "Introduction to Techniques of Literary Research and Analysis" is required for English majors.

4. Horner has since left the institution where these events took place.

Works Cited

Adams, Katherine H. *A History of Professional Writing Instruction in American Colleges: Years of Acceptance, Growth, and Doubt.* Dallas: Southern Methodist UP, 1993.

Aldridge, John W. *Talents and Technicians: Literary Chic and the New Assembly-Line Fiction.* New York: Scribner's, 1992.

Anson, Chris M. "Who Wants Composition? Reflections on the Rise and Fall of an Independent Program." O'Neill, Crow, and Burton 153–69.

Bakhtin, M. M. *Speech Genres and Other Late Essays.* Trans. Vern W. McGee. Ed. Caryl Emerson and Michael Holquist. Austin: U of Texas P, 1986.

Bawarshi, Anis S. "Beyond Dichotomy: Toward a Theory of Divergence in Composition Studies." *JAC: A Journal of Composition Theory* 17.1 (1997): 69–82.

Baxter, Charles. *Burning Down the House: Essays on Fiction.* Saint Paul, MN: Graywolf Press, 1997.

Beach, Christopher. *Poetic Culture: Contemporary American Poetry between Community and Institution.* Evanston, IL: Northwestern UP, 1999.

Beech, Jennifer, and Julie Lindquist. "The Work before Us: Attending to English Departments' Poor Relations." *Pedagogy: Critical Approaches to Teaching Literature, Language, Composition, and Culture* 4.2 (2004): 171–89.

Bell, Madison Smartt. *Narrative Design: A Writer's Guide to Structure.* New York: Norton, 1997.

Bell, Marvin. "Poetry and Freshman Composition." *College Composition and Communication* 15.1 (1964): 1–5.

Berger, James. "Ghosts of Liberalism: Morrison's *Beloved* and the Moynihan Report." *PMLA* 111.3 (1996): 408–20.

Berlin, James A. *Rhetoric and Reality: Writing Instruction in American Colleges, 1900–1985.* Carbondale: Southern Illinois UP, 1987.

———. "Rhetoric, Poetic, and Culture: Contested Boundaries in English Studies." *The Politics of Writing Instruction: Postsecondary.* Ed. Richard Bullock and John Trimbur. Portsmouth, NH: Boynton/Cook, 1991. 23–38.

———. *Rhetorics, Poetics, and Cultures: Refiguring College English Studies.* Urbana, IL: National Council of Teachers of English, 1996.

———. *Writing Instruction in Nineteenth-Century American Colleges.* Carbondale: Southern Illinois UP, 1984.

Bernstein, Charles. *A Poetics.* Cambridge: Harvard UP, 1991.

Berry, R. M. "Theory, Creative Writing, and the Impertinence of History." Bishop and Ostrom 57–76.

Bishop, Wendy. "The Literary Text and the Writing Classroom." *JAC: A Journal of Composition Theory* 15.3 (1995): 435–54.

———. "Places to Stand: The Reflective Writer-Teacher-Writer in Composition." *College Composition and Communication* 51.2 (1999): 9–31.

————. *Released into Language: Options for Teaching Creative Writing.* 2nd ed. Portland, ME: Calendar Islands Publishers, 1998.

Bishop, Wendy, and Hans Ostrom, eds. *Colors of a Different Horse: Rethinking Creative Writing Theory and Pedagogy.* Urbana, IL: National Council of Teachers of English, 1994.

Bizzaro, Patrick. "Research and Reflection in English Studies: The Special Case of Creative Writing." *College English* 66.3 (2004): 294–309.

————. *Responding to Student Poems: Applications of Critical Theory.* Urbana, IL: National Council of Teachers of English, 1993.

————. "Should I Write This Essay or Finish a Poem? Teaching Writing Creatively." *College Composition and Communication* 49.2 (1998): 285–97.

Bizzell, Patricia. "'Contact Zones' and English Studies." *College English* 56.2 (1994): 163–69.

————. "Marxist Ideas in Composition Studies." *Contending with Words: Composition and Rhetoric in a Postmodern Age.* Ed. Patricia Harkin and John Schilb. New York: Modern Language Association, 1991. 52–68.

Brodkey, Linda. "Modernism and the Scene(s) of Writing." *College English* 49.4 (1987): 396–418.

Burke, Kenneth. *A Grammar of Motives and a Rhetoric of Motives.* Cleveland: World Meridian, 1962.

Caesar, Terry. "Getting Hired." J. Williams 241–63.

Cain, Mary Ann. *Revisioning Writers' Talk: Gender and Culture in Acts of Composing.* Albany: SUNY Press, 1995.

Clark, Timothy. *The Theory of Inspiration: Composition as a Crisis of Subjectivity in Romantic and Post-Romantic Writing.* New York: Manchester UP, 1997.

Connors, Robert J. "Afterword: 'Advanced Composition' and Advanced Writing." Shamoon et al. 143–49.

Conroy, Frank. "The Writer's Workshop." *On Writing Short Stories.* Ed. Tom Bailey. New York: Oxford UP, 2000. 80–89.

Crowley, Sharon. *Composition in the University: Historical and Polemical Essays.* Pittsburgh: U of Pittsburgh P, 1998.

————. *The Methodical Memory: Invention in Current-Traditional Rhetoric.* Carbondale: Southern Illinois UP, 1990.

————. "Reimagining the Writing Scene: Curmudgeonly Remarks about *Contending with Words.*" *Contending with Words: Composition and Rhetoric in a Postmodern Age.* Ed. Patricia Harkin and John Schilb. New York: Modern Language Association, 1991. 189–97.

Delany, Samuel R. "Remarks on Narrative and Technology; or, Poetry and Truth." *Technoscience and Cyberculture.* Ed. Stanley Aronowitz, Barbara Martinson, and Michael Menser, with Jennifer Rich. New York: Routledge, 1996. 255–77.

Dodd, Wayne. *Toward the End of the Century: Essays into Poetry.* Ames: U of Iowa P, 1991.

Emig, Janet. "Uses of the Unconscious in Composing." *College Composition and Communication* 15.1 (1964): 6–11.

Fehrman, Carl. *Poetic Creation: Inspiration or Craft.* Trans. Karin Petherick. Minneapolis: U of Minnesota P, 1980.

Fenza, D. W. "Creative Writing and Its Discontents." *Writer's Chronicle* March–April 2000. Available at <http://awpwriter.org/fenza1.htm>; accessed 13 June 2001.

———. "Tradition and the Institutionalized Talent." *AWP Chronicle* 24.4 (1991): 11, 14–20.

Foerster, Norman. *The American Scholar: A Study in* Litterae Inhumaniores. 1929. Port Washington, NY: Kennikat Press, 1965.

———. *The American State University: Its Relation to Democracy.* Chapel Hill: U of North Carolina P, 1937.

Foti, Veronique M. *Heidegger and the Poets.* Atlantic Highlands, NJ: Humanities Press, 1992.

Foucault, Michel. "What Is an Author?" *The Foucault Reader.* Ed. Paul Rabinow. New York: Pantheon, 1984. 101–20.

Fromm, Harold. *Academic Capitalism and Literary Value.* Athens: U of Georgia P, 1991.

Fry, Paul H. *A Defense of Poetry: Reflections on the Occasion of Writing.* Stanford: Stanford UP, 1995.

Galef, David. "Words, Words, Words." Herman 161–74.

Gioia, Dana. *Can Poetry Matter?* Saint Paul, MN: Graywolf Press, 1992.

Goggin, Maureen Daly. "The Tangled Roots of Literature, Speech Communication, Linguistics, Rhetoric/Composition, and Creative Writing: Selected Bibliography on the History of English Studies." *Rhetoric Society Quarterly* 29 (1999): 63–88.

Goodheart, Eugene. *Does Literary Studies Have a Future?* Madison: U of Wisconsin P, 1999.

Graff, Gerald. *Beyond the Culture Wars: How Teaching the Conflicts Can Revitalize American Education.* New York: Norton, 1992.

———. *Clueless in Academe: How Schooling Obscures the Life of the Mind.* New Haven, CT: Yale UP, 2003.

———. *Professing Literature: An Institutional History.* Chicago: U of Chicago P, 1987.

Haake, Katharine. *What Our Speech Disrupts: Feminism and Creative Writing Studies.* Urbana, IL: National Council of Teachers of English, 2000.

Halden-Sullivan, Judith. "The Phenomenology of Process." *Into the Field: Sites of Composition Studies.* Ed. Anne Ruggles Gere. New York: Modern Language Association, 1993. 44–59.

Heidegger, Martin. *Being and Time.* Trans. John Macquarrie and Edward Robinson. New York: Harper and Row, 1962.

———. *Being and Time.* Trans. Joan Stambaugh. Albany: SUNY Press, 1996.

———. *On the Way to Language.* Trans. Peter D. Hertz. New York: Harper and Row, 1971.

———. *Poetry, Language, Thought.* Trans. Albert Hofstadter. New York: Harper and Row, 1971.

———. *The Question Concerning Technology and Other Essays.* Trans. William Lovitt. New York: Harper and Row, 1977.

———. *What Is Called Thinking?* Trans. J. Glenn Gray. New York: Harper and Row, 1968.

Heller, Michael. "The Uncertainty of the Poet." *American Poetry Review* 24.3 (1995): 11–16.

Herman, Peter C., ed. *Day Late, Dollar Short: The Next Generation and the New Academy.* Albany: SUNY Press, 2000.

———. "Introduction: '60s Theory/'90s Practice." Herman 1–23.

Holden, Jonathan. *The Fate of American Poetry.* Athens: U of Georgia P, 1991.

Horner, Bruce. *Terms of Work for Composition: A Materialist Critique.* Albany: SUNY Press, 2000.

Kalamaras, George. "Getting Past 'Killer Dichotomies': Reinscribing the Institutional Relationship of Composition and Creative Writing." Paper presented at convention of the CCCC, Phoenix, 15 March 1997.

Kameen, Paul. "Rewording the Rhetoric of Composition." *Pre/Text* 1.1–2 (1980): 73–93.

Kercheval, Jesse Lee. "The Gates of Heaven: Writers and Tenure." *Chronicle of Higher Education* (27 June 1997): A56.

Kinneavy, James L. "The Process of Writing: A Philosophical Base in Hermeneutics." *Journal of Advanced Composition* 7.1–2 (1987): 1–9.

Kinzie, Mary. *The Cure of Poetry in an Age of Prose: Moral Essays on the Poet's Calling.* Chicago: U of Chicago P, 1993.

Koethe, John. *Poetry at One Remove.* Ann Arbor: U of Michigan P, 2000.

Krell, David Farrell. Introduction. *Nietzsche.* By Martin Heidegger. 2 vols. Trans. David Farrell Krell. San Francisco: Harper Collins, 1991. x–xxvii.

Lauterbach, Ann. "The Night Sky." *American Poetry Review* 25.3 (1996): 9–17.

———. "The Night Sky II." *American Poetry Review* 25.6 (1996): 9–15.

———. "The Night Sky III." *American Poetry Review* 26.2 (1997): 19–25.

———. "The Night Sky IV." *American Poetry Review* 26.4 (1997): 35–42.

Lentricchia, Frank, and Thomas McLaughlin, eds. *Critical Terms for Literary Study.* Chicago: U of Chicago P, 1990.

Lindemann, Erika. "Freshman English: No Place for Literature." *College English* 55.3 (1993): 311–16.

Mahala, Daniel, and Jody Swilky. "Geographical Designs: Rethinking Reform in the Humanities." *JAC: A Journal of Composition Theory* 21.1 (2001): 97–127.

———. "Remapping the Geography of Service in English." *College English* 59.6 (1997): 625–46.

McClatchy, J. D. *White Paper: On Contemporary American Poetry.* New York: Columbia UP, 1989.

McFarland, Ron. "An Apologia for Creative Writing." *College English* 55.1 (1993): 28–45.

McHugh, Heather. *Broken English: Poetry and Partiality.* Hanover, NH: UP of New England, 1993.

———. Preface. *Hinge and Sign: Poems, 1968–1993.* By Heather McHugh. Hanover, NH: UP of New England, 1994. xiii–xv.

Mehta, J. L. *Martin Heidegger: The Way and the Vision.* 1967. Honolulu: U of Hawaii P, 1976.

Miller, Richard E. "Composing English Studies: Towards a Social History of the Discipline." *College Composition and Communication* 45.2 (1994): 164–79.

Miller, Susan. *Rescuing the Subject: A Critical Introduction to Rhetoric and the Writer.* Carbondale: Southern Illinois UP, 1989.

———. *Textual Carnivals: The Politics of Composition.* Carbondale: Southern Illinois UP, 1991.

Miller, Thomas P. *The Formation of College English: Rhetoric and Belles Lettres in the British Cultural Provinces.* Pittsburgh: U of Pittsburgh P, 1997.

Monroe, Jonathan. "Poetry, the University, and the Culture of Distraction." *Diacritics* 26.3–4 (1996): 3–30.

Moxley, Joseph, ed. *Creative Writing in America: Theory and Pedagogy.* Urbana, IL: National Council of Teachers of English, 1989.

Murphy, James J., ed. *A Short History of Writing Instruction from Ancient Greece to Twentieth-Century America.* Davis, CA: Hermagoras Press, 1990.

Myers, D. G. *The Elephants Teach: Creative Writing since 1880.* New York: Prentice-Hall, 1996.

North, Stephen. *The Making of Knowledge in Composition: Portrait of an Emerging Field.* Montclair, NJ: Boynton/Cook, 1987.

North, Stephen, with Barbara A. Chepatis, David Coogan, Lale Levinson, Ron Maclean, Cindy L. Parrish, Jonathan Post, and Beth Weatherby. *Refiguring the Ph.D. in English Studies.* Urbana, IL: National Council of Teachers of English, 2000.

O'Dair, Sharon. "Academostars Are the Symptom; What's the Disease?" *Minnesota Review* n.s. 52–54 (Fall 2000): 159–74.

———. "Stars, Tenure, and the Death of Ambition." Herman 45–61.

Ohmann, Richard. *English in America: A Radical View of the Profession.* New York: Oxford UP, 1976.

Oliver, Mary. *A Poetry Handbook.* San Diego: Harcourt Brace, 1994.

Olson, Gary A. "The Death of Composition as an Intellectual Discipline." *Composition Studies* 28.2 (2000): 33–41.

———. "James Kinneavy and the Struggle over Composition." *JAC: A Journal of Composition Theory* 19.4 (1999): 536–39.

———. "Struggling over Composition." *JAC: A Journal of Composition Theory* 20.2 (2000): 454–55.

O'Neill, Peggy, Angela Crow, and Larry W. Burton, eds. *A Field of Dreams: Independent Writing Programs and the Future of Composition Studies.* Logan: Utah State UP, 2002.

Ong, Walter J. "Writing Is a Technology That Restructures Thought." *Literacy: A Critical Sourcebook.* Ed. Ellen Cushman, Eugene R. Kintgen, Barry M. Kroll, and Mike Rose. Boston: St. Martin's, 2001. 19–31.

Ott, Hugo. *Martin Heidegger: A Political Life.* Trans. Allan Blunden. New York: Basic Books, 1993.

Perelman, Bob. *The Marginalization of Poetry: Language Writing and Literary History.* Princeton: Princeton UP, 1996.

Perillo, Lucia. "When the Classroom Becomes a Confessional." *Chronicle of Higher Education* (28 November 1997): A56.

Perloff, Marjorie. *Radical Artifice: Writing Poetry in the Age of Media.* Chicago: U of Chicago P, 1991.

Piirto, Jane. *"My Teeming Brain": Understanding Creative Writers.* Cresskill, NJ: Hampton, 2002.

Radavich, David. "Creative Writing in the Academy." *Profession* (1999): 106–12.

Rasula, Jed. *The American Poetry Wax Museum: Reality Effects, 1940–1990.* Urbana, IL: National Council of Teachers of English, 1996.

Revell, Donald. "Better Unsaid: On Poetic Fragments." *American Poetry Review* 25.4 (1996): 29–30.

Richardson, Mark. "Who Killed Annabel Lee? Writing about Literature in the Composition Classroom." *College English* 66.3 (2004): 278–93.

Richter, David H. Introduction. *The Critical Tradition: Classic Texts and Contemporary Trends.* Ed. David H. Richter. New York: St. Martin's, 1989. 1–14.

Riebling, Barbara. "Contextualizing Contexts: Cultural Studies, Theory, and the Profession—Past and Future." Herman 175–97.

Ritter, Kelly. "Professional Writers/Writing Professionals: Revamping Teacher Training in Creative Writing Ph.D. Programs." *College English* 64.2 (2001): 205–27.

Rose, Mike. *Lives on the Boundary.* New York: Penguin, 1989.

Russell, David R. *Writing in the Academic Disciplines, 1870–1990: A Curricular History.* Carbondale: Southern Illinois UP, 1991.

Safranski, Rüdiger. *Martin Heidegger: Between Good and Evil.* Trans. Oswald Ewers. Cambridge: Harvard UP, 1998.

Santos, Sherod. "Eating the Angel, Conceiving the Sun: Toward a Notion of Poetic Thought." *American Poetry Review* 22.6 (1993): 9–13.

———. *A Poetry of Two Minds.* Athens: U of Georgia P, 2000.

Schmertz, Johanna. "Identity Wars: 'Passing' through the Lit/Comp Gap." *READER: Essays in Reader-Oriented Theory, Criticism, and Pedagogy* 47 (Fall 2002): 61–82.

Scholes, Robert. *Textual Power: Literary Theory and the Teaching of English.* New Haven, CT: Yale UP, 1985.

Schreiner, Stephen. "A Portrait of the Student as a Young Writer: Re-evaluating Emig and the Process Movement." *College Composition and Communication* 48.1 (1997): 86–104.

Seitz, James. *Motives for Metaphor: Literacy, Curriculum Reform, and the Teaching of English.* Pittsburgh: U of Pittsburgh P, 1999.

Shamoon, Linda, Rebecca Moore Howard, Sandra Jamieson, and Robert A. Schwegler, eds. *Coming of Age: The Advanced Writing Curriculum.* Portsmouth, NH: Boynton/Cook, 2000.

Shelnutt, Eve. "Notes from a Cell: Creative Writing Programs in Isolation." *Creative Writing in America: Theory and Pedagogy.* Ed. Joseph Moxley. Urbana, IL: National Council of Teachers of English, 1989. 3–24.

Shetley, Vernon. *After the Death of Poetry: Poet and Audience in Contemporary America.* Durham, NC: Duke UP, 1993.

Spanos, William V. *Heidegger and Criticism: Retrieving the Cultural Politics of Destruction.* Minneapolis: U of Minnesota P, 1993.

Tate, Gary. "A Place for Literature in Freshman Composition." *College English* 55.3 (1993): 317–21.

Trimbur, John. "Literacy and the Discourse of Crisis." *The Politics of Writing Instruction: Postsecondary.* Ed. Richard Bullock and John Trimbur. Portsmouth, NH: Boynton/Cook, 1991. 277–95.

Villanueva, Victor. "Preface to the First Edition." *Cross-Talk in Comp Theory: A Reader.* Ed. Victor Villanueva. 2nd ed. Urbana, IL: National Council of Teachers of English, 2003. xiii–xvi.

Watkins, Evan. *Work Time: English Departments and the Circulation of Cultural Value.* Stanford: Stanford UP, 1989.

Weiss, Theodore. Interview by Reginald Gibbons. *American Poetry Review* 30.3 (2001): 33–40.

Wenderoth, Joe. "Obscenery." *American Poetry Review* 26.2 (1997): 29–35.

Wilbers, Stephen. *The Iowa Writers' Workshop: Origins, Emergence, and Growth.* Iowa City: U of Iowa P, 1980.

Williams, Jeffrey J., ed. *The Institution of Literature.* Albany: SUNY Press, 2002.

———. "Introduction: Institutionally Speaking." J. Williams 1–15.

Williams, Raymond. *Keywords: A Vocabulary of Culture and Society.* Rev. ed. New York: Oxford UP, 1983.

Winterowd, W. Ross. "Emerson and the Death of *Pathos.*" *JAC: A Journal of Composition Theory* 16.1 (1996): 27–40.

———. *The English Department: A Personal and Institutional History.* Carbondale: Southern Illinois UP, 1998.

Wolin, Richard, ed. *The Heidegger Controversy: A Critical Reader.* 1991. Cambridge: MIT Press, 1993.

Worsham, Lynn. "The Question Concerning Invention: Hermeneutics and the Genesis of Writing." *Pre/Text* 8.3–4 (1987): 97–244.

Yood, Jessica. "Writing the Discipline: A Generic History of English Studies." *College English* 65.5 (2003): 526–40.

Young, Richard, and Maureen Daly Goggin. "Some Issues in Dating the Birth of the New Rhetoric in Departments of English: A Contribution to a Developing Historiography." *Defining the New Rhetorics.* Ed. Theresa Enos and Stuart C. Brown. Newbury Park, CA: Sage, 1993. 22–43.

Index

Conference on College Composition and Communication (CCCC), 111–13, 163–65, 172n4

confessional rhetoric, 146–48

Connors, Robert J., 97

Conroy, Frank, 17

conscious territorialism, 106–14

contemporary literature studies, 41, 45–46, 48–63, 150–52

"Contrary Impulses: The Tension between Poetry and Theory" (Koethe), 56–57

craft, definition of, 65–67, 83

craft criticism, 30; and academic literary criticism, 36–39, 42–44; composition studies, 78–81, 86–88; contemporary landscape, 45–46, 48–63; contemporary literature studies, 151–52; definition, 33–36; descriptive examples, 46–63; and disciplinary boundaries, 94–96; fiction writing, 45–46, 48, 58–63; first-year composition courses, 134–38; function, 63–64; and Heidegger, Martin, 70–74; historical background, 39–45; ideological focus, 47–48; poetry, 48–58, 70–74, 81–86, 139–48

creative nonfiction, 172n2

creative writing: alliance with composition studies, 98–101, 104, 107, 110–14, 127–28, 133–39; classroom dynamics, 114–15; as complement to literary studies, 19–20; contemporary landscape, 45–47; criticisms, 18, 41–42; disciplinary boundaries, 1–7, 19–21, 31–32, 94–96, 127–28; divergence theory, 116; essential components, 13; faculty hiring changes, 157–63; and first-year composition courses, 134–39; historical background, 10–12; innate versus learned ability, 14–17, 67, 115–16, 118–20; institutional criticism, 88–94; integration into curricula, 153–54; integration of genres, 154–56; introductory courses, 139–49; multiple genres, 11–12; process theory, 75–81; scholarly analysis, 12; structural reform, 25–27, 98–101, 127–67; teachability, 13–14, 111, 119; theoretical discourses, 58–60; theoretical discourses of change, 129; as true literature, 42. *See also* composition studies; craft criticism; poetry

"Creative Writing and Its Discontents" (Fenza), 18–20

Creative Writing in America: Theory and Pedagogy (Moxley), 119

Critical Terms for Literary Study (Lentricchia & McLaughlin), 151

Critical Tradition: Classic Texts and Contemporary Trends, The (Richter), 42–43

criticism, definition of, 35–36

Cross-Talk in Comp Theory (Villanueva), 9–10

Crowley, Sharon, 4, 5–6, 98, 101, 108, 134

cultural studies, 104–5, 146–47

Cure of Poetry in an Age of Prose, The (Kinzie), 15

Day Late, Dollar Short (Herman), 107–8, 110

Defense of Poetry: Reflections on the Occasion of Writing, A (Fry), 117

Delany, Samuel R., 62

disciplinary boundaries, 1–7, 31–32, 94–96, 111–13, 122–24, 127–28

disciplinary discourses of change, 22–24

disciplinary integration, 165–66

divergence theory, 116

Dodd, Wayne, 81–82, 120–21

Does Literary Studies Have a Future? (Goodheart), 106

"Dysfunctional Narratives, or: 'Mistakes Were Made'" (Baxter), 61

Elephants Teach, The (Myers), 25, 40, 98

Emig, Janet, 101–3

enframing, 72

English studies: binary categorizations, 33; disciplinary boundaries, 1–7, 31–32; faculty hiring changes, 157–63; German model, 99–100; historical background, 21–22, 40–45; innate versus learned ability, 119–20; institutional boundaries, 122–24, 127–28, 132–33; institutional criticism, 112–13; integration of genres, 154–56; structural reform, 22, 24–27, 98–101, 127–67; terminology issues, 30–31; territorialism, 103–14, 130–31; theoretical discourses of change, 129–30; writing-about-literature courses, 149–53. *See also* composition studies; creative writing; literary studies

essence of technology, 70–71, 96, 134
expressivism, 116

faculty hiring changes, 157–63
Faulkner, William, 84
Fehrman, Carl, 66–67
Fenza, D. W., 18–20, 56, 60, 110–11
fiction writing, 16–17, 45–46, 48, 58–63. *See also* craft criticism
Field of Dreams: Independent Writing Programs and the Future of Composition Studies, A (O'Neill, Crow, and Burton), 27, 130–31
first-year composition courses: and creative writing, 134–39; historical background, 9; and literary studies, 6, 108; multiple genres, 136–37; and poetry, 102, 135–39; process theory, 81; structural reform, 133–39. *See also* composition studies
Foerster, Norman, 98–101, 165–66
forestructure, 79–80
formal criticism, 43–44
formalism, 120–22
formal verse, 50
Formation of College English, The (Miller, Thomas P.), 21, 131
Foti, Veronique, 73
Foucault, Michel, 14–15, 30, 59
free verse, 50, 53, 81–83, 120–21
Fry, Paul H., 117–18

Galef, David, 107
genre criticism, 47, 74–75, 81–86
George, Stefan, 73
"Getting Past 'Killer Dichotomies': Reinscribing the Institutional Relationship of Composition and Creative Writing" (Kalamaras), 111
"Ghosts of Liberalism: Morrison's *Beloved* and the Moynihan Report" (Berger), 36–37
Gibbons, Reginald, 29–30, 45, 106
Ginsberg, Allen, 89
Gioia, Dana, 48–52, 148, 170n5
Giroux, Henry, 123
Goggin, Maureen Daly, 21
Goodheart, Eugene, 106
graduate programs, 172n3
Graff, Gerald, 23, 26, 40–41, 98, 132

Haake, Katharine, 58–60
Halden-Sullivan, Judith, 86–88
Hass, Robert, 54, 84
Heidegger and the Poets (Foti), 73
Heidegger, Martin, 55, 65, 67–96, 78, 134, 171nn2–3
Heller, Michael, 121–22
Herman, Peter C., 107
Hinge and Sign: Poems, 1968–1993 (McHugh), 86
History of Professional Writing Instruction in American Colleges: Years of Acceptance, Growth, and Doubt, A (Adams), 40
Holden, Jonathan, 45, 51
Horner, Bruce, 31, 159
humanism, 53

"Identity Wars: 'Passing' Through the Lit/Comp Gap" (Schmertz), 113–14
independent writing departments, 130–31
innate versus learned ability, 14–17, 67, 115–16, 118–19
inner process, 17
institutional-conventional wisdom, 13–20, 29–30, 42–48, 54–63, 66–67
institutional criticism, 47–48, 55–57, 74–75, 88–94, 106–9, 112–13
Institution of Literature, The (Williams, Jeffrey J.), 109–10
interviews, 11–12
introductory creative writing courses, 139–49
Iowa Writers' Workshop. *See* University of Iowa; Wilbers, Stephen

Kalamaras, George, 111
Kameen, Paul, 78
Kinneavy, James L., 78–81, 111–12
Kinzie, Mary, 15–16
Koethe, John, 55–58, 118
Krell, David Farrell, 171n3

language, 29–30, 71–73, 77–78, 82–83, 85–90, 93–96
Language Poetry, 45–46, 48, 51–54, 81, 120–21, 127
"Language Writing and Literary History" (Perelman), 126
Lauterbach, Ann, 88–91, 94

Lentricchia, Frank, 151
Lindquist, Julie, 129
Linemann, Erika, 5
literary criticism, 43
literary studies: as complement to creative writing, 19–20; and composition studies, 101–3, 108–10, 113–14; disciplinary boundaries, 1–7, 31–32, 127–28; faculty hiring changes, 157–63; institutional criticism, 106–9; multiple genres, 150–56; and poetry, 124–27; politics in, 106; structural reform, 25–27, 98–101, 104–6, 110, 127–67; territorialism, 104–10; writing-about-literature courses, 149–53. See also craft criticism
Lives on the Boundary (Rose), 108, 166
"Love Lyric of a South Amboy Teenager" (Mayers). See "Close to Home" (Mayers)

Mahala, Daniel, 105
mainstream writers, 45–46, 48, 52–54, 81, 121
Making of Knowledge in Composition: Portrait of an Emerging Field, The (North), 9
Marginalization of Poetry: Language Writing and Literary History, The (Perelman), 124
"Marginalization of Poetry, The" (Perelman), 124–27
"Marxist Ideas in Composition Studies" (Bizzell), 123
McFarland, Ron, 12–13
McHugh, Heather, 84–86, 115–16
McLaughlin, Thomas, 151
metaphysics. See Heidegger, Martin
Methodical Memory: Invention in Current-Traditional Rhetoric, The (Crowley), 134
Miller, Richard E., 24, 25
Miller, Susan, 4, 32
Miller, Thomas P., 4, 21, 35–36, 131
Modernism, 53
"Modernism and the Scene(s) of Writing" (Brodkey), 59
Modern Language Association (MLA), 113, 163–65
Morrison, Toni, 36–37
Motives for Metaphor (Seitz), 135–36
Moxley, John, 119
Myers, D. G., 19, 24–25, 40, 41–42, 67, 98
mystery, in writing, 117–19
mystification, in writing, 117–18

"My Teeming Brain": Understanding Creative Writers (Piirto), 12

narrative writing, 61–62
National Council of Teachers of English (NCTE), 22
new course creation, 132–33
New Criticism, 43–44, 53, 139
New Formalism, 45, 48–54, 81, 120–21
"Night Sky, The" (Lauterbach), 88–91
North, Stephen, 9, 24, 26–27, 158, 163

"Obscenery" (Wenderoth), 54–55, 67–68
O'Dair, Sharon, 108–9, 172n3 (chap. 4)
Oliver, Mary, 15–16
Olson, Gary A., 111–13
Ong, Walter, 96
opposition, as catalyst for change, 123–24, 126–28
"Origin of the Work of Art, The" (Heidegger), 71
ostension, 117

pedagogical imperative, 10
Perelman, Bob, 124–27
Perillo, Lucia, 146–47
Perloff, Marjorie, 12
personnel. See faculty hiring changes
"Phenomenology of Process, The" (Halden-Sullivan), 86
Piirto, Jane, 12
Poetic Creation: Inspiration or Craft (Fehrman), 66
Poetics, A (Bernstein), 51–52
poetry: and authorship criticism, 81–86; confessional rhetoric, 146–48; contemporary audience, 68; contemporary landscape, 45–46, 48–58; as craft, 66–68, 144; and first-year composition courses, 102, 135–39; formalism, 120–22; as fragments, 84; and genre criticism, 81–86; genuineness, 54–55; and Heidegger, Martin, 67–77; innate versus learned ability, 15–16, 115–16; institutional criticism, 88–91, 94; and language, 29–30, 71–73, 82–83, 85–86, 88–90; and literary studies, 124–27; and McHugh, Heather, 84–86; mystification, 117–18; New Criticism, 43; and process theory, 75–77; revision process, 141–46; and rhetoric, 122;

and theoretical discourse, 56–57; and thinking, 75–77, 85–86; as true literature, 42; and truth-telling, 76–77, 82. *See also* craft criticism; creative writing
"Poetry and Freshman Composition" (Bell), 102
Poetry at One Remove (Koethe), 55–58
"Poetry at One Remove" (Koethe), 57–58
Poetry Handbook, A (Oliver), 15–16
portfolios, 133, 136, 150
"Portrait of the Student as a Young Writer, A" (Schreiner), 102–3
postmodernism, 53, 60, 85
privilege of unknowing, 7, 113
process criticism, 47, 74–81, 102
"Process of Writing: A Philosophical Base in Hermeneutics, The" (Kinneavy), 78–79
Professing Literature (Graff), 40–41
professional discourses of creative writing, 11–12, 45–47
professional organizations, 163–65
professional publication activity, 31, 35, 44
pseudo-formal verse, 50–51
publish or perish philosophy, 11

"Question Concerning Invention: Hermeneutics and the Genesis of Writing, The" (Worsham), 91
"Question Concerning Technology, The" (Heidegger), 70

Radavich, David, 21
Radical Artifice (Perloff), 12
Rasula, Jed, 45–46
"Remarks on Narrative and Technology, or Poetry and Truth" (Delaney), 62
Rereading America, Signs of Life in the U.S.A., 105
resistance, as catalyst for change, 123–24, 127
Responding to Student Poems: Applications of Critical Theory (Bizzaro), 118
Revell, Donald, 37–39
"Rewording the Rhetoric of Composition" (Kameen), 78
rhetoric: confessional rhetoric, 146–48; definition, 3; integration of genres, 154; and poetry, 122, 146–48
rhetorical criticism, 43–44
Rhetoric and Reality: Writing Instruction in

American Colleges, 1900–1985 (Berlin), 40
Rhetorics, Poetics, and Cultures (Berlin), 24, 26, 154
Richardson, Mark, 5–7, 169n1
Richter, David, 42–43
Riebling, Barbara, 108
romanticism, 115–16, 118, 121
Rose, Mike, 108, 166
Russell, David, 40

Santos, Sherod, 75–77, 78, 81, 85
Schmertz, Johanna, 113–14
scholarship, 12, 166
Scholes, Robert, 149
Schreiner, Stephen, 102–3
Seeing and Writing, 105
Seitz, James, 24, 26, 135–36
self-expression, 138
"Self-Reflections and the Scene of Writing" (Haake), 59
Shelnutt, Eve, 44
Shetley, Vernon, 12, 45, 51, 120, 170n6
social constructionism, 116–17
sonnets, 150–51
speech genres, 39–41, 82
staffing issues. *See* faculty hiring changes
Stafford, William, 54, 84
"Stillness" (Baxter), 61–62
"Stranger's Way of Looking, A" (McHugh), 84–85
structural discourses of change, 23–27
student writing evaluations, 133, 136, 146–49
Swilky, Jody, 105

talent, in writing, 120
Tate, Gary, 5
technological determinism, 120
technology, essence of, 70–71, 96, 134
tenure, 160–61
Terms of Work for Composition (Horner), 31
territorialism, 103–14, 130–31
textbook publication, 12
textual interpretation versus textual production: craft criticism, 34–39, 43–44; integration of genres, 153–56; process theory, 79–80; structural reform, 23–24, 110–11, 133; territorialism, 105
theoretical discourses of change, 22–23, 30, 56–59, 129–30, 132–33